PLANNING AND DESIGNING THE DATA WAREHOUSE

THE DATA WAREHOUSING INSTITUTE SERIES
FROM PRENTICE HALL PTR

Planning and Designing the Data Warehouse

Building, Using, and Managing the Data Warehouse

PLANNING AND DESIGNING THE DATA WAREHOUSE

Ramon C. Barquin
Herbert A. Edelstein
Editors

For book and bookstore information

http://www.prenhall.com

Prentice Hall PTR, Upper Saddle River, New Jersey 07458

Library of Congress Cataloging-in-Publication Data

Planning and designing the data warehouse / Ramon C. Barquin,
  Herb Edelstein.
    p. cm.
   ISBN 0-13-255746-0 (alk. paper)
    1.   Database design.   2.   Decision support systems.
  3.   Client/server computing.   I.   Barquin, Ramon C.
  II.   Edelstein, Herb.
  QA76.9.D26P54   1996
  658.4′038′028574—dc20   96–18788
                                            CIP

Acquisitions editor: *Mark L. Taub*
Editorial assistant: *Kate Hargett*
Production supervision: *Mary Sudul*
Cover design: *Anthony Gemmellaro*
Cover design director: *Jerry Votta*
Copyeditor: *James Gwyn*
Manufacturing manager: *Alexis R. Heydt*

© 1997 Prentice Hall PTR
Prentice Hall, Inc.
A Simon & Schuster Company
Upper Saddle River, New Jersey 07458

The publisher offers discounts on this book when ordered in bulk
quantities. For more information, contact Corporate Sales Department,
Prentice Hall PTR, One Lake Street, Upper Saddle River, NJ 07458.
Phone: 800-382-3419; FAX: 201-236-7141; email: corpsales@prenhall.com

All product names mentioned herein are the trademarks of their respective owners.

Printed in the United States of America

10 9 8 7 6 5 4 3 2

ISBN 0-13-255746-0

Prentice-Hall International (UK) Limited, *London*
Prentice-Hall of Australia Pty. Limited, *Sydney*
Prentice-Hall Canada Inc., *Toronto*
Prentice-Hall Hispanoamericana, S.A., *Mexico*
Prentice-Hall of India Private Limited, *New Delhi*
Prentice-Hall of Japan, Inc., *Tokyo*
Simon & Schuster Asia Pte. Ltd., *Singapore*
Editora Prentice-Hall do Brasil, Ltda., *Rio de Janeiro*

Contents

Series Foreword

P*lanning and Designing the Data Warehouse* is the first volume in the Prentice Hall series on data warehousing. As Series Editor, I wanted to put down my thoughts on what we would like to accomplish with this series of books.

Data warehousing is still very much an emerging technology. Some refer to it as an approach, a movement or even a set of technologies. Whatever the result of this taxonomic exercise, it is obvious that there is a strong need for a clearer vision of what data warehousing as a discipline is and where it is going; more rigorous definitions of its various components; a common vocabulary for enhanced usage; a better understanding of the skills needed to properly undertake the different functions involved. Furthermore, how does data warehousing relate to other disciplines within information systems technology? Does it fit best within computer science, management information systems, information engineering or some other such denomination? What business role does it play within an organization? What successful implementation strategies can be identified? In short, there are a significant number of questions that must, and will be, answered as data warehousing matures and blossoms.

Through this series we also expect to address some of the key technical problems that data warehousing practitioners are facing. Whether it be the issues related to data warehousing architecture, data warehouse database design, metadata repositories, data mining algorithms, or other specific topics, we will bring the top experts in the field to share with us their best knowledge and experience.

Like other such endeavors, there is a substantial number of management considerations involved in data warehousing. From critical success factors to financial considerations, from cost accounting mechanisms to staffing issues, this collection will deal with them.

Ultimately, our goal is to present as complete a reference source as possible for individuals and organizations involved in planning, designing, building, managing and using data warehouses.

It is not a simple goal, nor an easy challenge; but it is convergent with The Data Warehousing Institute's mission.

As President of The Data Warehousing Institute, I am in the fortunate position of being able to draw on the resources of the Institute to address the demands of being the editor for this Prentice Hall series on data warehousing. The Institute is committed to expanding the use of this technology and enhancing data warehousing professionalism. As such, it runs a growing set of educational and technical programs that have become groundbreaking in their quality and scope. In the process, the Institute has brought together within its "faculty" some of the top experts in the field and has identified the pioneering "case studies" where organizations have implemented successful data warehouses. In short, there is a very strong cross-fertilization between the Institute's activities and the issues we will be addressing in future volumes of this series.

We are convinced of the importance of data warehousing as an agent of change within the information systems industry; and we are pleased to be at the leading edge.

Ramon C. Barquin, Editor
President, The Data Warehousing Institute

Foreword

This book is organized to present the reader with a collection of articles and essays written by data warehousing practitioners who have been pioneers in the field. The articles, consolidated in one volume, focus on how to plan and design a data warehouse project. It is a very necessary attempt to capture the state of the art in what is an extremely volatile field.

The book is divided into four sections: *1) Introduction; 2) Planning the Data Warehouse; 3) Designing the Data Warehouse; and 4) Some Case Studies.*

The *Introduction* intends to provide the background and position the book. To that effect, Barquin's "A Data Warehousing Manifesto" opens the mainstream of the book by giving a bit of history, some definitions, and underscoring the basic process of data warehousing itself; as well as stating the basic purpose and programs of The Data Warehousing Institute.

Alan Paller, Director of Education and Research for The Data Warehousing Institute, and the intellectual father of "A Roadmap to Data Warehousing," presents this widely circulated and popular document that serves as a framework for the discipline. In the "Roadmap" he identifies the principal components of data warehousing and places the many hardware and software tools within their appropriate boxes.

The "Roadmap" is followed by Herb Edelstein's "An Introduction to Data Warehousing," which is truly the defining article introducing the key concepts and vocabulary for the rest of the book.

The *Planning the Data Warehouse* section addresses the earliest stage of data warehousing initiatives. It is kicked off by Ellen Levin's piece on "Developing a Data Warehousing Strategy." In this elegant and well-written article, Ms. Levin, an experienced practitioner and consultant in the field, describes a methodology to develop an enterprise-wide data warehousing strategy as an essential prerequisite for a successful project.

Data warehouses need to be justified and sold to top management. Without this support it is highly unlikely that any such project can have a long-term positive impact on an organization. Leading us through this maze is "How to Justify the Data Warehouse and Gain Top Management Support," by Doug Neal, a senior consultant with ATKearney. Doug, who has been doing Decision Support Systems (DSS) work for many years, has now applied his intellect and experience to the problem at hand, and comes up with a series of questions to assist the new practitioner through this sensitive but key part of the process.

Carol Burleson and David Tabler form a remarkable team. Together they implemented one of the first and most successful data warehouses within the federal government at the Naval Surface Warfare Center Dahlgren Division. Their work there has led them to honors and awards, and now they have been also named Fellows of The Data Warehousing Institute. Based on their experience, they give us "Data Warehousing: Putting it All Together," which is a nuts-and-bolts account of how you implement a data warehousing project.

The latter part of the section is "Ten Mistakes to Avoid for Data Warehousing Managers," by Barquin, Paller and Edelstein. This brief piece was the result of an Institute research project with IS managers and professionals doing data warehousing work. First published as a booklet by the Institute, it also appeared in *Application Development Trends.*

Designing the Data Warehouse starts where *Planning* leaves off. The design process now forces rigor and methodology into any discipline. Pieter Mimno, a highly respected and heeded independent consultant, starts out by addressing the fundamentals in his "Data Warehousing Architectures."

This is followed by "Database Design for Data Warehouses: The Basic Requirements," by Bob Rumsby and Glen Livingston, from Red Brick Systems. This piece lays out the different approaches to data warehousing database design providing the pros and cons of each. In particular it addresses the multidimensional vs. relational database controversy.

"Choosing the Right OLAP Technology," by Neil Raden, Archer Decision Systems, is a fascinating article by one of the field's foremost experts. In this piece he delves into the origins of the data warehousing process and does an excellent job of looking at the different on-line analytical processing tools that vie for adoption in today's data warehousing environments.

The final article in this section is "Metadata Repositories: The Key to Unlocking Information in Data Warehouses." In the article, Duane Hufford, an experienced consultant with AMS, and chair of The Data Warehousing Institute's Metadata User Council, delves into the ways and byways of the basic navigational instrument within the data warehousing environment.

The book closes with two specific case studies. In the first, Burleson and Tabler give us additional detail on their installation through "Data Warehousing at NSWCDD: A Case Study." In the last, Mark Poole, the architect of Harris Semi-conductor's Integrated Yield Management System, describes their award-winning alert system in "Alarming Profits at Harris Semi-conductor: A Case Study."

Ramon Barquin and Herb Edelstein, Editors

Acknowledgments

Many folks have assisted in the birth of this volume, the first one in this series on data warehousing.

The concept for this book was a direct result of The Data Warehousing Institute's 1995 Annual Conference. This groundbreaking event was the first conference fully dedicated to data warehousing where pioneers in the field had the opportunity to talk at length about what they had done, and answer questions from the large contingent of I/S professionals facing the challenging tasks of planning, designing and building data warehouses for their own organizations. The providers of hardware and software products and the theoreticians have an important role to play, but only from those that have been in the trenches can you really expect to learn what it's like to be in war.

This book, hence, must acknowledge the immense contribution made by the band of pioneers who led the charge in the Institute's first Annual Conference. Thanks go to Diane Brown, Jim Wells, Carol Burleson, David Tabler, Peggy Bennett, Narsim Ganti, Tom Smith, Jane Griffin, Larry Meador, Rich Franklin, Mark Harris, Chris Lane, Boris Bosch, Charles Sellers and Carol Rapking.

To them, and to all data warehousing pioneers: Thank you!

About the Data Warehousing Institute

The Data Warehousing Institute has two goals: (1) expanding effective use of data warehousing technology and (2) enhancing the careers of data warehousing managers and staff. It does this through sharing information about best practices and about lessons learned by data warehousing pioneers. It conducts courses, offers tips and techniques, provides references to outstanding speakers, consultants, and system integrators; and it conducts annual data warehousing user conferences where experienced data warehousing managers share the lessons they have learned about what works and what doesn't.

DATA WAREHOUSING USER CASE STUDIES

Organizations could avoid unnecessary delays and mistakes if they could find people who had already resolved the problems they are now facing. Our collection of user case studies helps Institute Associates by providing useful knowledge and a link to other users who may be willing to discuss their experiences. The case studies are a growing, living collection, constantly being augmented, edited, and pruned by each Special Interest Group (SIG).

SPECIAL INTEREST GROUPS

Institute Associates find significant value from communicating with other data warehousing practitioners who share their specific subset of issues, problems, tools, etc. The SIG groupings are organized by industry. At the 1995 Annual Conference, SIGs were launched in health care and manufacturing. The Institute is also launching SIGs in finance, government, telecommunications, wholesale/retail, and public utilities. Proposals for additional SIGs are expected.

DATA WAREHOUSING AWARDS

The "Best Data Warehousing Projects" awards help identify good models to follow.

DATA WAREHOUSING ELECTRONIC FORUM

Associates of The Data Warehousing Institute may gain access to Institute staff and other Associates through an electronic forum maintained in a widely accessible on-line service. Information about new announcements in data warehousing, new case studies, new consultants and system integrators added to the list, and "Best Data Warehousing Projects" can all be accessed through the forum. An up-to-date list of data warehousing conferences and resources is also maintained. In addition, the forum facilitates moderated broadcasts of messages from members to other members.

ANNUAL TRAINING CONFERENCE

Each year in January, teams of data warehousing practitioners come together to attend a dozen well-designed, in-depth half-day and full-day courses on key data warehousing methodologies and technologies. The courses are also offered in-house for requesting organizations. These courses are taught by a faculty whose members consistently win extraordinarily high ratings in conferences and seminars throughout the world.

REGIONAL AND INTERNATIONAL TRAINING PROGRAMS AND CONFERENCES

The Data Warehousing Institute conducts in-depth courses and conferences in many cities in the U.S. and around the world. These programs bring the top-rated speakers from the Annual Conference and the Annual Training Conference to people who were not able to attend. Many of the courses and conferences are hosted by a local company, government agency, or association. The host organization receives low-cost admission to the program. If you would like more information about hosting such a program, e-mail tdwi@aol.com, and indicate "co-hosted programs" in the subject line, or call the Institute at 301-229-1062.

THE DATA WAREHOUSING INSTITUTE ANNUAL CONFERENCE

Each summer, several hundred data warehousing managers and their staff meet to share experiences and to find practical solutions to the challenges they face. About half the delegates are experienced data warehousing practitioners; the other half are in the evaluation or pilot phase.

THE JOURNAL OF DATA WAREHOUSING

A quarterly technical journal of case studies and in-depth articles on data warehousing will begin February, 1996.

PARTICIPATING IN THE DATA WAREHOUSING INSTITUTE PROGRAM

The Data Warehousing Institute has an Associate's program currently numbering close to 500 participants. You can become an Associate by participating in an Annual Conference, a Training Seminar, or any other of the Institute's formal activities. Associates share a private electronic forum, receive a subscription to *The Journal of Data Warehousing*, and get reduced rates on Institute publications, conferences, and courses. When appropriate, Associates contribute case studies of their warehousing activities and the lessons they learned, help with special interest group activities, and share their knowledge at Institute workshops, conferences and in *The Journal of Data Warehousing*.

About the Authors

DR. RAMON C. BARQUIN

Dr. Barquin is president and founder of The Data Warehousing Institute, as well as of Barquin and Associates, his own consulting firm. He specializes in developing information system strategies, particularly data warehousing, for corporations. His presence in the information technology industry has spanned four decades and three continents. He had a long career with IBM covering both management and technical assignments, including overseas postings and responsibilities in Asia and Latin America. Afterwards, he served as President of the Washington Consulting Group, where he had direct oversight for the performance of several major federal information systems' contracts. An electrical engineer and mathematician by training, he holds a Ph.D. from MIT. The author of over 75 technical and management publications, he has held faculty appointments at MIT, the Chinese University of Hong Kong, and the University of Maryland. An acknowledged expert in the field of data warehousing strategies, he has assisted a number of organizations looking for guidance on data warehousing initiatives. Some of his clients include the FAA, CIGNA, EMC, IBM, NASDAQ, the U.S. Army Reserve Command, the U.S. Coast Guard, the FBI and others. Dr. Barquin is also the editor for the Prentice Hall book series on data warehousing and the co-editor of the two volumes in the series: *Planning and Designing the Data Warehouse* and *Building, Using, and Managing the Data Warehouse*.

HERBERT A. EDELSTEIN

Herbert A. Edelstein is a co-founder and president of Two Crows Corporation, a company that specializes in data mining solutions. He is an internationally recognized expert in data warehousing, data mining and electronic document management. He consults to both computer vendors and users on these topics and has been invited to chair and keynote numerous conferences. He is also a widely published author on data warehousing and image management topics, and was technical editor for the Codd and Date Relational Journal. He is currently serving as Technical Director for the Data Warehousing Institute and is Conference Chairperson for their annual conference.

Mr. Edelstein has degrees from the University of Maryland, Johns Hopkins University, and Carnegie-Mellon University. He is a member of AIIM (the Association for Image and Information Management) and of the ACM (the Association for Computing Machinery).

ALAN PALLER

Alan Paller is Director of Education and Training for the Data Warehousing Institute, co-author of "Ten Mistakes to Avoid for Data Warehousing Managers" (TDWI, 1995) and author of "The EIS Book: Information Systems for Top Managers" (Irwin, 1990). He is widely known for his research on the challenges and opportunities in the relationship between CEOs and CIOs and on the "clandestine costs of client server computing."

ELLEN J. LEVIN

Ellen Levin is presently associated with the consulting firm of Barquin and Associates, an organization specializing in the development of data warehousing strategies. With over 25 years in information management disciplines, she focuses on strategies, techniques, and solutions for maximizing information assets in support of business goals. Her assignments at major corporations, such as Mobil, USF&G, Freddie Mac and INTELSAT, have included both managerial and technical responsibilities related to information resource management.

DOUGLAS NEAL

Douglas Neal is a Principal with the Strategic Information Technology Practice of the management consulting firm of ATKearney. Mr. Neal's work focuses on the intersection of strategy, business operations, and technology. His recent efforts have been in the area of using data warehousing and modeling techniques to assess the performance potential of organizations and to build systems that help executives and operational staff achieve their potential.

CAROLYN L. BURLESON AND DAVID E. TABLER

Carolyn L. Burleson and David E. Tabler each have over 20 years of experience in Information Technology and are pioneers in the field of data warehousing. Since 1992, Carol and David have been responsible for implementing and evolving what has been called "one of the most innovative data warehouses in the federal government." They have been actively writing, speaking, and consulting on data warehousing and related subjects since 1994.

PIETER R. MIMNO

Pieter Mimno helps government agencies and commercial organizations plan and implement data warehouses and enterprise-wide client/server systems. He is one of the most highly rated teachers in the field and the author of several books and numerous articles. He is on the faculty of The Data Warehousing Institute and is the editor of the James Martin/McGraw-Hill Productivity Series. Pieter holds undergraduate and graduate degrees from the Massachusetts Institute of Technology.

GLEN LIVINGSTON

Glen Livingston is vice president, sales operations and programs, Red Brick Systems, Inc., Los Gatos, California. He is responsible for sales operations, indirect channel sales worldwide and technical services, including consulting, training and the Red Brick Systems Technology Center.

BOB RUMSBY

Bob Rumsby is a senior technical writer with Red Brick Systems, Inc. in Los Gatos, California. He writes and edits Red Brick Warehouse software documentation, including SQL reference materials and installation guides for MPP platforms.

DUANE HUFFORD

Duane Hufford is a senior principal at American Management Systems. He has worked on a variety of systems development and data administration projects for the Department of Defense, Army and Navy organizations focusing on improving data documentation and quality and making data more accessible. These projects include leading the design and development of dictionaries to support data standardization and management of data warehouses, conducting training on data administration concepts and procedures, and helping organizations develop data administration policies and procedures. He speaks at professional gatherings concerned with data administration and has written articles for publications such as Auerbach, Data Management Review, and Database Advisor.

NEIL RADEN

Neil Raden is the co-founder of Archer Decision Systems, a firm that provides consulting, system integration, project management, and development services, particularly in the areas of data warehousing, DSS, and database marketing. Neil has been actively consulting in this field for over 15 years. His expertise is in understanding the role of decision support in an enterprise and the challenges associated with creating and supporting an enabling architecture.

MARK POOLE

Mark Poole is Manufacturing Systems Manager at Harris Semiconductor in Melbourne, Florida. He has 13 years of experience in client/server systems and software that automatically collect manufacturing data, provide control and reporting mechanisms, and offer comprehensive data analysis tools for a worldwide user community. Mark's accomplishments have been recognized in the Wall Street Journal, Information Week, and Software Magazine. He holds a BSEE degree from the University of Missouri and an MBA from the University of Arkansas.

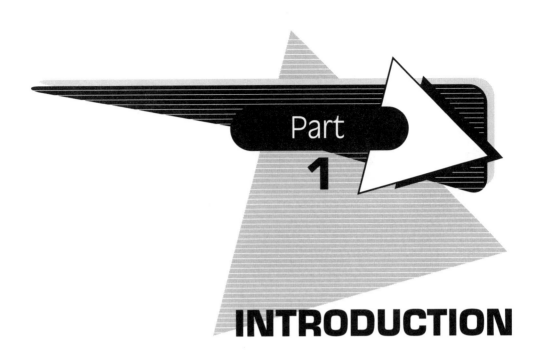

Part 1

INTRODUCTION

Chapter
1

A Data Warehousing Manifesto

Ramon C. Barquin

President
The Data Warehousing Institute

INTRODUCTION

Data warehousing is taking the information industry by storm, and it is now poised to transform it. It is becoming the standard choice for delivering information to users throughout the enterprise; and the data warehousing pioneers leading the charge are becoming the new heroes within their enterprises. Furthermore, it is only the latest and most important manifestation to date of our attempts to glean insights and meaning from the universe of observations we gather on a daily basis.

Why is this happening? Because the broad need for competitiveness is rapidly converging with the availability of new client/server technologies and parallel database machines. These technologies and machines can harness the transactional data assets of an organization and enable decision-making grounded on an enterprise-wide or department-wide information base. At the center of this revolution is the concept of the data warehouse which provides the infrastructure and enabling technology for business process reengineering and other mission-critical decision support and client-support systems.

While some enterprises have been using data warehouses for a few years now (under this name or another) the recent growth has been staggering. Recent survey data show that the vast majority of *Fortune 1000* firms have started data warehousing projects over the last 24 months. And the growth is now escalating as client/server computing increases, as it has in the past few years.

What is a data warehouse?

It has been said that data warehousing is a journey and not a destination. What does this really mean? For starters it necessitates a step back into definitions. A data warehouse is usually defined to be a subject-oriented, integrated, time-variant, and non-volatile collection of data in support of management's decision-making process.[1]

However, the data warehouse itself does not data warehousing make. This has been at the root of one of the major problems data warehousing has had to contend with since its inception. People often take issue with the term "data warehouse" as having a static connotation. It engenders thoughts of hoarding, storing items for no other purpose. Often people think of it in archival terms or as an electronic museum. Yet nothing could be further from what data warehousing as a discipline attempts to accomplish; which is precisely to get information out of what have been called "jailhouses" and into the hands of the users who can utilize it to make improved decisions about their business operations.

---

[1] This definition is from Dr. William Inmon, founder of PRISM Solutions, Inc. He has been the primary driving force in the development of the data warehousing concept since the early years of this decade.

So let us focus not on the data warehouse but on the data warehousing process itself. What is data warehousing? Here is a suggested definition: *Data warehousing is the process whereby organizations extract value from their informational assets through the use of special stores called data warehouses.*

Furthermore, data warehousing is the continuation of the age old process of obtaining meaning from a collection of data points or observations. Daniel Boorstin gives some fascinating insights into these data points and operations through his essay, "The Age of Negative Discovery," in his book *Cleopatra's Nose*.[2] Boorstin points out that "for most of Western history interpretation has far outrun data."[3] He also says, "The modern tendency is quite the contrary, as we see data outrun meaning."[4]

He attributes this "outrun" to the advent of the "mechanized observers" or machines that generate such vast numbers of observations, or data points, and make it essential that we learn to navigate these oceans of data. The essential insight in all this has to do with the importance of negative discovery.

In other words, discovering that which is not and hence allowing us to discard all data, through analysis, that does not move the ball forward in terms of providing a better understanding of our reality.

These insights tie very directly to our concept of data warehousing. Not so much in terms of the tool, the data warehouse, but rather the process of finding meaning from observations, knowledge production, and insight engineering.

Data warehousing will eventually give way to a term that more effectively describes the true nature of the discipline.

---

[2] Boorstin, Daniel J., "The Age of Negative Discovery," *Cleopatra's Nose: Essays on the Unexpected*, Vintage Books, New York, pp. 3–17.

[3] Boorstin, op cit., p. 12.

[4] Boorstin, op cit., p. 8.

WHAT HAS LED TO DATA WAREHOUSING?

Let us expand on a point we made earlier. Data warehousing has been around for some time. Any organization with minimal competence has been trying, over the last few years, different approaches to harmonize and clean their databases, migrate systems, develop enterprise data models, etc. Furthermore, analysts in many organizations have been putting together, often just in their own hard drive, extracts—tables and roll-ups of data that allows them to obtain answers to specific questions being asked by management.

What is different today is that there has been an explosion of tools that have allowed this process to blossom in a way that organizations can now methodically develop their departmental, functional and enterprise-wide data warehouses; going from the experimental phase that characterizes the early stages of adoption of an innovation, to that of wide acceptance and dissemination in which we are today.

We are here as a result of technology. In the early days of the information revolution, most organizations had one computer. Occasionally, very large organizations might have had more than one, but they were specialized to do very focused applications. This centralization allowed substantial power to concentrate in the hands of the "Data Processing (DP) Manager" or "Vice President for Information Processing." The computer installation was a thing to behold, and it was usually put in a glass bowl for everyone to admire from the outside. This was the era of school children touring the computer installations of community-minded organizations. But the primary focus of the DP shop was to develop and run the applications essential to operate the business. Billing, accounts receivable, accounts payable, general ledger, and inventory systems were paramount. And the focus of technology was on how to capture transactions ever faster and faster. And, as a necessary consequence, how to store these records ever more efficiently. The thrust of research and development was on faster processing and more efficient storage.

In the midst of all this, demand for computing was growing and from everywhere in the organization requests were heard for the implementation of new applications. Unfortunately, the difficulties involved in maintaining the existing applications in large and complex organizations often precluded almost all new application development.

Enter the Personal Computer (PC)! In the late 1970s and early 1980s the PC made its revolutionary appearance in the corporate world. With it arrived the era of the end user, where almost any individual, department, or function could start to develop and install their own key applications at a fraction of the time and effort of what putting them on a mainframe might have entailed. With these developments, of course, also came the creation of the databases necessary to run and operate these functional applications.

In the heyday of the PC revolution, we also recall the tremendous diversity of hardware and software platforms that ensued. Soon, even the least complex organizations started to have different databases that had been developed using different standards, database management systems (DBMSs) and often different data models and definitions. With the advent of network technologies, many users started to gain access to these disparate systems through the installation of LANs (Local Area Networks) or WANs (Wide Area Networks).

In the early days we used to speak of an organization's "computer." Today, of course, we know that what we have is a network of networks throughout which processors and databases are shared as resources interacting to accomplish the information processing needs of the enterprise.

This is precisely where data warehousing comes in. It has been increasingly important to be able to obtain a comprehensive and integrated view of the enterprise for the purpose of making decisions about business and how it can improve. The many disparate and most frequently incompatible data bases that resulted from the decades of haphazard systems growth within these organizations has made this process very difficult. In addition, the mergers and acquisitions of the 80s has added substantially to the patchwork cacophony of many enterprises' information systems' resource.

Many anecdotes abound of CEOs trying, and not being able, to get answers to relevant questions, such as: How many 25- to 30-year olds in the Los Angeles metropolitan area bought TV sets from us over the last 5 years? How many active policies has our insurance company issued to retired military personnel in Nebraska since 1975? Which have been our best selling products for German women over the last 10 years? What specific components of our fleet's jet engines have had the largest number of unscheduled maintenance incidents over the last 5 years?

As these difficulties appeared, many enterprises, and the individuals within them, started to experiment with different approaches to extract value from the data their organizations had accumulated over the years. Many were disappointed to find that not only did they have major media compatibility problems, where in many cases they were unable to recover historical information, but even worse, that they could not bring together and harmonize current data resident in diverse systems, for all the reasons we have reviewed.

Even when they could access one single database that may have significant information of particular use, the issue of interfering with the performance of operational systems was in itself a major problem. Hence the emergence of this movement toward extracting data from the operational systems—and in the process, cleaning and transforming it into a new format—and aggregating it in special stores for purpose of analysis.

As this process evolved and perfected itself, these stores began to be called data warehouses; they were defined; and—most important—a plethora of new tools emerged to allow organizations to move into data warehousing in a major mode.

WHAT IS THE PROCESS AND WHERE IS IT GOING?

The next 24 months will surely be a critical period for enterprises in information-intensive industries. Tighter markets and new technology will force these enterprises to invariably transition to a new information paradigm. The main competitive advantage will come from a firm's ability to bond with its clients to ensure loyalty, and the key to this will be relevant, accurate, and timely information made available to managers and analysts as they need it.

This is important, because many large organizations, as we have said, have long been data rich and information poor, resembling informational wastelands incapable of providing useful business intelligence to management—either because of incompatible databases and dysfunctional networks or as a result of ambiguity of definitions leading to irrelevant data. The advent of targeted decision systems, enabled through data warehousing, however, heralds the emergence of a new linchpin of an enterprise's business command center.

Most organizations present some subset of the characteristics described above. Its market, under attack from both traditional and non-traditional competitors, must be able to extract maximum value from its information resources in ways that allow precision marketing, identification of hidden business opportunities, quick detection of new trends in the marketplace, and/or response to key events inside the organization.

When an organization has a solid information system infrastructure in place, the focus is now on enhancing the decision support capabilities for end-users of targeted information resources. This approach usually points to the building of data marts, or departmental data warehouses, that might later be integrated into an enterprise-wide data warehouse.

We are now moving toward a strategy of empowering end-users by giving them the information they need, when they need it. These end-users should also be provided with the ability to drill down and massage information with better OLAP (on-line analytical processing) and data mining tools and have full use of multimedia to enhance their ability to act effectively on information and decision support systems. These strategies will eventually help to enhance the ability to resolve issues with which these end-users are tasked. For this, of course, the enterprise should have a sound model that provides a solid starting point from which to handle critical processes; object libraries (or their equivalents); points of maximum business leverage; and all such other important factors. From here, it is a small step to a data warehouse.

Organizations moving in this direction, should discuss and answer the following questions. First, they would be well served with the development of an enterprise-wide data warehousing strategy, so as not to run the risk of developing a new layer of stovepipe applications through multiple unrelated and incompatible data marts. As an enterprise moves towards a data warehouse, it will need to think through what to put in that warehouse. The principal task will be determining what to extract from legacy systems, how to extract it, transform it, and invariably, clean it. Beyond that, and in order to truly start adding value, it'll be advisable to look at innovative non-traditional internal and external data. Explore the Internet and examine relevant external commercial data bases or news feeds. Look at block by block census information with a Geographical Information System (GIS), video clips and/or specially commissioned market research.

Then one must choose middleware, the software that links the end-user's programs in their PCs with the data warehouse. There are many possible choices and every major vendor has their own recommendation. Product selection is the critical decision issue in this step of a data warehousing project.

Where will you store the data? Here one must deal with design issues before moving to implementation. But depending on the plan, one may decide to go toward a multidimensional database or stick with relational databases. As is happening more frequently, go to a ROLAP (relational OLAP) tool to give multidimensional views from your relational databases. Furthermore, what servers will you use? What storage devices? And how much hardware will you need? In any case, it will be necessary to think through the growth prospects of the warehouse, and even plan a hierarchical storage approach for archival retrieval some years down the road.

Navigating through the data warehouse—that is, knowing what information is there, and how to find it—is the single most important factor leading to the success or failure of the project from the perspective of your end-users. One may have an excellent architecture, and great response times, but if nobody can find what they're looking for, what good is the data warehouse? Hence, the importance of the metadata repository, or the information about information. There are some excellent products available in the marketplace today that can go a long way to assist you with the metadata question. But there is no substitute for common sense. There is also the need for some level of standards in this area. Today, many products generate their own metadata with no uniformity in format whatsoever.

End-users will need to apply the data warehouse to their specific tasks. The tools for the development of applications, the decision support and executive information systems are, again, a critical aspect of a data warehouse. Furthermore, a data warehouse without a DSS/EIS front end to assist end-users in making decisions about the business of the business, is probably an unsuccessful data warehouse. There are a large number of products that can be resorted to here. Power-builder, Pilot Lightship, FOCUS, SAS/EIS, and Comshare are some of the more traditional software tools for building decision support systems.

Alerts are potentially one of the most valuable features that can be obtained from a data warehouse. Once you are up and running, specific variables that define the health of systems or processes can be tracked within the data warehouse, and alerts or alarms can be programmed to "go off" if values go beyond specified thresholds. This can be extremely valuable to management, since early detection and notification is very important in minimizing the cost of fixing almost any business problem.

How is the information delivered to end-users? There are many different approaches, of course, and they need not be mutually exclusive. Traditional well known spreadsheets, such as Lotus 123 or Excel, or even word processors, can be utilized. You can go to your users via the Internet, if you wish, assuming you can handle the integrity and security concerns. But more specific software packages are also available, as will be described in other parts of this volume.

In addition, a successful data warehousing operation needs both process and system management components. There are solid tools in place now that can do many of these tasks as we will describe later on in the book.

In any case, you must decide whether you can justify a data warehouse; and if so, then look at your hardware, software and people. Do you have enough hardware capacity for both normal operations as well as peaks? If not, how are you going to handle them? Do you have the right people to staff a data warehouse with? Should you outsource? If keeping an inside staff, what training do you need?

Even as you're building the data warehouse you should be thinking about issues related to controls and auditability. System integrity and security will also be important issues that no single vendor has a total answer for.

THE DATA WAREHOUSING INSTITUTE

The Data Warehousing Institute (TDWI) was born to address the growing need for quality education and training, with a practitioner's focus, in a vendor-neutral setting. This was important for several reasons. In the early days of any technology, you have a very limited set of sources from which to learn. Usually these sources are in the development labs of the firms that are working on early product applications or the halls of academia.

Once these prototype products are out in the market, of course, pioneering users commence the process of buying, installing and testing their application in a production setting. At this point the market wants to know not just about the features and prices of these products, but also what results the early users have obtained. And, because they are looking for unbiased opinions, they want to hear from real live users and not necessarily from the vendors whose interest is served by selling the product.

Furthermore, in the specific case of data warehousing, there were a number of questions in which only those individuals and organizations that had been in the trenches, building and using data warehouses, could realistically answer. How do you justify the data warehouse to your management? How much does it really cost to build one? Can you design and build it with your current staff or must you bring in outside consultants? How much time from conception to full production? Can you build the data warehouse with existing tools? How do you make it mission critical within your own enterprise?

The Institute was founded to focus precisely on these types of issues, and provide a neutral forum where all stakeholders in the process could come together for education, training, and discussion through a variety of programs and activities. Hence, it runs an Annual Conference and Annual Implementation Conference, both of which are international in scope; as well as some regional or country specific training events. It has launched Special Interest Groups (SIGs) by vertical industries to assist the application of data warehousing in transportation, finance, distribution, health care, public sector, energy and other settings.

The Institute's "Best Data Warehousing Projects" contest is an annual event where specific organizations showcase their data warehousing applications and winners are selected by a panel of Institute judges based on specific criteria.

Publication plays an important role in the Institute's programming. First of all, in order to establish some order in the morass of competitive offerings in the data warehousing marketplace, we published the *1995 Data Warehousing Roadmap,* a wall poster, followed in 1996 by the booklet, *Data Warehousing: What Works?,* which incorporated a diverse number of cases where data warehousing was being used successfully to address real problems around the world.

We launched the *Journal of Data Warehousing* in the Spring of 1996, with Dr. Hugh Watson (University of Georgia) as its editor. The quarterly is intended as the Institute's principal communications vehicle for its associates; and where the debate will take place defining terms, discussing standards, and establishing the academic and intellectual rigor necessary for the legitimate incorporation of this discipline into the world's body of knowledge.

At the same time, of course, we joined forces with Prentice-Hall to publish a series of books on data warehousing with the objective of having it eventually become the seminal reference source for this discipline.

There are many other programs: TDWI's home page on the World Wide Web, the Metadata Users Council, The Data Warehousing Institute's Fellowships, and others. The programs constitute the core components of TDWI's data warehousing campaign.

THE DATA WAREHOUSING INSTITUTE'S CAMPAIGN

Hence, we feel confident asserting that data warehousing is the catalyst that will lead the information industry into its next evolutionary stage—knowledge production. We at The Data Warehousing Institute are committed to leading the effort in this transformation.

What then must be done? We have already embarked on a campaign consisting of five parts, which we envision taking place over the next three years.

1. Laying the common ground
2. Winning the hearts and minds
3. Showing what works
4. Teaching what and how to do it
5. Ensuring quality

Laying a common ground means establishing a shared base of understanding for data warehousing. We need agreement on goals and objectives for the data warehousing community, but also at the very least on vocabulary and definitions.

Winning the hearts and minds entails proselytizing and winning over converts to our team, the data warehousing team. This is the team that will empower knowledge workers by allowing them to obtain maximum yield from the informational assets of their own organizations.

Showing what works is the identification of successful examples of data warehousing, the dissemination of the information of these case studies, and the "best practices" they exemplify.

Teaching what and how to do it involves the development of the training and educational programs to transfer the skills necessary to implement the technology.

Ensuring quality means professionalizing data warehousing and establishing the necessary standards, possibly including the certification of data warehousing managers and professionals.

This campaign will be essential to advance data warehousing as the principal agent of change for information technology to achieve its full potential.

CONCLUSION

As we have already recounted, several years ago the concept of data warehousing was introduced as an experimental approach precisely to empower the embattled analyst by facilitating timely access to focused, relevant, and accurate business intelligence. The results have been remarkable. Since the early years of this decade, hundreds of data warehouses have been successfully built to the high acclaim and testimonials of managers, users, and practitioners alike. The data warehousing process allows knowledge workers to target specific subject areas and extract valuable insights from these information gold mines that they have been unable to exploit in the fast. Furthermore, data warehousing has now gone beyond the experimental stage reserved for pioneers and early adopters and has turned the corner into broad expansion and dissemination.

The Data Warehousing Institute expects to be leading the charge in many aspects of this transformation. In the process it has initiated a solid set of programs, publications and other communications vehicles with which to carry out its campaign. We believe it has importance much beyond its narrow technical domain. Its true importance lies precisely in that data warehousing, and its associated disciplines, are the enablers of knowledge discovery and insight engineering. It is the seed of a new scientific method with which to explore the oceans of observational data points that we must navigate to discover new worlds. Data warehouses are, in brief, knowledge production machines.

Cybernauts of the world, unite! The future holds great potential.

A Roadmap to Data Warehousing

Alan Paller

The Data Warehousing Institute

"Data Warehousing is a journey, not a destination."

. . . and this chapter provides the roadmap to help illuminate the paths available to those who are setting out on the data warehousing journey.

WHICH WAREHOUSE WILL YOU BUILD?

Road maps are valuable for travelers who have an idea where they would like to travel, so we begin with a review of the choice of categories of data warehouses that one might build. Medium and large organizations are currently deploying data warehouses in most or all of these categories.

We use a two-stage approach to categorizing data warehouses. First, we show the categories defined by the type of information users need and the computing environment in which the warehouse will operate. Second, we show how the size of the project budget and the locus of responsibility for that budget, affect the types of warehouses that are being built.

Computing Platforms for Data Warehouses

The first two decisions that will define your data warehouse project are (1) whether to acquire new computers or use existing hardware and (2) what information needs the new system is designed to meet. See Table 2–1.

Table 2–1

	Why is the information needed?	
How busy are the operational computers?	For real-time transaction-based decisions	For pattern-based decisions
Processing power is available on existing equipment	Virtual data warehouse (1)	Enterprise data warehouse and/or data mart (3)
Additional hardware is required	Operational data store (2)	

The term "virtual warehouse" describes the time-tested environment in which users gain query access to operational systems (1). This approach continues to provide value in organizations that have sufficient processing power on their mainframes and departmental transaction systems. Some retail organizations, for example, perform transaction processing at night and have excess capacity during the day. But as the benefits of data mining and complex historical pattern analysis become better understood and as the number of potential users grows from a dozen to a thousand, new equipment becomes inevitable. Thus in time, most organizations will migrate part or all of their data warehousing activities to computers dedicated to the data warehousing/data mining task. When operational data is mirrored on a separate computer for decision support, it is called an operational data store (2). When extensive historical data is maintained, well beyond that in the operational system, the new system is usually called a data warehouse or a data mart (3).

The data warehousing manager cares about which questions are going to be asked because the question defines the data that will be maintained in the system. For decisions that rely on status information (e.g., Do we have enough units in stock to offer a special discount?) you build an operational data store. For decisions that require historical analysis (e.g., Can we offer this client a gift suggestion based on the types of gifts he/she bought last year) or on complex pattern analysis (e.g., Which promotional offers to which clients in which months are most likely to maximize profits?) you build a data warehouse or data mart. The operational data store provides access to real-time or near-real-time transaction data (1 and 2), while the data warehouse or data mart requires access to large volumes of transactions recorded over many months or years (3).

Money Matters

For those who have made the decision to build a data mart or data warehouse, the choice between the two is usually not controlled by technological considerations. Rather, the controlling factors are size of budget and the responsibility for that budget. See Table 2–2.

Table 2–2

	Who has the budget?		
Budget	User Department	IS Department	Combination
under $1 million	Data Mart	Pilot Project	Data Mart
$1 to $10 million	Data Marts and Distributed Data Marts	Mixture of Techniques	Distributed Data Marts
more than $10 million	Distributed Data Marts	Enterprise Data Warehouse	Multi-Tiered Data Warehouse

Multi-Tiered Data Warehouse

Where the Information Systems (IS) Department controls a large budget (over $10 million) for their projects, organizations are attempting to create enterprise-wide data warehouses. Where budgets are smaller or where control is in user departments, data marts and distributed data marts become far more common. The differentiator between a data mart and an enterprise data warehouse is the focus. Data marts are usually single-department warehouses containing a small number of subject areas. Enterprise data warehouses are grand schemes to bring all decision-making data together from across the organization.

Multi-tiered data warehouses are combinations of enterprise data warehouses and data marts. The data marts are fed from transaction systems through the enterprise data warehouse and also from data that has never been in transaction systems.

Distributed data marts are collections of departmental data marts, sometimes centrally managed, but without a central core of data. They occur when multiple departments decide to build data marts independently.

Whichever approach you take—enterprise data warehouse, data mart, distributed data marts, or a multi-tiered data warehouse—you'll face a series of questions. The remainder of this article describes the questions and the types of answers that are available for each of them.

STRUCTURE OF THE ROADMAP

Each segment of the roadmap contains answers to questions that may arise when you are planning and implementing your data warehouse. Here they all are together:

1. How do you justify the warehouse?
2. Data origination and migration:
   Where do the data originate?
   What extracts the data, transforms it, and cleans it?
   What middleware links the sources with the warehouse?
3. Database management, hardware and networking:
   In what database are the warehouse data stored?
   On what computer systems are the data stored?
4. Information analysis and delivery:
   How do people find the information they need?
   What special techniques speed the retrieval?
   How is the data delivered to end users? Query and reporting systems? Multi-dimensional database sys-

tems? Relational On-Line Analytical Processing (OLAP) systems?
What development tools create applications for an Executive Information System (EIS) and a Decision Support System (DSS?)
How is value added through alerts?
5. Management:
What manages the process?
What manages the systems?

Now let's look at each question.

How Do You Justify the Warehouse?

The easy but half-witted way to justify a warehouse is to use generalizations. The most common are:

To save money;

To speed information retrieval;

To become more competitive;

To improve productivity through improved access to information;

and, the all time favorite for this type of system,

To improve decision making.

Each of these claims has been made by thousands of technologists on behalf of tens of thousands of proposed new projects, all long before data warehouses were invented. Senior management—at least those who were awake for the past two decades—is rightfully skeptical when they hear such claims.

Facing the skeptics, some data warehousing planners have found more specific justifications for their projects that seem a little closer to the mark. They say that their data warehouses are being built to:

Lower the cost of information access overall

Improve customer responsiveness through better information

Identify hidden business opportunities

Perform precision marketing or mass customization

These claims sometimes get the money approved. As good as they sound, however, they too lead to confusion and ultimately to dissatisfaction. They are simply too general.

The long-term solution to the justification challenge is to link the data warehousing initiative to an essential business objective that has already been chosen by top management. Then you demonstrate how the warehouse will help the organization accomplish the objective. A data warehouse that is tightly linked to an important business objective will, if it meets its promises, maintain its economic justification as long as the objective exists and will be looked at as a model for a solution to other key business objectives that rely on effective use of information.

Data Origination and Migration

If the goal of a data warehouse is to make an organization's information readily available for mining and analysis, then an important leg of the data warehousing journey involves finding the information that will be used, developing methods of acquiring and cleaning that information, and automating the process of moving that information into a staging area where it is available for immediate use. Experienced data warehousing managers report that the bulk of the unexpected costs in their projects were consumed in data cleaning and transformation. Three questions are generally asked: (1) Where do the data originate; (2) What extracts the data, transforms it, and cleans it; and (3) What middleware links the sources with the warehouse?

Where do the data originate?

The easy answer is "in transaction systems" and certainly some warehouse data comes from those systems. But other data comes from external sources such as market research companies, departmental PCs, and a wide variety of other sources. If your plans encompass only the relatively simple numeric and character data contained in transaction systems, then you will not be ready to respond when users' information needs go beyond transaction data. Documents are the most important type of information that demand attention from data warehousing managers—and documents include not only formatting of text and graphics, but also the history and collaboration of information that make documents relevant and respected.

To be included in this box of the road map, a data source simply needs to be in wide use in business or government.

What extracts the data, transforms it, and cleans it?

Data transformation, replication, and cleaning tools promise to automate the movement of information from legacy data sources into relational databases. Each type is described below. However, data in original sources usually has at least two problems that must be solved before it can be useful in a warehouse: (1) multiple names for the same customer and/or supplier of other business entities and (2) overlapping or confusing codes and definitions. In addition, internal consistency and just plain accuracy problems can damage the value. These problems are not easy to solve and transformation and cleaning tools do not automatically eliminate them. Transformation and cleaning tools do, however, reduce the manual effort involved in solving the problems.

There are three principal types of data acquisition, transformation, and cleaning products: data copying and replication tools, code generators, and data cleaning tools. They solve complementary problems; many large data warehousing sites use all three:

- Data copying and replication tools make exact duplicates of data. Replication tools, usually purchased from the database vendor, move data from relational databases to relational databases, so they don't solve the problem of acquiring data from non-relational sources. Bulk data copy tools can move data from non-relational sources into relational databases and often do it very quickly. Neither of these tools, however, transform or clean the data, though some replication tools are gaining this capability.

- Data transformation tools extract information from both relational databases and non-relational sources.

They convert codes, aggregate, and calculate derived values. They function by creating new programs (they are sometimes called code generators) that run regularly to extract and change the data. Upon seeing how they work, many companies decide that they can write their own programs to do the same thing. Do-it-yourself, using COBOL, SAS, Focus, or other widely used languages, works well for small projects, but for large projects with seven or more data sources and/or continuing user demands for new data, the automation offered by these tools can more than pay for them in just a few months.

- Data cleaning tools help solve the very difficult problem of bringing together information about customers or suppliers when the original records used different spellings for their identification. Data entry clerks may enter a name in a wide variety of formats (AT&T ATandT and ATT are just three of the more than 60 ways this company's name has been spelled). Using increasingly sophisticated algorithms (and knowledge), data cleaning systems assist companies in automating the transformation of formats and spellings into a common format. They can pay for themselves very quickly simply from the decreased postage costs for duplicate mailings, and they can help companies get closer to their customers.

To be included in this box, a software product must be used primarily for replication, code generation, or data cleaning. Tools such as COBOL, Natural, Focus, and SAS are included because they are often used in lieu of specialized tools.

What middleware links the sources with the warehouse?

Data warehousing users interact with programs on their PCs while the data they want is usually stored on another computer. Middleware connects the two programs so that their incompatibilities are invisible to the user. For organizations that decide to build a virtual data warehouse (where the data remains in the transaction systems and users have query access), a sophisticated type of middleware makes non-relational information available to SQL queries. However, performance of these systems does not usually satisfy harried knowledge workers so they are used for batch reporting and downloading more frequently than for real-time queries. Other middleware connects query tools with relational databases and allow one PC to get data from others as well as from database servers.

To be included in this box, tools must either be database gateways or they must offer other intelligent functions that help connect databases with tools.

Database Management, Hardware, and Networking

The largest component of the tools budget for data warehousing is invested in hardware and database management. Thus the questions in this section are central to the warehousing decision process.

In what database are the warehouse data stored?

The great debate of 1995 was whether to store critical data warehousing information, needed for rapid retrieval, in relational databases or in specialized structures called multi-dimensional databases. The specialized structures offer very rapid access; the relational databases offer the confidence of well-understood management, back-up, and recovery. End-users—especially senior managers—like the speed and are the principal force behind the MDD (multi-dimensional database) successes. However, when databases get too large (something over 10 gigabytes) MDD performance actually lags that of a relational database. Furthermore, new developments in 64-bit and parallel hardware and in database indexing technology are making relational databases faster and faster (see The Data Warehousing Institute's "Trends Shaping Data Warehousing In 1996" for details on these performance improvements).

Many organizations use a dual approach in which most data are stored in relational databases and specialized data are stored in multi-dimensional databases. This dual approach is being encouraged by the merger of multi-dimensional database software vendors into relational database management companies. The acquiring database management vendors can provide integration between the two and allow "drill-through" from multi-dimensional data to the underlying information in the relational database.

To be included in this box, software must either be a relational or multi-dimensional database or an older style of database with such a large user community that people use it for data warehousing just because it is available and because people know how to use it.

On what computer systems are the data stored?

Successful data warehouses and data marts can be found on mainframes, on UNIX/RISC (Reduced Instruction Set Computer) systems, and on Intel-based computers. What is not well understood, however, is how to calculate the size of the machines that are needed for data warehousing. Demand for data warehousing is unpredictable. Much of the demand emerges from people and departments that showed no interest in data warehousing when it was first proposed. Thus the initial estimates of computing power needed for data warehousing are usually wrong—so wrong that organizations must often buy an entirely new large computer within a few months after a successful data warehouse begins.

To be included in this box, a computer must be in common use as a server for data warehousing.

Information Analysis and Delivery

How do people find the information they need?

Once a data warehouse is populated with any reasonable amount of data, finding the right information is a challenge for users. When users have trouble finding what they want, or worse, when they find the wrong information, they will, at best, avoid the data warehouse. At worst, they will actively try to destroy it. Hence, good user help for finding information is a critical success factor in data warehousing.

To be included in this box, a tool must have specific functions that assists users in identifying the information they want and/or in helping users ensure the information they found is the right information from the correct source.

What special techniques speed the retrieval?

A few months after a data warehouse goes into operation, the number one job of data warehousing managers and technologists becomes improving query performance. Users have come to expect fast response, but as data and usage expand, the system isn't able to respond as quickly as it did during the demonstration phase. One common option is to buy additional hardware and many data warehousing managers do that, but there are other approaches to performance improvement. This box lists many of them, from statistical query optimizers to bit-mapped indices to smart summary table-makers and smart storage systems. Because of the critical role that performance plays in the reputation of a data warehouse, every vendor has developed technology that improves performance. There are always trade-offs, however, and benchmarking your load is probably the only sensible way to understand the differences among the various approaches.

How is the data delivered to end users? Query and reporting systems? Multi-dimensional database systems? Relational OLAP systems?

The largest category of products in data warehousing comprises the tools that sit on the desktop or on servers and help users retrieve and analyze the data in the warehouse. More than 150 vendors offer such tools in many sub-categories. The trade-offs between those sub-categories—reporting systems, managed query systems, OLAP tools, and relational OLAP tools—are complex and are at the heart of the service that your data warehouse provides to its users. Issues abound. Should the tools deliver information through proprietary desktop software (that must be updated by the data warehousing manager) or through widely available web browsers? Should the tools allow direct access back to the detailed data?

We will cover these and related trade-offs in a thorough analysis at another time.

To be included in this box, a tool needs to be capable of extracting information from one or more of the common databases used for data warehousing and deliver that data to users who make *ad hoc* requests.

What development tools create applications for EIS and DSS?

Ad hoc requests are a small part of the ultimate use of a data warehouse. Packaged queries and packaged reports with preplanned analytical functions are much more widely used—especially after the warehouse has been operational for several months. To create these systems customized to answer specific questions—often called executive information systems and decision support systems—technologists must develop software. They do that using the C or C++ language or they use one of the many client server development tools that have gained popularity over the past decade.

To be included in this box, a product must have a programming language or procedure that allows developers to create custom information delivery systems that extract data from databases and deliver it on desktop computers.

How is value added through alerts?

Though *ad hoc* requests and regular reports are the primary delivery vehicle for most data warehouses, a growing contingent of users is moving toward exception reporting or alerts. Alert systems monitor specific indicators or combinations of indicators and send out emails or other notices whenever values exceed pre-specified ranges. When an alert system is well synchronized with the key objectives of a department or business, it can be of enormous value to the business managers and to the career of the data warehousing manager who created it.

To be included in this box, a software product must have trigger or intelligent agent technology that monitor indicators in the data being maintained in a data warehouse.

Management

What manages the process?

The least well developed technology of data warehousing is management. Some tools exist and they are quite innovative but most of the hard problems of managing very large databases are not well understood or solved. Tools in this category are primarily metadata management facilities and data movement monitors.

What manages the systems?

Systems and network management are mature technologies with a wealth of strong products. These tools provide security, network monitoring, backup, console automation, and more. To be included in this box, a product must offer system and/or network management and be in widespread use on UNIX systems and other computers used for data warehousing.

THE BOTTOM LINE

Data warehousing is far more than copying data from a mainframe to a UNIX or NT computer and giving users easy access to the data. Modern data warehouses have management infrastructures, rich user access methods and alerts, performance boosters, and custom applications all designed to make the information a powerful tool for business.

In such a complex field, a well-designed architecture can be of great value. On the other hand, too much emphasis on architecture can get in the way of effective business planning. The roadmap outlined here (and available as a periodically updated wall poster) offers a balance between too much and too little architecture. It also provides a common framework for discussion of changes to the warehouse and for assessment of the appropriateness of new tools that emerge from the vendors.

An Introduction to Data Warehousing

Herb Edelstein

Two Crows Corporation

Since the advent of commercial computing in the 1950s, businesses have been searching for the ability to provide management with the information it needs to run the business more effectively. For decades, Management Information Systems meant little more than enormous reports of various corporate activities. In the 1960s the arrival of database management systems (DBMSs) were going to increase the availability of information by centralizing it in a corporate data store that could be easily accessed for information. The difficulty of using early DBMSs such as IBM's IMS or Cullinet's IDMS for query purposes, coupled with their intrinsic lack of flexibility, made them unsuitable for true decision support, and even the development of the more flexible relational model of DBMS wasn't enough.

Complicating the problem was the fact that companies didn't really have a centralized data store. Rather, they had different databases, typically with different database management systems, supporting a multitude of applications. Even where there was a "corporate database" there were other databases as part of applications such as a contract management system, an inventory system, a human resources system, etc. When management needed answers that required data spanning these databases, they were often disappointed that it was impossible to get those answers.

Data warehousing has changed all this. At last, information is available that allows knowledge workers to make informed decisions in doing their jobs, regardless of into which database the data was originally collected. Furthermore data warehousing does this without significantly reducing the performance of a company's transaction systems. Many data warehousing queries involve retrieving enormous amounts of data and joining many large tables. It is impossible to perform these operations without materially reducing the rate at which transactions can be processed.

A data warehouse does this by collecting the data from the different application databases and storing them in a common, integrated database. Not only is current data consolidated from transaction databases, but historical data from these applications is also part of the data warehouse. As we shall see later on, integrating these disparate databases is a very difficult task.

USES OF A DATA WAREHOUSE

A data warehouse has three primary uses. First, it is used for the presentation of standard reports and graphs. While such reporting has always been a part of transaction applications, data warehouses extend it and make it easier by allowing data from different transaction systems, which has already been consolidated into the warehouse, to be used in reporting.

Second, they also support a type of query and reporting called dimensional analysis, which greatly simplifies looking at data summaries across a number of important attributes called dimensions. It also facilitates comparing results across different dimensional values, especially time periods.

This capability is very useful when trying to answer questions about why something happened as opposed to what happened. For example, "Why were sales up in the New England region but not in the Mid-Atlantic?" or "Why are we over budget?" It helps answer these questions by enabling the knowledge worker to investigate a hypothesis through successive interactive query of the database at ever greater detail and from different dimensional viewpoints.

Lastly, the data warehouse is a key enabler of an exciting new technology called data mining. Data mining automatically recognizes patterns in the data to help you describe existing data and predict future behaviors based on current characteristics. Essentially, it is a way of answering questions you did not know enough to ask.

DATA WAREHOUSES VS. TRANSACTION SYSTEMS

Traditional transaction applications and data warehousing applications are poles apart in their design requirements and operational characteristics. It is important to understand these differences to avoid the trap of designing a data warehouse as if it were an on-line transaction processing (OLTP) application.

OLTP applications are organized about the transactions they perform, such as entering orders, updating inventory, or moving money between accounts. On the other hand, a data warehouse is organized about a particular subject, such as the customer or product. For example, customer information may reside in an order entry application, an accounts receivable application, a customer service application, and a credit authorization application. There is also additional information about former customers that resides in archived files. When designing the data warehouse to ease the access to customer information, all of this data will be consolidated into a single customer data warehouse.

Another difference is that the number of users of a data warehouse tends to be smaller than for an OLTP system. It is not uncommon for a single OLTP system to have hundreds if not thousands of users simultaneously entering transactions, whereas most data warehouses have at most a few hundred users and frequently well under one hundred.

In part, the smaller number of users stems from the nature of a transaction in an OLTP system, which tends to be short and accesses relatively few records. Quite often, the transaction uses the primary key of the record to be updated and has no need to access any other records. It's not surprising to find OLTP systems performing such short transactions at a rate of hundreds of transactions per second with each transaction being completed in less than a few seconds.

However, the data warehouse query may need to look at many rows, even an entire table of one billion rows, to get its answer. Finding an answer may require joining five or more tables, each with tens or hundreds of million rows. It's not surprising that response time may be measured in minutes or hours for these queries and that even a small number of users with the right (or wrong) workload can tie up quite a large machine.

Another factor is that OLTP databases tend to be smaller than data warehouses. This is not surprising in that the data warehouse is not only consolidating data from multiple OLTP databases, but keeping the data around rather than purging it every month or so. There is also the historical data that is part of the data warehouse to add to its bulk. Thus, a 50 gigabyte OLTP database would be considered quite large and a terabyte OLTP database unheard of. Data warehouses commonly range in size from a few gigabytes to hundreds of gigabytes, with an increasing number that contain a few terabytes of data!

Another difference is that an OLTP database design is a highly normalized data structure consisting of many tables each of which tends to have a relatively small number of columns. Data warehouses will have fewer tables, because they are devoted to particular subjects, but many of those tables will have a large number of columns. This is because of the large amount of attributes pertaining to the entities in the warehouse and because the tables are often denormalized to improve performance. Furthermore, because of the historic data, the tables have many more rows than the corresponding transaction database tables.

The presence of historic data also points out another element that distinguishes data warehouses from OLTP systems—the importance of time as an attribute of entities. While most transactions include a date or time for an occurrence, in a data warehouse, this time value plays an important role in aggregating and comparing values, and looking at trends. Furthermore, rather than being summed just for the few periods that a transaction system keeps its data, the warehouse data may go back for years.

One of the most significant differences is that warehouse data is updated in batch periodically as opposed to the continuous updating of transaction systems. Each update to the source transaction systems becomes part of an input stream that must be processed and added to the data warehouse. Typically, this is done every night or once a month, although other periods (such as quarterly) are also used.

Keep in mind that while OLTP applications are radically different from data warehousing applications, there are applications that partake of the characteristics of both. For example, customer service applications may require a consolidated data warehouse that includes historic as well as current product and customer information, while at the same time needing to process the collection of transactions that make up a customer service request. Additionally, a customer service system may have a large number of interactive users. Consequently, the developer will need to simultaneously address many of the problems of both an OLTP system and a data warehouse.

What Makes Data Warehousing Difficult

From these differences it's easy to see that the sources of difficulty in data warehousing are very different from the those in OLTP systems. This has occasionally led OLTP developers to mistakenly assert that data warehousing is an easier application because it doesn't require managing concurrent updates from hundreds of users all demanding instantaneous response, nor managing the administrative complexities of logs and failure recovery.

But data warehousing has its own set of problems that make it a far from easy application to implement.

First is the sheer size of the database involved. What may be simple with 100 megabytes of data is difficult with 100 gigabytes of data. Even something so seemingly straightforward as a database backup is complicated when the time to backup exceeds the time between updates, or when the periodic updates to the warehouse are so voluminous that they can't be done in the time available.

Second is the database design problem. An OLTP design tends to be relatively stable, because the transaction definitions are stable. However, a data warehouse design is under constant pressure to adapt to changing requirements.

These changes come from two sources. First the source databases may change, new sources may be added, or old sources deleted. The second source is more common and more important. The data warehouse design is based on a careful analysis of user requirements. But the answers to queries often veer off in unanticipated directions, requiring information, calculations, summaries, or data structures that are not in the warehouse. Thus the warehouse design needs to be organic in that it constantly evolves to meet the new user demands.

The third reason is by far the most challenging, and that is the problem of integrating data from many sources as well as historic data. The quality of the data and the variations in its form are the toughest obstacle to building good data warehouses. We'll examine this topic in more depth in a latter section.

DATA WAREHOUSE COMPONENTS AND ARCHITECTURES

Now that we know what a data warehouse is, we need to examine the components of a data warehouse and how they are organized.

A data warehouse is made up of:

- data migration tools which access the source data and transform it;

- metadata repositories that describe the data warehouse;

- a warehouse data store that provides rapid access to the data;

- a collection of tools for retrieving, formatting, and analyzing the data; and

- tools for managing the warehouse environment.

An enterprise data warehouse collects all the information about a number of subjects (such as customers, products, sales, real estate, or personnel) that span the entire organization. Because of its size, central location, and database design, it may be appropriate to subset the data warehouse based on the needs of particular groups. Therefore, these subsets, or data marts, may be copied from the enterprise data warehouse on to other computers as data warehouses in their own right.

Data marts (Figure 3–1) are data warehouses in their own right, and may be as large (or even larger) than the data warehouse that spawned them. They are built to meet particular focused needs. For example, the West region may only care about data that pertains to them and would like to work with that geographic subset. The Marketing Department might only care about customer, product, and sales data, and wants that subject subset. A group in the Marketing Department needs to do data analysis that is best supported by a dimensional structure, so a data mart with the data structures and summaries appropriate for multi-dimensional analysis is set up for them. Because of summarization, this last example could grow larger than the source data warehouse.

In some cases, the size of the enterprise might result in a very large and complex enterprise data warehouse that requires years to build. Therefore, some companies have started building the data marts first, so that they can benefit much sooner from data warehousing. They intend to take a "bottom up" approach to building their enterprise warehouse as opposed to a "top down" approach as described above.

Figure 3–1   Types of Data Warehouses

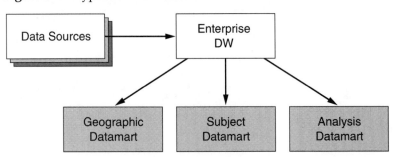

However, there is a potential problem that the data marts will prove difficult to integrate if they are not designed from the beginning to mesh. The same inconsistencies that plague a data warehouse constructed from transaction systems or other legacy databases can arise from uncoordinated data marts. Unfortunately, planning the data marts to mesh may prove almost as difficult as building the enterprise data warehouse to start with.

In addition to the types of data warehouses, the architecture must also address which computers the warehouse data reside and where the calculations will be performed. There are five main variations.

Typically, the enterprise data warehouse data is structured to be as flexibile as possible in order to answer the entire spectrum of current and future requirements. This usually means a standard relational DBMS and an entity relationship type of design, with some summaries and denormalization added for performance. This kind of data warehouse design is sometimes called an atomic data warehouse.

The data warehouse application is a client-server application. The role of the client in all the variations generally includes managing the user interaction and formatting and reporting data retrieved from the warehouse.

However, desktop applications may also need to perform all the complex calculations and summaries that go beyond the capabilities of the warehouse DBMS's SQL. This two tier architecture (Figure 3–2) is sometimes called a "fat client" approach because of the heavy demands made on the client computer.

Figure 3–2 Two-Tier Architecture

Desktop

User interface
Data analysis
Report formatting
Summarize
Calculate

Data Warehouse

Calculate
Summarize
Summarized data

© Two Crows Corporation

When doing dimensional analysis, the client software may require the data to be structured as a star schema that simplifies both the software operation and the user view of the data. The data for this may be either in a data mart (Figure 3–3) or the data warehouse itself.

Figure 3–3 Three-Tier Architecture

Desktop

User interface
Data analysis
Report formatting
Summarize
Calculate

Star Server

Calculate
Summarize
Summarized data

Data Warehouse
Datamart

Calculate
Summarize
Summarized data

© Two Crows Corporation

It is becoming increasingly common to add an application server between the client and the warehouse to improve performance and reduce network traffic in what is called a three tier architecture (Figure 3–4). This application server manages the interaction with the warehouse, performs the necessary calculations, and sends results to the client. The client remains responsible for managing the user interaction and formatting and reporting resulting data, but requires less horsepower due to the reduced calculations and database server interaction. As in the two tier architecture, the application server may go directly to the data warehouse or to a data mart with a star schema.

Figure 3–4   Three-Tier Architecture

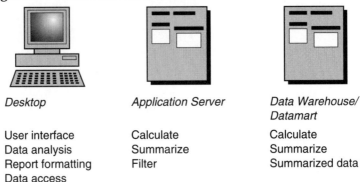

Desktop	Application Server	Data Warehouse/ Datamart
User interface	Calculate	Calculate
Data analysis	Summarize	Summarize
Report formatting	Filter	Summarized data
Data access		

© Two Crows Corporation

The last variation in a three-tier architecture is a special type of DBMS called a multi-dimensional database (MDD) that stores the data in a special structure designed to facilitate dimensional analysis (Figure 3–5). We'll look more closely at MDDs in a latter section.

Figure 3–5   Three-Tier MDD Architecture

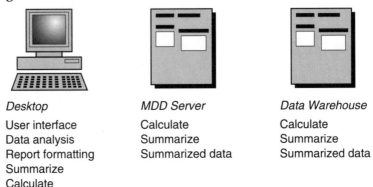

Desktop	MDD Server	Data Warehouse
User interface	Calculate	Calculate
Data analysis	Summarize	Summarize
Report formatting	Summarized data	Summarized data
Summarize		
Calculate		

© Two Crows Corporation

DATA QUALITY

As was indicated above, one of the most difficult problems in building a data warehouse is to ensure the quality of the data. The old computer aphorism "garbage in, garbage out" (GIGO) was never more true than in the case of data warehouses, where a few wrong answers can have a major effect on a company if they result in wrong decisions. Once knowledge workers lose confidence in the warehouse, its effectiveness is severely undermined.

When integrating data from multiple transaction systems and from archived data, the quality problem becomes obvious. Virtually everybody's first data warehouse project surprises them with the bad data they find.

For example, within a single database there may be missing values, such as not recording the price of a sale or incorrect values, such as a product color of yellow when yellow was never used in manufacturing the product. Records may reference other records that are not there, such as a sales order referencing a nonexistent salesperson. Data may be inconsistently recorded within a database, such as the full name of a company or its commonly used abbreviation.

The problem is worse when trying to reconcile differences between databases. As in a single database, there will of course be inconsistent values. But what makes the problem more difficult is the differences in the way data is defined and used or data heterogeneity.

For example, two fields will have the same name but refer to different things (homonyms), such as cost meaning the price of an item or the selling price of a collection of items. A related problem is synonyms in which the same thing is called by two different names, such as two fields named color and colour or grade and class. Different units may be used to measure things such as price in U.S. dollars or British pounds. Another problem may be that relationships are different. For example, one database breaks sales down by regions and states whereas another breaks sales down by regions, districts, and states.

It is important to recognize that no matter how thorough you are in looking for quality problems, somewhere in the many gigabytes of data you are migrating, there will likely be problems that you miss or that are totally undetectable. A number of companies have introduced vary useful tools to help detect quality violations, but expect some problems to slip through.

Not only is finding all the data quality problems difficult, but correcting the problems may be impossible because the correct information is no longer obtainable. This is particularly evident with older data. In such cases, it will be necessary to develop consistent policies such as default values that make the users aware of potential problems, while not stopping them from doing the queries and analysis they need to do.

DATA MIGRATION AND LOAD

The process of migrating data from the source database to the data warehouses is really made up of two very different operations. First is the problem of initializing the warehouse and second is the problem of periodically updating it.

To initialize the data warehouse, the first step is to extract the desired data from the source databases. This can be done by writing a custom program or using a data extraction tool. The next step is to detect and fix the quality problems.

The data must then be mapped to the data warehouse data structure. The warehouse database design will have removed the differences in data names, attributes, and relationships, so you will have to carefully establish the correspondences. For example, multiple fields with different names will supply values for a single field in the data warehouse.

As part of the warehouse design, certain calculations will be defined, such as "xprice = price * qty". In addition certain summaries will have been defined, so common calculations do not have to be repeated. For example, rather than recalculate monthly and daily sales whenever the data is retrieved, the totals may be calculated and stored for faster response.

The load process may involve some preprocessing steps, such as sorting the data and performing any calculations or aggregations. The amount of time to load the data can be quite long, even with parallel computers, given the volumes of data, the number of calculations, and the need to build indexes.

All of these steps need to be performed when updating the data warehouse. What makes that problem more difficult is that this batch update must be performed in a limited window of opportunity when the warehouse can be taken off-line.

Some people advocate rebuilding the warehouse every time you update it. Indeed, if there is a change to the data structure or the database has lots of summaries to be recalculated, a rebuild may be necessary. But the penalty is making the warehouse unavailable for as much as 12 hours or even considerably more for large warehouses.

Therefore, it is desirable to extract only the changes from the source databases and apply those to the data warehouse. This is a complex task because pulling off only the changed data is not easy, using only change data can obscure quality problems (such as incorrect references), and updating the data warehouse, including performing the necessary calculations to change aggregates, is harder than simply loading it (and may not be shorter).

However, with care and planning, incremental updates of the warehouse are often successful.

METADATA

One of the most important tools in migrating data, managing the warehouse, and using the warehouse is the metadata repository. A metadata repository is a database that describes various aspects of the data in the data warehouse. Despite its importance, it is one of the least understood and least mature aspects of data warehousing. This is in part because of all the different uses of metadata and consequent variety of repositories. Metadata can be divided into two broad categories: administrative metadata and end-user metadata.

Administrative metadata contains description of the source databases and their contents, the data warehouse objects, and the transformations required to move data from the sources into the data warehouse. It will also contain operational information such as a history of the migrated data, what organizations were responsible for the source data creation, what happened during the migration, what data has been purged or is scheduled to be purged, who is using data and in what way, as well as a host of other things.

The end-user metadata helps users create their queries and interpret the results. For example, a user may need to know information about where the data came from, what kinds of transformations it underwent, what other names it is known by, or what business policies were in effect at various times when the original data was generated. The user may also need to know the definitions of the warehouse data as well as descriptions of it and consolidation hierarchies for dimensions.

Most products in the data warehousing arena have their own unique metadata repositories. There are no real standards for metadata, and it is not clear that with the variety of tools out there that any standards will ever be successfully promulgated. However, some tools can read other tools repositories to populate their own.

MANAGING THE DATA WAREHOUSE

Managing the data warehouse can generally be divided into two categories of tasks—data administration and process administration.

One of the first tasks in data administration is capacity planning. A data warehouse has a very large database with numerous, complex queries being performed against it. It is important to properly size the data storage, I/O capacity, and CPU capacity. The amount of source data going into the data warehouse can easily grow, as can the amount of storage, especially when moving from an atomic warehouse design to a highly summarized database. In one example, about 200 megabytes of atomic data grew into 43 gigabytes of multidimensional data!

The large amount of data will require careful physical database design, including partitioning data across multiple I/O subsystems so that the warehouse data DBMS can retrieve data in parallel. The number and capacity of these I/O subsystems must be adequate to keep the data warehouse performance from being choked.

It is less common for a data warehouse to be CPU bound, but you should still gauge the adequacy of your compute engine, especially in a two tier architecture that places a large calculation burden on the warehouse DBMS that is also getting plenty of data from a well designed I/O.

Once you have sized your storage needs, you must continue to manage it. For example data warehouse users may need frequent access to the last two years data, and less frequent access to the prior three years. It may be cost effective to establish a hierarchical storage management system in which the infrequently used data is stored in "near on-line" storage such as an optical disk juke box or tape juke box.

It is also important to establish purging rules for a data warehouse. Because the warehouse contains historical data, many people think that you should never get rid of any data because someday you may need it. However, data storage, while relatively cheap, is still not free. More importantly, data kept past its useful and legally mandated life may someday be required for discovery proceedings. No matter how innocuous the data is, the cost of providing it may be an unwelcome expense.

Another important aspect of data administration is security. Integrating data from many different systems makes it much easier for your knowledge workers to find out information about your business, but it also makes it much easier for people whom you would rather not have this information to get it. Bank robber Willie Sutton is famous for supposedly saying he robbed banks "because that's where the money is," and people may come to your data warehouse because that's where the information is. Therefore you must be especially cautious in guarding the warehouse.

It is also necessary to maintain a backup copy of the data warehouse to protect against unfortunate accidents such as head crashes, fires, flood, or other natural disasters. Even if all the data is available to recreate the data warehouse, you don't want to undergo either the cost or the burden.

Data administration is also responsible for tracking who is using the data and how the data is being used. This is important information for tuning the system as well as for helping designers better understand how the system is being used in practice.

Process administration ensures that all the things that have to happen for the warehouse to stay accurate and up-to-date are occurring. This includes monitoring the update process, such as the changes from the source databases, validating the quality of the new data, making sure that the existing warehouse hasn't been corrupted, and subsetting the enterprise data warehouse into the appropriate data marts.

These operations require sequencing events to make sure that they occur and coordinate both people and computer programs. Not surprisingly, workflow software, which was developed to provide this functionality for other applications, is beginning to find a home in data warehousing.

WAREHOUSE DATA STORE

The data warehouse data may be stored in:

- existing transaction databases (either relational or non-relational);
- copy databases from transactional databases;
- relational databases; or
- multi-dimensional databases.

Some people have tried to use database gateways to access existing transaction databases like the warehouse data store (sometimes called virtual data warehouses), but this is not a good idea. It usually doesn't perform well on the warehouse queries, there are many unanswerable queries, and the source database performance is reduced. This is because, as we saw above, transaction processing is incompatible with the query burden of data warehousing. Furthermore, if those queries need to gather data from multiple databases connected over a wide area network, the amount of data transferred will be so great that performance will be totally unacceptable in the vast majority of cases. Furthermore, neither the source data nor the historical data has been properly integrated with the inconsistencies resolved or the quality problems addressed, making it difficult to get good answers, or even any kind of answer in many cases.

Taking a single transaction database and creating a query copy is very commonly done, and addresses the application incompatibility. In those cases where your queries can be satisfied with the copied data, the solution is adequate. However, the problems for which people build consolidated, integrated data warehouses can not usually be solved by this method.

In general, the warehouse data store is a relational database, especially in the case of an atomic database where the queries are best solved by an entity-relationship design, even one in which the data structure has been denormalized for performance reasons. This is true for both enterprise warehouses and data marts.

However, an important question that arises is what kind of database should be used for multi-dimensional analysis: a relational database or a special purpose database called a multi-dimensional database (MDD)?

Multi-dimensional views of a data store (Figure 3–6) allow users to look at the details and aggregates of business measurements in a data warehouse by the attributes of those measurements. Measurements (or facts) are the numbers that quantify what the business process is doing, such as dollar sales, unit sales, or number of employees. The lowest level of detail (or granularity) is the minimum level of aggregation appropriate. Typically data is stored at the detail level or aggregated by the day, week, or month.

Dimensions are the attributes that describe the measurements such as product, sales unit, or time. These dimensions may have hierarchical relationships such as:

- product: category, packaging, brand
- sales unit: region, state, office, person
- time: Year, quarter, month, week, day

Measurement may be described by as many as 20 dimensions, but users typically only work with two to four at a time.

Figure 3–6 Multidimensional Views

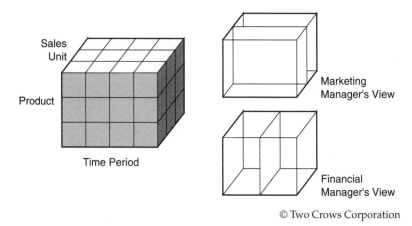

There are two primary reasons for advocating an MDD: speed and special operators for doing multi-dimensional analysis. However, relational databases in conjunction with multi-dimensional analysis tools can often supply the needed speed and operators, without sacrificing the generality of the relational model. Relational databases used in this fashion frequently require a particular style of database structure called a star schema.

As of this writing, there are many good tools of both types that can solve a wide range of multi-dimensional problems.

WAREHOUSE DBMS PERFORMANCE

Given the large size of data warehouses and the emphasis on queries as opposed to updating, what can be done to speed up response time and allow the DBMS to serve more users?

The first part of the answer is to improve the software with better access methods and the access optimizers to use them. Virtually all relational databases support B-tree and sequential access as fundamental access methods and some also support hashed access to data. While these methods are adequate for transaction applications that are dealing with only relatively small tables and result sets and for which the transactions are well known in advance, they begin to break down in data warehouses where the tables and result sets are very large and you don't know your query ahead of time, so you don't have the proper indexes.

One possible improvement is to add a type of index called a bit-map which allows many queries to be resolved in the index and can provide a real speed increase. Unfortunately, bit-maps are not useful all types of data, and an optimizer must be able to use mixed indexes.

Another possibility is to add index structures that speed up star joins or to allow frequently performed joins to be pre-defined.

The key to success with these kinds of index structures is the sophistication of the optimizer.

Another approach is for the DBMS vendor to redesign the storage structures of the relational database from scratch and customize them for data warehousing. Since the data warehouse needs to be a different database from the source databases, using a special purpose DBMS adds the most performance with only a small price to pay of administering a new DBMS. This has been done with both relational DBMSs, which are applicable to a broad range of data warehouse problems, and with multi-dimensional databases, which are limited to multi-dimensional analysis.

Beyond modifying the software, it is possible to use parallel hardware in conjunction with parallel DBMSs. The fundamental idea behind parallel hardware is that through assembling standard building blocks you can achieve scalability that is as close to linear as possible. Linear scalability means (roughly) that if you double the number of building blocks you double the size of the database and keep response time the same (scale-up) or you can double the number of building blocks and halve the response time (speed-up). Not surprisingly, bigger hardware is more expensive.

DBMSs take advantage of parallel hardware in a number of common ways. They will allow you to partition the data across I/O subsystems and retrieve it in parallel, search it in parallel, load and index it in parallel, and back it up in parallel.

There are substantial differences in hardware and software approaches for doing this, but since the goal is scalability of the warehouse, the effectiveness with which they achieve the goal can in principle be measured. In practice, the sizes of the databases are so large and there are so many variables in using parallel hardware and software that benchmarking is an expensive and time consuming task.

Of course, new index methods or specialized databases should be able to take advantage of parallel hardware for maximum scalablility.

CONCLUSION

Data warehousing is not a single solution, application, product, or architecture. Rather it is a collection of techniques and technologies that together can provide a pragmatic and systematic approach to dealing with the problem of end-user accessibility to information that has been distributed across an organization. As organization requirements grow and change, the data warehouse must evolve with them.

Delivering on the promise of data warehousing is not quick, cheap, or easy. It requires the dedication and hard work of both information systems professionals and knowledge workers to achieve success. But, for those companies that build good warehouses and make effective use of them, the payoffs are enormous. The insights into your business will result not only in great savings but improved revenue and more satisfied customers.

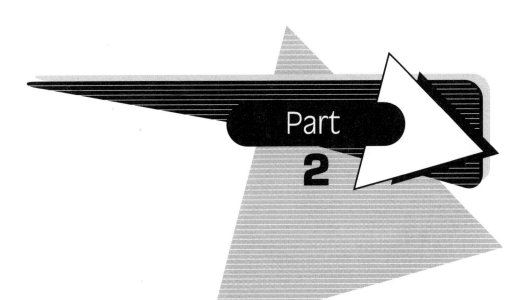

Part 2

PLANNING THE DATA WAREHOUSE

Developing a Data Warehousing Strategy

Ellen J. Levin

Barquin and Associates

INTRODUCTION

Business, government, and educational organizations are undertaking data warehousing projects in order to satisfy the information needs of their users. A number of these efforts have been "point" solutions, which address specific, often narrow requirements of a single department. While providing immediate benefit, they do little to help organizations escape from the stovepipe approaches of the past, and in fact, create further barriers to supporting the integrated organization of the future. As organizations engage in business process reengineering efforts, they find that their existing systems prevent them from looking at the business in an integrated way. One solution for them is to build decision support solutions to provide an integrated view of the business after-the-fact. These solutions, if viewed as isolated efforts alone, will not meet the organization's continuing requirements. What is needed, preferably before embarking on a series of unintegrated efforts, is an overall plan or strategy to address data warehousing requirements.

Developing a data warehousing strategy provides the opportunity to align data warehouse efforts to the organization's business strategies and goals. The data warehousing strategy establishes a framework for future development and helps to gain consensus on common objectives. It helps to manage expectations regarding what will be built and when, and places the data warehousing efforts within the systems environment. It establishes key infrastructure requirements to ensure that users needs are met successfully. As a communication vehicle, it helps to promote data warehousing concepts, to establish common terminology, and to obtain management commitment. As a road map it helps ensure coordination and integrated development.

Within this discussion, the definition of a data warehouse is consistent with accepted industry usage:

> A data warehouse is a subject-oriented, authoritative, integrated database of historical data reflective of changes over meaningful time periods structured to facilitate query and analysis in support of management decision making.

This paper is divided into two sections: (1) the process of developing the data warehousing strategy and (2) the contents of the data warehousing strategy document.

DATA WAREHOUSING STRATEGY DEVELOPMENT PROCESS

Development, writing, and presentation of the strategy should take no longer than three months. The exact timeframe will vary based on the size of the organization, number of interviews, previously documented architectural efforts, technology situation, urgency of the sponsor, and size of the team. If it appears that the strategy effort will extend beyond this estimate, the strategy development project should be rescoped, the level of detail raised, and some components deferred to a next phase. Any effort that extends beyond three months runs the risk of losing management attention and interest.

Objective

The objective of the data warehousing strategy study is to assess the extent to which the information needs of the organization to support strategic decision making are being satisfied and to recommend a course of action in the area of data warehousing that addresses these needs. The initiative should facilitate the creation of a suitable architecture that will enable the timely capture and dissemination of strategic information for decision support purposes. In describing a vision of the future, with steps to get there, the strategy recommendations should take advantage of new technology, including client/server based tools, in order to provide a centralized data store with data distributed based on functional profiles.

Strategy Team

The study team should be comprised of 2 to 4 individuals, but may be larger, depending on the scope and objectives of the study; for example, if the strategy effort is to include the evaluation and selection of technology platforms, additional resources and time must be planned for this activity. The individuals conducting the strategy study should have a thorough knowledge of data warehousing, based on education and relevant experience. If the data warehousing strategy is conducted by outside consultants, one of the full-time team members should be an individual from the organization who knows the business and the major systems that support it.

Strategy Study Activities

The data warehousing strategy development project consists of two phases:

- gather requirements
- develop recommendations

Gather Requirements

- Conduct interviews with key business people to determine information needs. If possible, group facilitated sessions are to be preferred over individual interviews because they shorten the interview period and help to build organizational consensus for the effort.

- Survey the documentation related to current legacy systems to determine existing operational systems that are likely to be sources for the data warehouse and major reporting or decision support systems.

- Review existing architectural documents such as an enterprise data model, system dataflows, and technology architecture. Look at reporting requests, pending projects, and periodic reports.

The requirements that are gathered should address the five categories shown in Figure 4–1.

Develop Recommendations

Based on an understanding of business organization priorities, information needs, and the data, application, and technology environments, recommend a course of action for data warehousing. Present the recommendations to the sponsor and gain support to proceed.

DATA WAREHOUSING STRATEGY DOCUMENT

Figure 4–2 displays the chapter topics for the data warehousing strategy document. Each part is discussed in the following pages.

Executive Summary

This section concisely summarizes the key recommendations pertaining to the data warehousing strategy. The section should emphasize the rationale for data warehousing, stressing qualitative business benefits that can be expected, especially as they relate to strategic business initiatives. It includes technology and organizational requirements, costs, and indicates incremental results to be achieved within acceptable timeframes. The executive summary concludes with a request for management actions or approvals in order to proceed with the next steps.

Figure 4–1 Data Warehousing Requirements Gathering

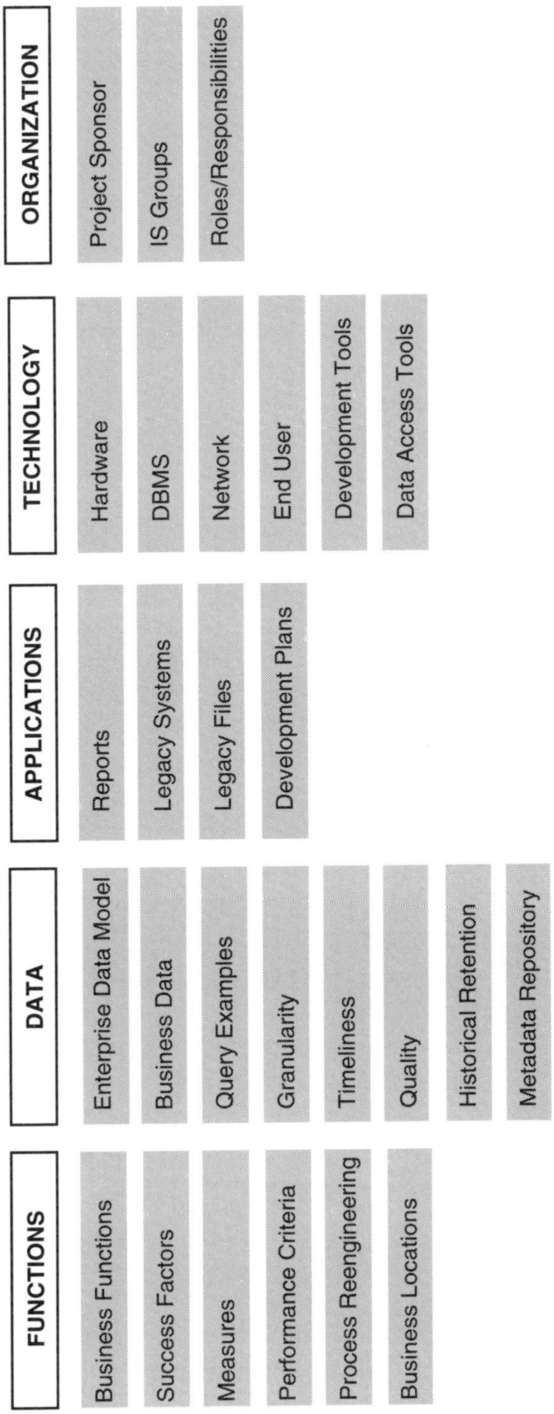

ORGANIZATION	TECHNOLOGY	APPLICATIONS	DATA	FUNCTIONS
Project Sponsor	Hardware	Reports	Enterprise Data Model	Business Functions
IS Groups	DBMS	Legacy Systems	Business Data	Success Factors
Roles/Responsibilities	Network	Legacy Files	Query Examples	Measures
	End User	Development Plans	Granularity	Performance Criteria
	Development Tools		Timeliness	Process Reengineering
	Data Access Tools		Quality	Business Locations
			Historical Retention	
			Metadata Repository	

Figure 4–2: Data Warehousing Strategy Table of Contents

Data Warehousing Strategy Table of Contents
1. Executive Summary 2. Current Assessment 3. Data Architecture 4. Technical Architecture 5. Organizational Requirements 6. Development Process 7. Timeline 8. Proof-of Concept Project 9. Management Considerations

Current Assessment

This section summarizes the findings resulting from the interviews and other requirements gathering.

Management Priorities

Management priorities consist of business subject areas that must be addressed to support strategic decision making and effectively manage the organization. These should be summarized from the interviews or facilitated sessions. Based on the information gathering sessions with business people, it should be possible to cite specific functional areas and information needs that might be addressed. List the query examples provided by interviewees. The queries should illustrate decision support requirements and demonstrate why consolidated data is needed to support strategic analysis. Queries should cross subject areas, e.g., Insurance Policies and Claims, in order to make comparisons that the organization may have had difficulty doing previously.

- analyze seasonal buying patterns to forecast fuel inventory levels

- respond faster to customer inquiries on balances for multiple accounts

- determine the profitability of different product lines by comparing product costs vs. sales or insurance policies vs. claims

- support cross-selling of products to potential customers

- identify patterns for mortgage risk assessment

- ensure a rapid response to questions critical to public safety

A conceptual subject area data "map" (Figure 4–3) can be produced to provide a picture of major subjects and dimensions of importance to the business.

Figure 4–3: Data Subject Map

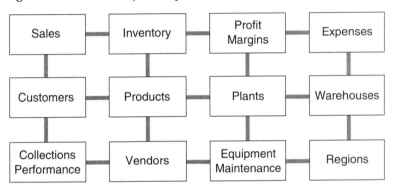

Granularity (Level of Detail)

Indicate the business need for data at the lowest individual level of transactions to support data mining. State the requirements for lightly or highly summarized aggregated data that will support a strategic perspective, such as trend analysis of key measures.

Data Quality

Data quality describes the correctness and completeness of data. Within the timeframe of the strategy study, it is generally not feasible to assess data quality from a detailed perspective. However, business users and legacy system experts can provide an indication of problem areas in order to anticipate the difficulties that will have to be addressed in building the data warehouse. This section of the strategy report may be a good place to discuss business data stewardship.

Data Consistency and Integrity

Data consistency pertains to common data structure, definition, and domain values across systems. This characteristic allows meaningful comparisons, valid numeric results, and analysis without time-consuming and error-prone manual reconciliation. Business users can provide valuable insights in this area.

Data Access

One aspect of effective data access is that individuals initiate requests for and receive data directly from data sources to incorporate into functional activities, rather than via intermediaries. The strategy should indicate the current methods by which business users obtain data, as well as anticipated data access improvements with data warehousing. Another aspect of data access is data security. Differentiate between data accessible internally and data available to external customers.

Usage Patterns

Identify the number and types of users or requesters of data including users internal to the organization and external customers. Estimate the degree to which data warehouse data will be shared or local based on the organizational structure, geographical locations, and functional specialization. This will influence the client/server topology. Indicate the frequency that data will be requested.

Timeliness and History

For most decision support needs, data current as of the prior day is usually sufficient, but less frequent loading or refreshing of data, such as weekly or monthly, may be adequate. Based on user input, indicate the historical data requirements. These will vary from one type of business to another and may be driven by legal requirements, but significant history is often required to facilitate trend analysis and comparisons.

Data Sources

Indicate the major data sources for the data warehouse, and any special considerations pertinent to them. In some organizations, establishing the authoritative data sources for each subject area may be controversial, and the need for resolving differences should be advised. A representative list of external sources that will be included in the data warehouse should be provided.

End-User Workstation Tools

Indicate the end-user workstation tools in use, whether they are sufficient to meet the organization's needs, and the level of user sophistication to utilize them.

Data Warehouse Architecture

This section describes the key components recommended for inclusion in the architecture. Business users and even information systems professionals may have difficulty understanding why the data warehouse is needed in addition to transactional systems. Each of the components of a generic data warehousing model should be discussed in the context of the particular organization's needs. A graphic model tailored to the particular organization and labeled with the known technology components is helpful for depicting the interrelated components that need to be considered. It is important to communicate that the data warehouse is part of the system landscape, existing along with specific source operational systems. The architecture should be flexible to accommodate changes in source systems and changing access techniques. Figure 4–4 depicts a conceptual data and system architectural model; each of its components are discussed in the following section.

Data Warehouse

The data warehouse is at the center of the discussion. It is a consolidated, subject-oriented data resource that can be shared across the organization. Historical, time-based data is structured to emphasize the ways that business wants to analyze data. Data in the data warehouse documents changes over time, supports trend analysis, and compares one period to another. The data warehouse comprises several levels of detail and granularity in order to meet the needs of various user groups. The lowest level of detail exists in order to support "data mining" of data and to provide "drill-down" capability. Subsets of relevant data and summary data exist within the data warehouse architecture; they do not necessarily reside in a single physical data store, and in fact, performance and technology will probably dictate separate, distributed, and replicated data stores, but this is transparent to the end user.

Figure 4–4: Data Warehouse System Architecture

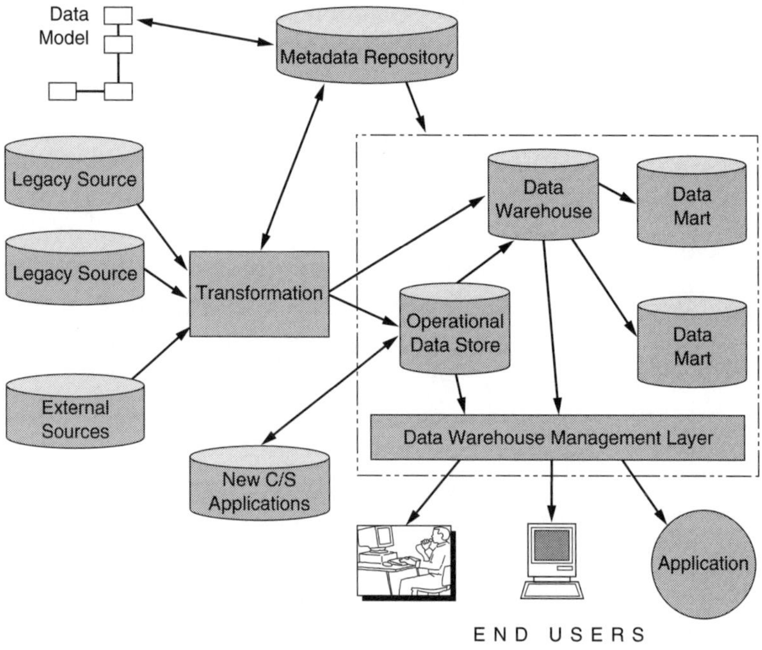

Source Systems

The data warehouse is built using data from internal operational systems and also from external databases. Often, several source application systems will be required for populating facts and reference data in a subject area. In some environments, as new operational systems are developed, a consolidated, operational database becomes the source for the data warehouse. In practice, most organizations will supply their data warehouse from multiple data sources.

The data warehouse is not a replacement for operational systems. Operational systems will continue to support day to day transactions, while the data warehouse will support strategic decision making. Data needed for purely operational day to day activities, but of little value for decision support, will not be included in the data warehouse.

Data Model

The data warehouse is based on a comprehensive and consistent data framework, exemplified by a data model, data definitions, and physical database structures. An enterprise data architecture ensures the ability to perform comparisons across application systems. A common data description defines the data elements in the operational systems, data warehouse, and user directory. For the data warehouse, the normalized design is modified to include elements of time, summaries, and derivations; redundant structures are added for ease of understanding and performance, and external data is included.

Database designs for transaction processing and data warehousing are different. Transaction processing database structures are normalized, complex, and tuned to facilitate update performance and to enforce data integrity. Data warehouses are "read-only" and optimized for query, reporting, and simplified understanding of the data. The database design will contain denormalized, pre-joined data structures that organize data in a way that reflects business user perspectives. One such technique, known as the "star schema," separates data into "facts" and "dimensions."

Transformation

Programs must be developed to select, extract, clean, and convert data from source system structures into consistent target warehouse data structures. Then the data must be loaded. The extract and transformation programs may be developed by conventional coding methods or, increasingly, with the use of automated productivity tool designed for this purpose. The data warehouse is populated on a frequency that meets the organization's needs.

Warehouse data will reflect the quality of the data in the source systems. In order for individuals to "trust" the data,

data needs to be precertified and validated for quality before inclusion in the data warehouse. Some improvements are possible in the process of extracting and transforming data by defining default values, error tests, and transformations to consistent structures and data domain values.

Metadata Repository

A metadata repository is used to store data models, the definitions of data elements for consistent reuse, business transformation rules, and source and target database descriptions. It also includes business data views developed for end user presentation. Metadata is accessible to systems professionals and business users.

Decision Support Applications

Decision support applications will use data from the data warehouse. These systems may include analytical applications in areas such as inventory forecasting, profitability analysis and staff deployment. Often termed "data mart," this is a specialized type of data warehouse containing a subset of data sourced from the data warehouse and "prepackaged" to support a particular functional business area. Data marts, because they contain lesser amounts of data than the full data warehouse, may provide superior performance and a less complex view of the data suited to a particular user group.

In some cases decision support applications will create "official" derived data. This data can be captured and provided to the data warehouse in a controlled way for sharing by others in the organization.

Warehouse Management Layer

The strategy should address the mechanisms for managing and controlling access to the data warehouse. Discuss the feasibility of building a user directory from the metadata repository that employs business data element names and descriptions and that functions like a library "card catalog." Administrative tools that monitor performance and usage, provide a consistent view of shared data, and minimize support might be implemented. Discuss the role of middleware to establish and manage business views that help insulate the business user and applications from changes to physical data structures and that support data security.

End User Decision Support Tools

End user access tools reside on user workstations. These tools will be used by different groups in the user community, based on their level of sophistication and the need to perform complex operations. Wherever possible, end user tools should screen the business user from having to understand the query language. These tools range from basic query and reporting tools to managed query tools and multidimensional analytical processing tools.

Technical Architecture

In this section of the strategy study, technology platform and related tool requirements are addressed. In some organizations, major technology decisions may have been made without regard to data warehousing needs, but rather based on a more familiar on-line transaction processing (OLTP) perspective. Other organizations are committed to using existing platforms. For organizations where decisions have already been made and relational database management systems are in place, it may be practical to suggest that a proof-of-concept project be established that will validate the suitability of the particular technology platform for data warehousing.

Some organizations will be open to considering a new technical configuration, especially in the client/server arena, that will support data warehousing requirements. Since data warehousing is perceived as an opportunity area for many vendors, new product releases are continuing to evolve to address data warehousing needs. Given the complexity of such technical evaluation decisions in many organizations, it may not be feasible to make specific product recommendations within the timeframe and constraints of the data warehousing strategy. Instead, certain criteria for the technical platform can be proposed and a recommendation be made that the next step in the data warehousing process is to select, procure, and deploy the technical infrastructure. A test suit of the platform to be used is a necessary prerequisite for a proof of concept project. Figure 4–5 depicts the types of tools that need to be considered for the data warehousing environment.

Building and accessing a data warehouse must be viewed as both business-critical and complex. For this reason, it is essential to evaluate the need for these kinds of tools in order to help ensure a robust solution.

Figure 4–5   Data Warehouse Technology Categories

Platform	Warehouse Management	End User Tools	Metadata
Data Server	Data Modeling and Database Definition	Ad Hoc Query	Metadata Repository
Operating System	Data Reengineering and Cleaning	Managed Query	
DBMS	Extract and Transformation	Multidimensional Analysis	
Application Servers	Operations and Performance	Data Mining	
Network Protocols		Decision Support Applications	
Workstations			
System Utilities			

Hardware, Software and Communications Network

The technical platform must be examined in terms of scalability, load and query performance, maturity, portability, and cost. Large data warehouses, loading, complex query performance, and response time are all factors that may drive technical platform decisions. Estimates of data volumes are likely to be underestimated because of historical needs and redundant warehouse tables. As detailed user requirements are developed, data volumes, query frequency, and geographical distribution patterns should be confirmed.

- Hardware—Decisions must be made regarding the data server hardware platform: mainframe, SMP (Symetric Multiprocessor), or MPP (Massively Parallel Processor). Storage requirements, I/O bandwidth, and number of processors must all be considered.

- Operating System—Choice of operating system, such as MVS, UNIX or NT, is closely tied to hardware, and will have an impact on the availability of tools available for the selected environment.

- DBMS—The choices in this area are among standard function relational DBMS, special purpose relational DBMS optimized for queries, or proprietary multidimensional DBMS. Database replication services to address data distribution in a client/server environment and other mechanisms for moving data may be required.

- Application Servers/Workstations—A two-tier or three-tier client server topology must be selected based on user distribution, workload, and application development tools. User workstations may need to be upgraded and include a standard workstation configuration.

- Network Protocols—Standardization of network protocols may be required.

- Utilities—In this category are data/file transfer and loading, scheduling, and backup. Some specialized software may be required for scheduling and transferring data from mainframe and other data sources to the data warehouse.

Data Warehousing Management/Productivity Tools

Tools exist in the marketplace that address building and maintaining a consistent data warehouse that can easily react to changes in a cost-effective way. Some or all of these types of tools may be recommended for a robust data warehousing implementation. They can be categorized as follows:

- Data Modeling—Whether oriented toward data modeling only, or integrated within a CASE (Computer Aided Software Engineering) product, data modeling software tools support the design of target data warehousing databases through graphical representation and text descriptions. The documentation produced for the data structures should be used to generate physical database tables and should be included in a metadata repository/directory for organization-wide access.

- Data Reengineering and Structural Analysis—These tools allow for automated analysis of existing legacy data to identify functional dependencies, anomalies, and to generate relational database structures from legacy file structures. Use of these tools provides validation of old, often poorly documented legacy data structures, and helps provide a basis for standardization and restructuring. Some of these tools can assist with auditing data, measuring data quality, and assisting with data scrubbing.

- Extraction/Conversion Tools—These tools generate program code to select data from source systems, map and transform the data into the target structure, and create files for loading to the target database for one-time and ongoing loading. Tools in this category can deal with multiple data sources and file types in order to support the disparate data that needs to be consolidated into the data warehouse. Business rules are specified in the tools, and consistent program code generated. These tools often provide significant productivity benefits, produce standard well-structured code, and facilitate change management. Inherent in these tools is the creation of metadata that provides traceability for data from source to target, including derivation and summarization. When changes are required, they are specified in the transformation tool, and programs regenerated and tested.

- Warehouse/Directory Management—This area of tool support is receiving increasing attention. Tools in this category address comprehensive data warehouse management and operations. They address security, query performance monitoring at the data column level, and the creation and maintenance of business views of data. These subject-oriented business views provide an insulating layer between the business user or application and the physical database structures and can be organized into an enterprise-wide user directory similar to a library "card catalog." Because such an information catalog helps to communicate the contents of the warehouse, the need for specialized support is reduced and users can be more independent. Some end-user query tools address the creation of business views for individual user groups but do not have performance, security, and administration features.

End User Decision Support Tools

End user tools are key to the success of the data warehouse, because it is only through such tools that data can be accessed and turned into "information" of value. End user tools empower the business user and contribute to an effective organization. End user tools can be divided into five different categories, which overlap within the marketplace. An organization should consider the need for each type of tool in its environment, based on the complexity of analysis performed, and amount of Information Systems support required. What all these tools have in common are graphical user interface (GUI) features that help to increase user understanding. All of the tools should be able to work with standard workstation tools, including word processing, spreadsheet and statistical tools, and graphics packages.

- Ad hoc Query—These tools provide simple query and analysis functions. Users are very much on their own and need to understand relational principles and SQL.

- Managed Query—These tools provide a business layer between the end user and the database, translate cryptic physical names into meaningful business names, prejoin tables to present useful facts, and screen the user from needing to be expert in the SQL query language. They require set-up and administration by the information systems personnel, and this effort may be considerable.

- Multidimensional—Sometimes called On-line Analytical Processing (OLAP) tools, these support complex analysis of dimensional data. They may use either a proprietary database or relational DBMS structured with logical dimensions.

- Data Mining—These are tools that examine large amounts of detailed data in order to discover patterns and make connections among seemingly unrelated facts. They may be combined with data visualization features that portray data in graphic, sometimes three-dimensional, pictures that can be viewed from different perspectives.

- Applications—These are structured applications developed for a specialized purpose, such as forecasting, budgeting, and profitability analysis. Custom developed applications may be able to access data warehouse data directly, while proprietary package solutions often need to extract data from the data warehouse and import the data into its own data stores. Some of these types of applications overlap with multi-dimensional analysis tools. If separate data stores are built, these applications may be termed "data marts."

Metadata Repository

Management/productivity tools and end-user access tools create their own metadata. Synchronizing all metadata is a significant effort that needs to include logical and physical elements, transformation rules, business data views, and other relevant structural information for inclusion in one place. One approach is to utilize existing metadata repositories and apply extensions to accommodate data warehousing requirements.

A repository contains definitions and descriptions of data, indicates the physical systems where the data is used, shows the relationships among system objects such as programs, procedures, tables and data elements but does not show the actual values of transactional facts or reference data. A repository is a key tool in managing the interrelationships of components in a complex system environment, including data warehousing.

Organizational Requirements

In this section of the data warehousing strategy document, discuss the placement of the data warehousing team in the organization. Indicate the roles and responsibilities of the information systems organization and the business user organization. Indicate staffing levels, skills, and training required.

With client/server technology, graphical user interfaces, and user-friendly query tools, the role of IS is changing. Rather than developing custom reports, IS will increasingly focus on developing database structures designed for query performance; maintaining business data views that insulate users from physical database complexity and change; consulting with users on the best way to utilize powerful end-user tools; and building decision support applications that enable business users to be as self-sufficient as possible.

To help ensure successful rollout of the data warehouse, and its effective use, adequate staff should be assigned to support ongoing operations. From an internal "behind the scenes" perspective, these activities include network configuration management, production operations, database loading, backup, performance monitoring, business view development, and maintenance and enhancements. From an external or customer perspective, staff needs to be available to respond to user requests for assistance. Wherever possible, staff levels can be kept to a minimum by use of automated tools to support specific areas.

The data warehouse team should be comprised of individuals who contribute a mixture of skills. Not all individuals need to be full-time for the life of the project. The number of resources will depend on the scope of the project and the magnitude of the new technology that is to be introduced. Figure 4–6 summarizes data warehouse team roles.

Figure 4–6   Data Warehousing Roles

Role	Primary Responsibilities
Warehouse Manager	• Establish data warehouse strategy • Plan and manage data warehouse • Communicate warehousing objectives
Data Architect	• Develop enterprise data model • Analyze data requirements • Design data warehousing data structures • Define business data views
Metadata (Repository) Administrator	• Define metadata standards • Manage metadata repository and user directory
Database Administrator	• Create physical database structures, monitor load, and query performance
Business User	• Describe data • Specify business rules • Test transformation results
Applications/ Process Analyst	• Develop decision support applications
Source Applications Systems Specialist	• Define legacy systems data
Conversion Analysts/ Programmer	• Map source data to data warehouse • Create (generate) programs to select and load data
Technical/Tool Support Specialist	• Support technical configuration
Training Specialist	• Provide training in accessing data warehouse
Production Support	• Monitor source systems jobstreams and data warehouse loading

Information Resource Management (IRM)

Data warehousing should be managed by an information resource management (IRM) organization, or similar group accountable for establishing data sharing principles and procedures that help ensure high quality, consistent data. Within IRM, a data warehouse team establishes guidelines and standards, manages growth, builds and supports the data warehouse population, and consults with users in their access to the data. To help ensure consistency, there is centralized control of key functions. These include defining the data model; managing data quality, structural analysis and transformation methods, and tools; building, maintaining, and tuning the physical data base; establishing and maintaining the semantic translations between physical data and business views and managing the metadata dictionary/directory; and establishing and maintaining security and access to the data warehouse.

In some organizations, data warehousing responsibilities are associated with business functional groups and not IRM or another other IS group. This approach can be successful in meeting the needs of a department but may not be successful when measured against integration objectives. The strategy document should address this issue, recommend whether the data warehousing effort should be done entirely under the control of IRM, or whether a core team of IRM experts should establish the framework and then serve as "consultants" to multiple data warehousing project teams.

Depending on the degree to which the data warehouse is built synchronously or synchronously with decision support applications, it is necessary to define roles and communications between application teams and the data warehousing team.

Business Users

Business users, as the consumers of data, define the strategic data requirements and priority information needs. They describe business data, business rules, business views, and provide feedback to the data warehouse team on performance, additions, and changes. They approve data sources and are accountable for source system data quality.

Applications Process Specialists

Applications process specialists address business logic, processing, and presentation of data. They develop or implement structured applications that address specific business functions and provide input to data requirements definition. They may participate on a data warehousing advisory committee that sets priorities and resolves cross-organizational data differences.

Source Application Systems Specialists

Source application systems specialists provide expertise on legacy systems. They understand data definitions and program code of systems used as sources for populating the data warehouse. Often involved in generating changes to source systems, they notify the data warehouse team through established change notification mechanisms of any source system changes that may have an impact on database structure, extract, and load programs for the data warehouse.

Technical Specialists

Technical specialists support the technical environment. They manage and support hardware platforms, both servers and client workstations, software products, and communications networks. They provide data storage capacity, backup and recovery, and system security.

Development Process

This section of the data warehousing strategy that will be followed to build the data warehousing environment. It forms the basis of a work breakdown structure or task plan for detailed project planning. It is a key section because of a need to counteract an unfortunate tendency in some organizations to trivialize the effort required to build a consistent and usable data source.

The strategy document is an opportunity to introduce the concept that the process used to build the data warehouse is an iterative methodology in which the organization continues to improve and extend the data warehouse based on changing business requirements. Starting with a minimal set of data that is required by the user, additional data is added in subsequent iterations.

The iterative development process, depicted in Figure 4–7 and discussed below, focuses primarily on the activities required to build the database to supply data in subject areas for a variety of analytical and strategic purposes. It assumes that identified business users will access the data through end-user workstation query tools. A separate task outline will also be required in order to build a structured decision support application system that would use the database to produce preformatted reports or perform controlled data manipulation such as forecasting, alert conditions, or other specialized functions using application development tools. In practice, some organizations may choose to merge the two efforts.

Figure 4–7 Data Warehousing Development Process

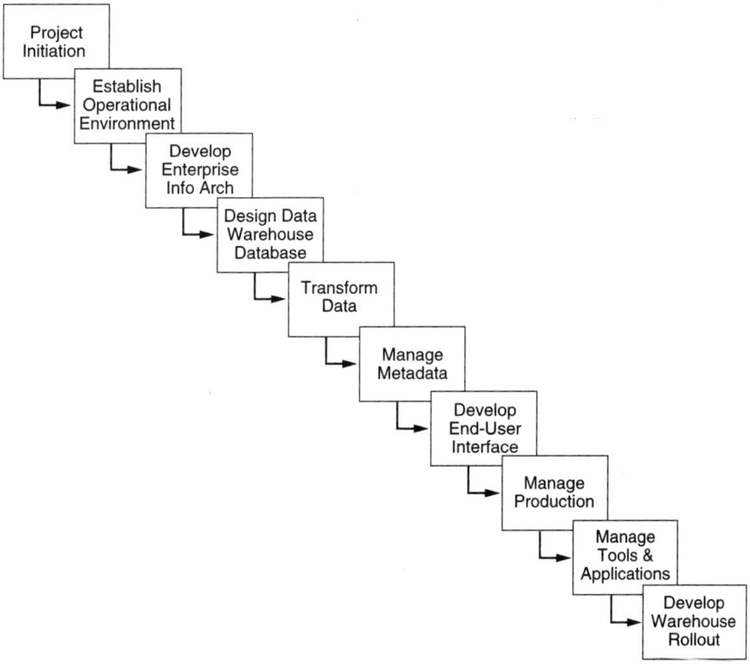

Initiate Project

This activity establishes mutual expectations for the project and produces the project plan. Its components include data scope, deliverables, technology infrastructure, resources, skills, team training, roles and responsibilities, methodology approach, change management process, issue resolution process, project tracking, and detailed project schedule.

Establish Technical Environment

This activity selects, acquires, and implements technical components and resources that will be required for the project, including platforms, DBMS, network communications, development tools, end user access tools and technical and operational personnel. Included in this activity are the establishment of service level objectives for availability, loading, maintenance, and query performance.

Develop an Enterprise Information Architecture

This activity establishes a conceptual framework or "big picture" that represents data shared across the organization. As a logical structure, this data model cuts across existing application systems and is irrespective of current physical system constraints. It adheres to the principle of data standardization for critical data shared across the organization and serves as the blueprint for incremental development of subject-oriented data warehouse databases. It will help to avoid unnecessary rework, ensure consistency, integration and communications across the organization, and prevent unmanaged redundancy.

If an enterprise data model exists, it can be easily leveraged. However, if the organization does not have an enterprise data model, there may be some reluctance to undertake this effort, often perceived as a time-consuming activity without tangible results. In order to realize the benefits of data warehousing, a practical approach should be taken to develop a high level conceptual framework and accomplish this activity within a limited timeframe.

Standards for metadata will need to be defined. Standards help to ensure understanding, promote reuse, and avoid redundancy and inconsistency.

Design the Data Warehouse Database

This activity develops a physical database structure for the data warehouse based on user requirements, focusing on a single major subject area, in contrast to the enterprise model. Facilitated sessions are held with 5 to 9 subject matter experts, analysts and managers representative of the organization to identify data requirements. In these sessions, determine data requirements and definitions, including facts (measures) and dimensions, examples of data access and analysis activities, the frequency of data snapshots, historical retention, data sources and data quality issues, and security. The major deliverable from this phase is a database design suitable for data warehousing. Hold follow-up sessions to validate the design, preferably with a prototype database and end user query tool.

Data Transformation

This set of activities determines and implements the programming logic to extract data from the source system, perform data cleaning, format data consistently, compute data derivations and summaries, and prepare the data for loading to the target warehouse structures. While data conversion from a single system to a new environment may appear to have minimal structural differences, data difficulties often occur in consolidating data after the fact from several legacy systems and from historical files. Historical loads and ongoing changed data capture will need to be addressed as separate programs and tested. Processing platforms, download, file transfer, and loading times are critical features to be tested.

Manage Metadata

This set of activities addresses the need to document, reuse, and communicate the meaning of data and its system component relationships. This step creates confidence in the data because the data's definition, origin and subsequent derivations are stated and available for inquiry. A metadata repository should be populated with keys and attributes, business data descriptions, physical data structures, source structures, mapping and transformation rules, frequency, derivation, summarization algorithms, data stewardship, codes, defaults, security requirements, changes, and limits of data over time. Metadata generated from multiple data warehousing tools must be coordinated.

Develop End-user Interface/Applications

This activity consists of building structured decision support query and reporting applications or implementing software packages that use warehouse data. This activity follows a typical software development lifecycle with prototyping and should be discussed relative to the organization's development process. The strategy document should address the degree to which data warehousing will take a synchronous or asynchronous development approach.

- Synchronous data warehouse development—The data warehouse is built to meet the needs of specific decision support. Business interest and sponsorship is high, which helps to ensure acceptance of the data warehouse. The danger in this approach is that the warehouse will have a narrow application view of data that does not facilitate subsequent efforts or long-term integration objectives.

- Asynchronous data warehouse development—The data warehouse is built separately from application efforts, based on an understanding of business data and information needs. This approach is known as the "build it and they will come" approach and is often driven by the information systems organization. Lacking a specific business driver, this type of effort, while it can reflect a global and integrated point of view, requires a lot of selling to encourage users to try it. With this approach, as users start to use the data warehouse, significant changes in order to reflect actual usage patterns and additional data requirements can be anticipated.

Try to adopt an approach that is somewhere between the two extremes, in order to ensure business involvement and to maintain a broad perspective on the data.

Manage Production Environment

The data warehouse must be managed like any other organization-wide system. It must meet quality requirements for acceptance in the production environment, including unit and integration testing. Programs that select and extract data from source systems on a periodic basis are included in the source system production job streams and scheduled according to the production management and scheduling standards within the organization. Warehouse production operations staff must be available to address problems and rectify them within the agreed service level timeframe. An automated notification mechanism must be implemented to notify warehouse users of any failures to provide data at the promised time. Performance monitoring, database maintenance, backup, and recovery are included in this group of activities

Attention to change management is paramount. Anticipate changes in source and target data in accordance with iterative data warehouse development. Source-to-target mapping and conversion programs will have to be revised and tested when this occurs and end-users notified. Wherever possible, the use of business data views helps mask physical database changes and provides a measure of stability.

Manage Decision Support Tools and Applications

This activity provides support for a standard set of end-user access tools, including maintenance and enhancement of structured decision support applications. Support for the technology infrastructure, including platforms, networks, and workstations is necessary, but might not be unique to the data warehouse, and should follow technical services and "HELP" desk practices.

Develop Warehouse Rollout

This activity addresses the tasks needed for successful integration of the data warehouse into the organization's workflow. It includes establishing an advisory committee, training, ongoing communications, and customer feedback. The use of user directories and end-user tools that mask the complexities of SQL will speed the education process. Some advanced users will need training in specialized decision support tools. A user guide needs to be developed to explain what the data warehouse is, state data issues, and indicate who to call for assistance. As much as possible, this information should be developed from metadata documentation and be delivered via on-line "help" or other automated mechanisms. Information sessions should be held at various levels of the organization to promote data warehouse understanding and use.

A program to introduce the data warehouse to the organization needs to be planned carefully and applied on an ongoing basis. This program will combine communications, training, incremental implementation, and support services. Through a series of written materials and presentation sessions, the goals and objectives of the data warehouse should be communicated to the organization. This communication should describe the concepts, benefits, projects, timelines, and plans for including different functional and geographical units. Care should be taken that the communications are consistent with realistic expectations for accomplishments.

Training sessions will be needed that are suitable for different levels of the organization—managers, analysts, inspectors, and other users. The training should include:

- data warehouse principles

- data availability

- business data views

- query and reporting techniques

- data access tools

- services and feedback

Development Timeline

This section of the data warehouse strategy suggests an implementation and development sequence suitable for the organization and reflects the iterative, phase oriented methodology. The requirement for addressing legacy systems transition and elimination is also discussed.

Implementation Sequence

The implementation sequence should be based on strategic level priorities for access to data subject areas. Since different organizational groups may compete to have "their" data included, a formal process may help in deciding priorities. The process may include a data warehousing advisory committee comprised of business users who rank and choose among priorities. Initially, a high level development sequence can develop based on the data warehousing strategy interviews and reflective of the findings in regard to:

- management decision making needs
- patterns of subject area demand
- lack of current access to data
- core system redevelopment plans
- data reconciliation and consistency
- responsiveness and processing cycle time
- eliminating non value-added processes
- eliminating redundant or obsolete systems

The implementation sequence should project 2 to 3 years ahead. Propose a proof-of-concept project in an initial subject area, followed by additional subject area implementations at 3 to 6 month intervals. Be sure to indicate tasks required to establish the infrastructure, such as technology configuration and warehouse management and access tools, as well as enterprise data model development/validation. Some of these phases may be done in parallel. Figure 4–8 depicts a conceptual view of data warehousing implementation.

Legacy Systems Replacement

Along with the data warehouse subject implementation sequence, indicate which legacy reporting systems and files are likely to be replaced and the approximate timeframe. Adequate time must be planned for transitions that involve business users of the existing systems as well as legacy applications support personnel. Additionally, the development sequence should address the replacement of data sources for the data warehouse with new operational applications and the possibility of supplying the data warehouse from an operational data store. Diagrams similar to those in Figures 4–9 and 4–10 can be used to show phased implementation. In Figure 4–9, data is transformed from legacy systems, consolidated operational data stores, and external sources. In Figure 4–10, data is sourced from operational data stores and external sources, and legacy systems have been eliminated.

Figure 4–8 Data Warehousing Implementation Sequence

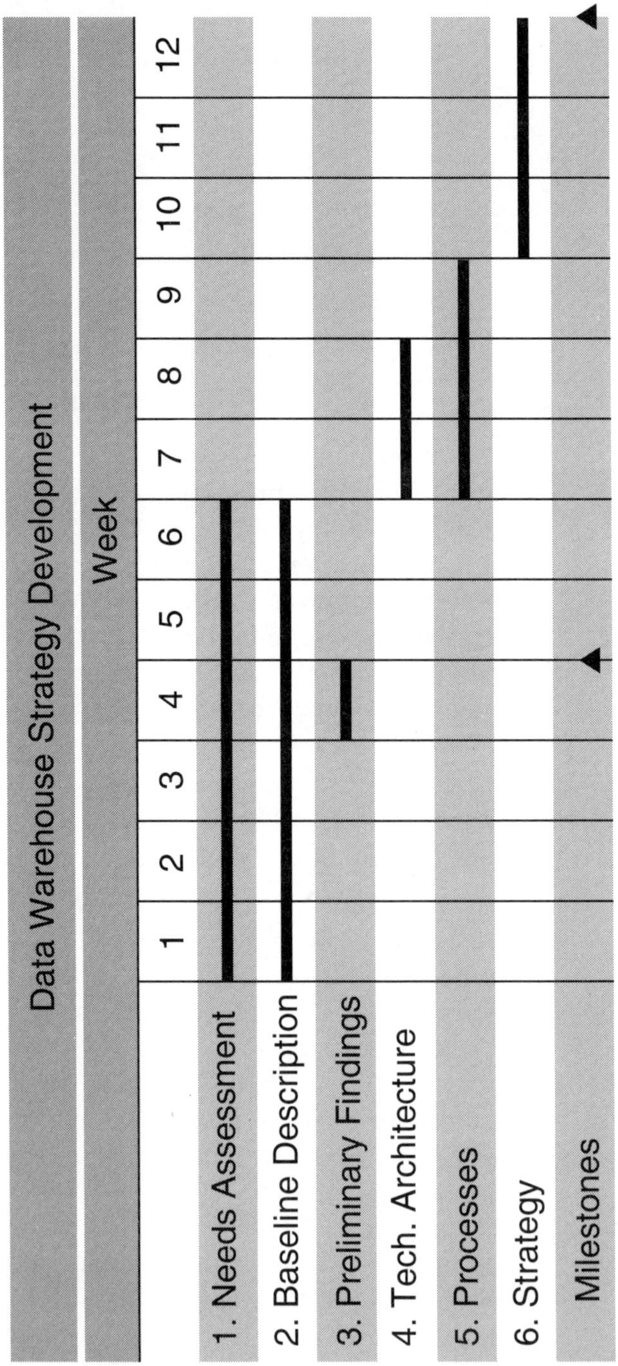

Figure 4–9 Initial Data Warehouse Implementation

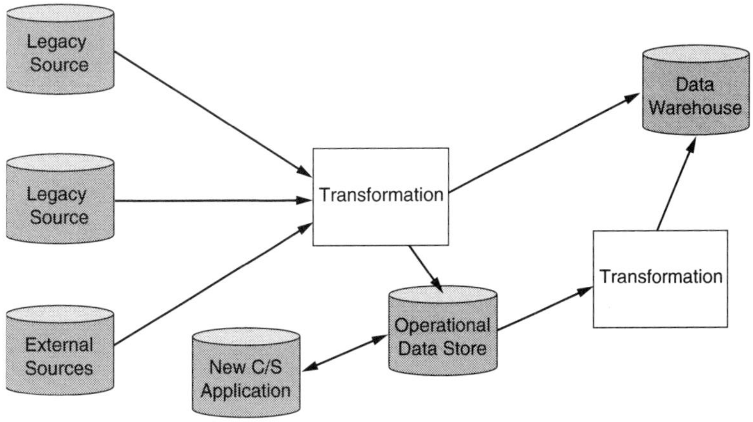

Figure 4–10 Target Data Warehouse Implementation

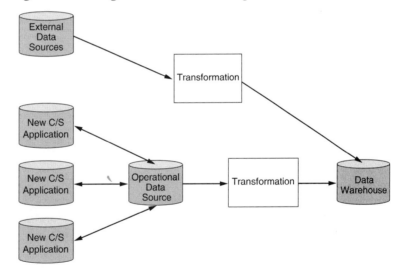

Proof of Concept Project

The purpose of conducting a proof of concept project is to develop and test the data warehouse in a controlled, limited environment in order to identify and correct any deficiencies in methods or tools wherever technically feasible. One major subject area should be chosen, which will encompass a few fact tables and a number of reference tables or dimensions containing descriptive attributes. Ideally, the proof-of-concept project should utilize the target technologies. To the extent possible, exercise the full data warehouse development process. Specify technology infrastructure support. At this stage begin the roll-out program to communicate to the organization.

Proof of Concept Project Success Factors

Determine the critical success factors for the project such as:

- Performance
- Functionality
- Ease of use
- Access to data using ad hoc queries and applications
- Flexibility
- Transparency

Project Implementation Plan

Develop a high level project implementation plan estimating scope, costs, time, and resources.

Management Perspective

This section includes objectives; benefits; critical success factors and performance measures; high level assumptions; risk factors with suggestions for mitigating risks; and a discussion on managing expectations. These items are drawn from the survey, findings, observations, and recommendations and help to solidify the environmental factors for a successful data warehouse implementation.

Data Warehouse Objectives

The objectives presented should address business problems and opportunities that exist. Objectives should enable the business users to visualize concrete improvements that data warehousing enables. Some examples of objectives are the following:

- Supports strategic decision making—The data warehouse will support strategic decision making by providing detail and summary data that can be used for trend analysis, performance measurement comparisons, statistical analysis, correlation among disparate facts, and other similar requirements.

- Supports integrated business value chain—Data warehousing supports a single source of authoritative, consistent, accurate, and timely data that cuts across traditional departmental applications. An opportunity exists to provide consistently-defined data and to reduce redundant efforts.

- Empowers workforce—Access to data empowers business users and improves analysis capabilities. It enables users to be more self-sufficient and reduces the dependence on time-consuming specialized report development. The data warehouse will enable organizational streamlining by simplifying dataflows enabled by better access to shared data.

- Speeds up response time to business queries—The data warehouse will enable faster response to business questions. Response times for data retrieval can be reduced from days to minutes.

- Data quality—A consolidated data store will eliminate reconciliation of inconsistent data. In the analysis and transformation of source data to the data warehouse, data quality improvements can be made.

- Document's organizational knowledge—A well-documented and centralized data store reduces organizational vulnerability caused by concentrating analysis expertise and the understanding of data in a few staffers with institutional knowledge.

- Streamlines systems portfolio—The data warehouse helps streamline operational systems by removing decision support functions and moving historical data out of operational systems into the data warehouse. Multiple overlapping of reporting data stores can be eliminated. Data warehousing can help to address legacy system deficiencies and support the transition to a new client/server platform.

Critical Success Factors

Critical success factors (CSFs) are criteria, which demonstrate that the data warehousing effort meets business needs. Only the most important CSFs should be included, along with performance measures that can be used to measure success. Figure 4–11 shows examples of data warehousing critical success factors and performance measures.

Figure 4–11   Examples of Data Warehousing Critical Success Factors

Critical Success Factor	Performance Measure
Provide a single source of consistent data	Eliminate the need for manual reconciliation among systems
Provide quick response to management queries	Reduce response time to management queries from several hours to minutes
Improve data timeliness	Provide summaries of sales activity current as of the previous day
Access to data by empowered workforce	Reduction by 50% of report requests to IS and corresponding increase in user-generated queries.

Assumptions

Assumptions address the understanding of the environment that underlie the strategy, such as functional scope and prerequisites. The assumptions should be confirmed before proceeding. If any assumptions are found to be unfounded or unclear, they need to be addressed before proceeding further. There are several categories of assumptions that need to be considered:

- Technical Assumptions
    - platform (database servers, operating system, DBMS, etc.) to be used
    - warehouse management/productivity tools to be employed
    - end-user access tool suite to be used
    - product procurement procedures and timing
    - vendor agreements in effect
    - configuration availability and installation schedules

- Scoping Assumptions
    - data model availability or development

- project subject boundaries
- anticipated source systems
- decision support application processes
- anticipated data volumes
- number of users

- Organizational Assumptions

  - warehouse team staffing level and skills
  - sponsor organization commitment
  - business user participation needed
  - training plan and responsibilities

- Management Assumptions

  - warehouse deliverable schedules/milestones
  - development process
  - budget
  - project tracking
  - issue resolution
  - administrative support

Risk Assessment

During the data warehousing strategy survey, identify the risk factors that can affect the successful introduction and use of the data warehouse and suggest a means of mitigating the risks. The categories of risk are similar to those in the area of assumptions: Technical, Scoping, Organizational, and Management. Figure 4–12 presents some examples of potential data warehousing risks and suggestions for mitigating them.

Figure 4–12:   Data Warehousing Risk Assessment Examples

Risk Area	Techniques to Mitigate Risk
Technical	
• New client/server platform	• Trained, dedicated technical support • Vendor partnership to share risk
• New extract & query tools	• Tool training • Vendor consulting • Proof-of-concept project
• Lack of experience with data warehousing database design	• Warehouse design training, consulting
• Unknown data volumes/capacity	• Proof-of-concept project

Risk Area	Techniques to Mitigate Risk
Scoping	
• Undocumented source system data, poor quality of source data	• Structure analysis tool, data pre-verification • Legacy application system specialist • Initiate metadata repository and data rationalization • Data quality program and data stewardship
• Data subject scope unclear	• Facilitated work sessions with user sponsors to agree on subjects, priorities • Track scope change requests
• Stovepipe perspective	• Global enterprise data model • Identify related information needs
• Mixed operational and data warehousing requirements	• Establish operational database and data warehouse
Organizational	
• Multiple uncoordinated data efforts	• Common architectural framework • Assign single accountability
• Limited experience of data warehousing team with business	• Increase analysis and design time estimates
• No user participation on project	• Stop project until users assigned
• IS-initiated project	• Obtain business sponsor/support
Management/Administrative	
• Delivery dates determined before scoping	• Negotiate reasonable subject scope • Identify incremental deliverables

Managing Expectations

It is important to set realistic expectations in the user and information systems community. Stress the need for an incremental approach in which high priority subject areas are addressed first. This means that not all data that is desired can be made available from legacy systems in the early stages. Additionally, some data that users would like is not captured in operational systems or is not available from external sources, so it will not be included in the warehouse. Based on past experiences business users may be skeptical and fear that changes and enhancements will take a long time, or perhaps never be addressed. To help ensure this does not happen, stress the importance of adopting the following practices:

- business participation
- productivity tools
- setting priorities
- manageable scope
- feedback mechanisms
- change management procedures
- release schedules
- dedicated data warehouse support team

CONCLUSION

In this paper an approach for developing a data warehousing strategy has been presented. The study team must gain a clear understanding of business information needs and priorities coupled with an assessment of how well the current systems environment can meet these needs. The strategy document presents a case for building a structured framework within which planned and coordinated data warehousing development can take place. The strategy document is also a sales tool for communicating data warehousing goals, objectives, and concepts to organization so that an effective dialogue can take place. It presents not only a vision of the future where business users can be self-sufficient in accessing critical data, but suggests concrete steps to be taken to reach this ideal.

Chapter

5

How to Justify the Data Warehouse and Gain Top Management Support

Doug C. Neal

ATKearney

As John Buie, a software sales executive with many years of experience in selling data warehouse projects, says, "Preparation is everything" when you meet with top management to gain their approval of your data warehouse effort. This chapter discusses a series of questions that you might ask yourself before the meeting to ensure that you are prepared. There are no simple answers. Each situation is different. You will need to come up with answers that work in your situation with your management team. However, it is much better to ask yourself questions now, before the meeting, while you have an opportunity to develop answers, than have to respond to these issues on the fly, during the meeting.

The topics covered by these questions reflect the experiences of many who have worked on data warehouses. They range widely and include a long section on how to tailor your presentation to the personalities of your management and a final question that speculates on what the data warehouse can become over time.

QUESTIONS FOR DATA WAREHOUSE BUILDERS

Question 1: Will your data warehouse effort be viewed by management as "just another Information Technology (I/T) project," or will it be viewed as a key supporting player in the successful execution of one or more parts of their corporate strategy?

Many executives have had the experience of being asked to approve an I/T project that did not seem to be in the best interests of the business. So, you need to be prepared to say how this one will be different. One of the best ways is to show how it does not exist in a vacuum but instead is a key supporting piece of a major corporate initiative or goal.

Examples of major initiatives might include:

- new market penetration

- understanding and achieving potential

- building a process for making and keeping commitments to Wall Street

- closing the gap with competitors

- moving to fact-based decision making

- sales force automation

- product and customer profitability

- corporate restructuring

Question 2: How can you find out what the corporate initiatives are that you might support?

There are a variety of sources within most organizations. Typically the best way is to identify individuals on the business side who can point you in the right direction. Be prepared to spend some time educating them as to the possibilities that a data warehouse can provide. Potential sources could include:

- strategic planners
- budget planners
- staff to the executives
- Business Process Reengineering plans
- consultants
- annual reports
- new initiative documents
- strategy documents
- board decisions
- regulatory board decisions
- adverse publicity

Once you have identified an initiative that could benefit from a data warehouse, you will need to educate the staff responsible for that initiative. Your goal should be to do a good enough job of demonstrating the benefits of having a data warehouse that they will help you argue your case to top management.

Question 3: Why do you have to be careful when you use the word "strategic" in the same sentence as data warehouse?

Many in senior management have had the experience of hearing technology side staff describe I/T investments as "strategic." Often, this occurred when the technology side staff were unable to find a way to link it to a cost savings or revenue enhancement but still believed that it was important for the corporation to do. Unfortunately, this sometimes came across as, "There's a pony under here somewhere, trust me." As a consequence, the word strategic must be used with great care. It is generally better to describe the data warehouse effort as a key support element or infrastructure that is needed to achieve a specific, already agreed upon strategic goal, such as increased market share through improved targeting of direct mail.

Question 4: What does the management team know about data warehouses before you give your presentation?

Don Connelly, Brigadier General, U.S. Army retired, said that people usually made one of two mistakes in making presentations to generals. They either assumed that the general knew nothing, or they assumed that the general knew everything. The truth, of course, is usually somewhere in between. The trick is to understand what their base of knowledge is and what their pre-dispositions are likely to be.

There is sometimes a cycle with new ideas that you have to watch out for. It starts with "What's a data warehouse?" and moves along to "We have to have one (whatever it is) because our chief competitor has one" and unfortunately often ends with "Oh, we had one of those. It didn't work and was a waste of time and money."

Before you go into a meeting with the management team you need to find out what their fact base is, where they look for information, and where they are in the life cycle of the idea of the data warehouse.

Question 5: Why can the data warehouse be a hard sell?

The data warehouse cuts across organizations, both organizationally and technically. This is a strength once it is installed and running, but it makes it difficult to generate initial support, since each part of the organization may look to other parts to provide initial funding and effort.

- Organizational issues—It's a horizontal play in a world where departments, I/T applications, and resources tend to be vertical stovepipes. That's why it helps to link the data warehouse to a strategic cross functional initiative, such as order to delivery.

- Technical issues—The data warehouse is an enabler. It is an infrastructure that consists of multiple capabilities of content, tools, training, and analytics that can be brought to bear on a variety of business problems.

It is not just a database, Local Area Network (LAN), Wide Area Network (WAN), or a big server. It is the combination of the capabilties that make the data warehouse valuable. The data warehouse cuts across the traditional communities of suppliers of these kinds of capabilities.

As organizations increasingly reach for cross functional solutions to achieve additional efficiencies and profitability, the data warehouse will become an easier sell.

Question 6: What kinds of justifications have others used?

The specific justifications that you use will depend on the initiatives that are on going in your organization and the personalities of the management. The justifications may evolve over time. However, it is much more powerful if you can link the data warehouse to initiatives that have a profit and loss (P&L) impact by increasing revenue, not just by reducing cost. Justifications that have been used successfully include:

- Data integration—The data warehouse may be the only place where data from separate organizational stovepipes can be combined to provide a complete view. This capability may make it possible, for the first time, to get an integrated view of the supply chain from raw materials to final consumer.

- Cost of current efforts—In many organizations there is a large and typically undocumented cost associated with producing reports that would be much easier with a data warehouse. This is sometimes called the "shadow data warehouse."

- Customer and product profitability—Understanding both your customers and your product costs are critical to becoming a lean and focused business.

- Competition is doing it—If the number one competitor in an industry segment is building a data warehouse, it is a good bet that others will follow on that basis alone.

- Common view and understanding of numbers, models, tools, and the business—There is a need to create consistent and widely understood numbers for business planning and monitoring. One vice chairman referred to it as "asterisk control," or the ability to have meetings without numbers that had asterisks attached to explain why one number was slightly different from another version of the same number.

A characteristic of all successful justifications is that the justification articulates a benefit that top management can relate to, not a set of features, especially ones that are technology based. In your justification, you need to be able to make clear why the data warehouse will be of benefit to them.

One of the best ways is to show how the data warehouse contributes to P&L through the revenue side of the business, such as through increased key account penetration or improved market targeting. After a number of years of focus on cost cutting, many firms are now looking to build top line growth. They see that profitable, but small companies, are being gobbled up and that only the larger firms have a chance of remaining independent.

An example of this is the following P&L driver diagram for retail banking. (See Figure 5–1.) Revenue is equal to the balances that customers have on deposit multiplied by the spread (the difference between the interest rate the bank pays the customers and the rate at which the bank can borrow). The balances are equal to the number of accounts multiplied by the average dollar balance per account. Depending on the nature of the area the bank is located in, it may be more productive to try to increase the number of accounts. If this is the bank's strategy, the data warehouse can be the place where data are assembled to enhance the targeting of a promotional campaign. If, on the other hand, the prospects for new customers are not good, the strategy may be to try to generate more business from existing customers. In this case, the data warehouse might be used to identify customer characteristics that would make them more likely to buy specific additional products. Or, the data warehouse could be used to track critical customer complaints, so that they could be dealt with before the customer was tempted to leave the bank.

Justifications that support revenue enhancing strategies will generate stronger and longer term support.

Figure 5–1: Simplified Retail Banking P&L Model

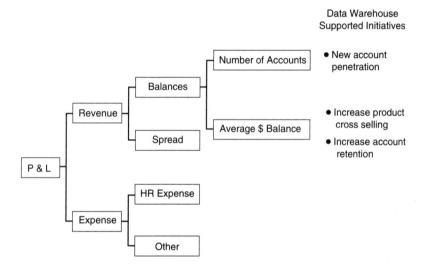

Data Warehouse Supported Initiatives

Question 7: How do you explain what a data warehouse is? Is it hardware, software, infrastructure, process, content, or what?

The whole notion of what a data warehouse is and can be is very much of a moving target. Initially, it will be more of a set of capabilities than a set of concrete results. It may be useful to think of it as an infrastructure that supports multiple corporate efforts. This can help build multiple constituencies that can be valuable in preventing the data warehouse from being too narrowly focused. A significant part of the value of a data warehouse is its ability to connect data from multiple sources. That capability can be hindered if the data warehouse is viewed as being in support of a single initiative. (See Figure 5–2.)

Figure 5–2: The Data Warehouse will provide consistent data, rules, frameworks, and models for multiple types of users and uses.

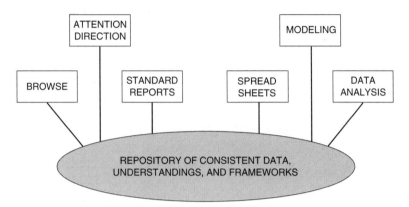

The data warehouse is unusual in that it may have quite a number of aspects, any one of which is emphasized at different times. (See Figure 5–3). Fundamentally, it is an infrastructure that makes use of other infrastructure elements, such as LANs and database servers. Additionally, it is the content, which may include data, voice, video, models, guesses, discussion groups, best practices, and requests for help. Going forward, it is likely to be viewed as both the client and server. Which aspect of the data warehouse you emphasize will need to depend on the purpose of the meeting.

As people gain experience and comfort in using a data warehouse, the types of tasks and sophistication will grow. To answer the question of what a data warehouse is, you need to specify where you are in terms of its evolution and application. The following are a series of steps that some data warehouse efforts have gone through.

Steps in Data Warehouse Capabilities Evolution— Key Characteristics

1. Status reporting—Access to legacy data and multi-dimensional repositories.
2. Attention setting—Focus on most critical items using attention direction mechanisms.

Figure 5–3:   Potential Data Warehouse Components

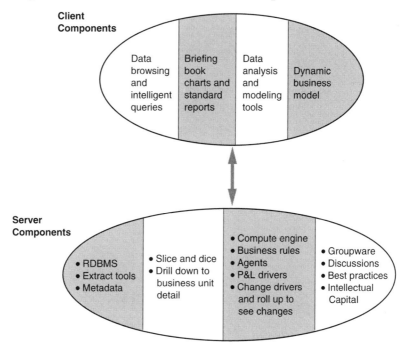

3. Information sharing—Addresses the need to share information, insight, and direction.

4. Business relationship modeling—Capture and use of "rules of thumb" and executive high level models of the business.

5. Process-driven dynamic modeling—Linking changes in financial results to changes in underlying physical processes.

From the perspective of the executive there will be similar changes over time. The most critical will be the change from using the Data Warehouse to understand the status quo to using the data warehouse to create the future. Change is now understood by top management to be an essential part of the future. They will support processes and capabilities that help them understand and drive changes needed by the organization. (See Figure 5–4.)

Figure 5–4: Steps in Data Warehouse Capabilities Evolution— Executive Mindset

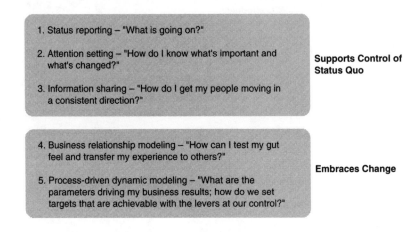

1. Status reporting – "What is going on?"

2. Attention setting – "How do I know what's important and what's changed?"

3. Information sharing – "How do I get my people moving in a consistent direction?"

Supports Control of Status Quo

4. Business relationship modeling – "How can I test my gut feel and transfer my experience to others?"

5. Process-driven dynamic modeling – "What are the parameters driving my business results; how do we set targets that are achievable with the levers at our control?"

Embraces Change

Question 8: How do you decide what to put in the warehouse and in what sequence?

A common problem with data warehouses is that when you conduct interviews and ask people what they want, they respond by saying, "Everything!" However, all data are not equally valuable. There needs to be a process that examines candidate data bases from the perspective of their potential business value. Business value is created by a chain that links data, definitions, models, analytics, and results. (See Figure 5–5.)

Figure 5–5: Business Value Chain from Data Warehouses

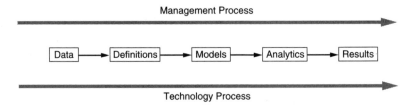

Management Process

Data → Definitions → Models → Analytics → Results

Technology Process

Organizations need to generate accurate, comparable, timely, and well understood numbers that can be traced back to their sources . . . end to end technology and management processes will be required.

To figure out what the priorities should be for inclusion in the data warehouse, it may be useful to start with critical business results and drive back down to the data. In this way the priority is clearly linked to a business result and is not just a consequence of what is available. (See Figure 5–6.)

Figure 5–6

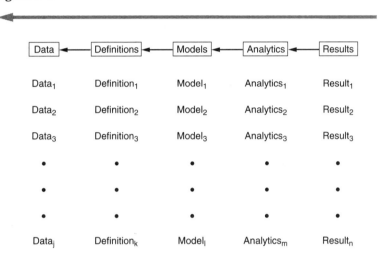

Driving back down the chain can help to identify the data that have the highest priority for inclusion in the warehouse. Each of these elements can be profiled in terms of content, dependency, priority, ownership, quality assurance, and technology

> **Question 9:** How big, in terms of people and resources, is the shadow of the data warehouse in your organization?

Many organizations have large staffs that perform painfully and manual tasks that would be greatly simplified and expedited with an effective data warehouse. Additionally, there would be means for capturing and repeating pieces of analysis so that they wouldn't have to start from scratch each time. Examples of the magnitude of this shadow data warehouse may be helpful in illustrating the need. For those who are not impressed by stories, Jane Griffin, president of Systems Techniques, Inc., has found it useful to conduct surveys to get a handle on the real cost. Often this cost is amplified by people using subscale tools and frequent manual data entry.

Additional costs can be inferred from the lack of a repository for models and analysis, which means that each new effort has to proceed from scratch. In other words, the separate processes of data, definitions, models, analytics, and results are not engineered end-to-end from both a process and technology perspective. This leads to relentless reinvention of the wheel and noncomparable results.

Question 10: Are you prepared to have them take control of the meeting?

Preparation includes being ready for the meeting to take other directions and to depart from your script. This means that you may have to dramatically shorten your presentation and bring things back to the topic through an effective and short summation.

If you have a sense of what is top of mind for the executives, you may be able to generate some likely scenarios that you can prepare for. One of the best ways to prepare is to ask your colleagues to help you role play the meeting and have it videotaped. It will certainly be embarrassing and painful to do, but such preparation can have very large benefits. Part of the evaluation in the eyes of top management is the extent to which you have thought through all the issues. Having first wrestled through them with your peers will help you look more calm and collected in front of top management.

Question 11: When will you be done selling to senior management?

When it is firmly embedded in the process of managing the company.

Question 12: Are the executives right to worry about how much time people will waste letting their fingers do the walking through the data warehouse?

- There is some historical evidence to justify that concern. Examples in several industries showed a huge spike in computer use immediately after the introduction of early data warehouses. Users did a great deal of exploring, often duplicating the work of others. This subsided once they were able to get a handle on the issues that were of concern to them. In some cases, this took a while because there were few road maps to guide them.

- While there is still an opportunity for this sort of surge, we now have enough experience to know that in addition to "on demand" (or at your fingertips) ad hoc information access, there is a large need for information alerts when key relationships have changed (information in your face). Increasingly, staff don't have the time to track everything they need to monitor. Increasingly intelligent agent software can track key relationships and generate alerts via color coded buttons, email, or voice mail when something has changed such as return rates, share of market segment, or delivery times.

- The second part is that we now know that the data warehouse is not just for data or even data about the data (metadata). The data warehouse is a read and write repository for the firm's best thinking, experiences, and models. A new user should be able to browse this first before sitting down to issue queries. Indeed, pre-stored queries and pieces of analysis, can be part of the data warehouse. This could range from sophisticated multi-dimensional models to Excel spreadsheets with the embedded query reissued at the touch of a button.

Question 13: Do you have a broad enough base of support so that the data warehouse does not become colored by the needs of just one group?

The data warehouse is fundamentally an infrastructure project that has the potential to support many corporate efforts. However, if you obtain support from only one group in the organization, you may find yourself making design and implementation choices that lessen the ability of the data warehouse to be all that it could be. This is a delicate balance because you need someone to help carry the ball and run with it. So you need their involvement, however, you cannot let them dominate the effort and create a "cult of personality" where the executive sponsor dictates all the details of the system, even to the extent of specifying color schemes.

> **Question 14:** Do you know the personalities, capabilities, and styles of the executives involved in the decision? Do you know how they learn and interact with others? Do you know what will bore them, interest them, or offend them? If the answer is no, you might want to consider the following:

Intelligence is not a single attribute. Educational psychologists, such as Thomas Armstrong, suggest that there may be at least seven important and distinct kinds of intelligence. People are rarely uniformly good across all categories. In fact, some may use one characteristic to compensate for a weakness in another area. For example, some are visually oriented and learn best from graphs and milestone charts. Others, do not see the patterns. They may be linguistically oriented, preferring narrative, detailed tables, and work breakdown structures. Many executives have a high level assistant who is well acquainted with the working style of their boss. These people are often the best source of information about what the right approach and level of detail should be.

In addition to cognitive capabilities, executives also have personalities. The nature of their personality may have a great deal to do with how you make your presentation and what you include in it. While you don't have time to conduct a complete analysis of the executives, you probably know or can find out enough to answer two questions: (1) Are they outgoing or reserved? (2) Are they intuitive or systematic?

John Brady, a management change consultant, uses the answers to these two questions to indicate which of 4 groups the executive belongs. His research indicates that advance knowledge of where the executive fits can have a big impact on how you should present your case for the data warehouse. For example, those executives who are outgoing and intuitive respond best to a big picture presentation that focuses on the end game, but always be sure to let *them* have the last word.

By contrast, those who are reserved and systematic want a formal presentation where you focus on facts and data, not opinions or stories. They do not want to be rushed. You need to be prepared for them to double check your assumptions. The good news is that once they have taken the time to draw a conclusion they will tend to stick to it.

Below is Brady's diagram showing the characteristics of each of the personality influence styles. (See Figure 5–7.) Following are descriptions of how to work with each of the four styles. (See Figure 5–8.)

Figure 5–7

Two questions to ask before a presentation to senior management:
1. How Outgoing or Reserved are they?
2. How Intuitive or Systematic are they?

Outgoing
Expressive/Eager
Eye contact is direct
Shares personal point of view openly
Concentrates on telling
Assertive gestures
Expansive expressions
Responds well to results and facts
Animated body language

Intuitive			**Systematic**
Decisive			Thoughtful
Random thinkers	Innovating Style	Initiating Style	Sequential thinkers
Big Picture			Accurate Picture
Situation orientation			Analytical
Plays hunches			Proof orientation
Likes new ideas			Plays system
Gets bored with repetition	Implementing Style	Integrating Style	Likes proven ideas
Always thinking of alternatives			Gets bored with stories
			Always thinking of end result

Reserved
Formal/cautious
Eye contact is indirect
Shares personal point of view modestly
Concentrates on listening
Controlled gestures
Thoughtful expressions
Responds well to relationship & teams
Conservative body language

Developed by John Brady, Brady & Associates, Management Change Consultants

Getting Results with the **INTEGRATING STYLE**

Description of INTEGRATING STYLE

The Integrating Style person is reserved and systematic. They will be thoughtful and cautious during conversations. They are most comfortable with facts and data. They prefer business talk to personal conversations. They usually listen more than they will talk. They are typically the perfect style for evaluating options in detail and providing research on advantages and disadvantages of a particular strategy. They are "systems" focused.

Dealing Effectively with the INTEGRATING STYLE

Dealing effectively with the Integrating Style person means providing detailed information for their consideration. They value calmness, patience, and intelligence. They react negatively to being pushed into a decision or being rushed. Highlight completeness and accuracy in your communications. They usually take a long time to decide, but will stick to a decision once they have made it.

Strategies for Simple, Quick, Effective Results·

- focus your facts and data
- be businesslike and formal until they invite a different approach
- be thorough and accurate
- be willing to explain the details and reasons for your recommendations
- allow them to draw their own conclusions
- avoid opinions, hype, or surprises
- avoid being pushy or over assertive
- encourage and allow them time by themselves to make a decision so they can check and cross-check the facts and data

Getting Results with the **INNOVATING STYLE**

Description of INNOVATING STYLE

The Innovating Style person is outgoing and intuitive. They will be open, talkative, and approachable. They are most comfortable with new ideas, creativity, and the opportunity to try something new. They are very interested in leading and directing new ventures or teams. They are typically the perfect style for start-up types of businesses and activities. They are visionaries.

Dealing Effectively with the INNOVATING STYLE

Dealing effectively with the Innovating Style person means providing support for their ideas and aspirations. They value newness, status, and creativity. They react negatively to people who will not listen to them, or cut them off. Highlight freedom, creativity, and newness in your communication. They decide quickly and will often change their minds just as quickly.

Strategies for Simple, Quick, Effective Results

- focus your conversation on ideas that are stimulating and exciting
- be attentive and listen (taking notes is optional)
- feed back to them what they said
- explore the vision, the big picture, and the grand end result
- allow them to take tangents
- avoid fine details, procedures, and confining rules of engagement (keep it broad)
- give them an opportunity to make a quick decision and let you deal with all the details
- always let them have the last word

Getting Results with the IMPLEMENTING STYLE

Description of IMPLEMENTING STYLE

The Implementing Style person is reserved and intuitive. They will be warm and attentive during conversations. They need rapport building relationship conversation before easing into business talk. They are very supportive and often will listen more than they will talk. They are typically the perfect style for teams, because they believe in team play and fairness. They are relationship focused.

Dealing Effectively with the IMPLEMENTING STYLE

Dealing effectively with the Implementing Style person means providing support for them personally, their team, and enhancing their relationships with others. They value fairness, equity, and loyalty to the team, group, department, and company. They react negatively to "pushy" people. Highlight people benefits, empathy, and consideration in your recommendations. They usually consult with others privately before making a decision and stick to it once a decision is made.

Strategies for Simple, Quick, Effective Results

- focus your conversation on people
- be warm, friendly, patient and support their relationship needs
- establish rapport before moving into business
- take the time to draw out their ideas and concerns (taking notes is optional)
- gently and tactfully explore areas of disagreement
- avoid topics that threaten the security of their team, department, or company, unless they open the subject
- avoid being pushy or over assertive
- encourage and allow them time to consult with others before they decide

Getting Results with the INITIATING STYLE

Description of INITIATING STYLE

The Initiating Style person is outgoing and systematic. They will be direct and to the point. They are most comfortable with the bottom line and people who promise and deliver results quickly. They are goal-, task-, and time-focused. They are typically the perfect style for tight deadline projects with high risk and reward. Their major desire is to control their environment.

Dealing Effectively with the INITIATING STYLE

Dealing effectively with the Initiating Style person means focusing on tangible results and well-planned activities. They value brevity and prefer a short menu of good alternatives so they can make the final decision. They react negatively to soft approaches, long stories, and missed deadlines. Highlight tangible results, "on time/under budget" approaches, and the bottom line. They decide quickly and will often change their minds as the situation changes.

Strategies for Simple, Quick, Effective Results·

- focus your conversation on tasks and results

- be business-like and formal (balance directness and tact)

- be quick and concise (taking notes is mandatory)

- feed back to them what they say and confirm your understanding of what they want

- encourage them to challenge your ideas and recommendations

- provide a well thought-out, short menu of recommendations (no more than three options) for them to choose from

- give them an opportunity to make a quick decision and let you deal with all the details

- always let them have the last word

Figure 5–8: Summary of Personality Influence Styles and How to Work with Each

Style	Description	Achieving Results
Integrating	Reserved and systematic—thoughtful, cautious, comfortable with facts, prefer business talk, evaluates options in detail, values calmness, patience, and intelligence. Perfect for evaluating options in detail and providing research on advantages and disadvantages of a particular strategy. They usually take a long time to decide, but will stick to a decision once they have made it.	• Focus your facts and data, provide details • Avoid opinions, hype, or surprises • Be businesslike, not pushy or over assertive • Be willing to explain the details and reasons for your recommendations • Allow them to draw their own conclusions • Allow them time by themselves to cross check facts and make a decision
Innovative	Outgoing and intuitive—open, talkative, approachable, comfortable with new ideas, wants to lead new ventures, values newness, status, and creativity. React negatively to those who do not listen to them or cut them off. Visionaries. Perfect for start-up types of business and activities. They decide quickly and will often change their minds just as quickly.	• Focus on ideas that are stimulating and exciting • Be attentive and listen (Taking notes is optional) • Avoid fine details, procedures • Explore the vision, the big picture, the end result • Always let them have the last word • Feed back to them what they said
Implementing	Reserved and intuitive—warm and attentive during conversation, wants rapport building before business talk, supportive, believes in team play, values fairness, equity, and loyalty to the team, group, department, and company. React negatively to pushy people. Relationship focused. They consult with others privately before making a decision and stick to it once a decision is made.	• Focus your conversation on people • Be warm, friendly, patient, supportive • Establish rapport before moving into business • Take time to draw out their ideas and concerns • Gently and tactfully explore areas of disagreement • Encourage them to consult with others before deciding

Style	Description	Achieving Results
Initiating	Outgoing and systematic—direct and to the point, most comfortable with the bottom line and people who promise and deliver results quickly. Goal, task, and time focused. Their major desire is to control their environment. They value brevity, and prefer a short menu of good alternatives so they can make their final decision. They decide quickly and will often change their minds as the situation changes.	• Focus on tangible results and well planned activities, not soft approaches or long stories • Be quick and concise, business-like and formal, present a short menu of options • Feed back to them what they said to confirm your understanding of what they want • Let them make a quick decision letting you deal with all the detail • Always let them have the last word • Taking notes is mandatory

Question 15: What are the components of an effective data warehouse? (See Figure 5–9.)

- Link to strategic objectives—These are the reasons for the data warehouse's existence. Without an explicit connection to the strategic objectives of the organization, it will be difficult to justify the effort that is needed to make a data warehouse successful.

- Training—Just because the data are available does not mean that people will know how to make effective use of the data warehouse. Most people are not trained in using facts to make decisions. In the past, facts were too costly and time consuming. People had to develop rules of thumb to get them through. Training will need to include how to think analytically, not just how to drive the tools.

- Client side tools—The data warehouse is incomplete with out a set of tools for access and manipulation of the data by multiple users for multiple purposes.

- Server side tools—The server can be more than a relational database and gateway to other sources. The server can store and execute complex, multi-dimensional models of the business. The server can be a place to build intellectual capital through discussions. The server can provide background search agents that track key relationships and e-mail deviations from expectation.

- The data warehouse infrastructure—The data warehouse makes use of enterprise infrastructures such as networks, dial-up capabilities, and servers. It is itself an infrastructure or enabling component for targeted efforts such as understanding business potential.

- Multiple types of content—The data warehouse is more than just numbers. It is an opportunity to capture, disseminate, and create new types of information, including models of the business, discussion groups, best practices for tool use, and analytic frameworks for thinking about business problems.

Figure 5–9: The Data Warehouse needs analytic frameworks to help users focus on business problems.

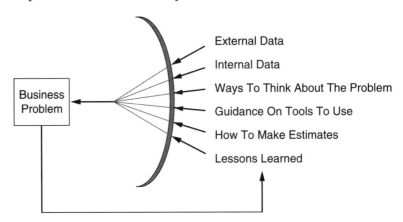

Question 16: Once they agree upon the need, how will top management know that you can do it?

- Milestones—The data warehouse needs to have a series of milestones for top management to review. In spacing your milestones, make sure they are far enough apart so that you can show real progress, but not so far apart that management will have forgotten about the project. Use the milestones to stimulate meetings to review progress to date and remind management of the importance of the effort.

- Pay as you see as you go—Try to avoid great leaps forward. Plan your warehouse in steps so that management can see benefits along the way. This lets them control the evolution of the data warehouse and not be faced with all or nothing decisions.

- Scalability—A common problem with data warehouses is that initial success leads to a sudden ramp up in demand, which causes the initial architecture to crash and burn. The best defense against this is to establish a scaleable architecture that can handle increased demand as needed.

- Flexible control—Going in, management may be very worried that information will get out and do them harm. You need to have mechanisms that can restrict access as needed, but not thwart legitimate use.

- Role of informal data—In addition to data about the data (metadata), the warehouse needs to store and grow ideas, ways of thinking about problems, and tutorials on tool use.

- Early success—The data warehouse is a long term effort. However, there should be some "low hanging" fruit, such as the integration of operational and sales data, which would provide some early success. Try to identify several of these areas before the project starts.

Question 17: Neil Raden, President of Archer Decision Sytems, asks how, as an organization, are you going to nurture and encourage people to use these facilities in new and innovative ways?

The data warehouse needs people to use it. These people should not be fettered by unnecessary security requirements. The culture needs to change so that the use of facts to make decisions is valued and so that innovative thinking about data is praised. Typically this has to start at the top of the organization. This is a key role for the champion of the data warehouse to perform. (See Figure 5–10.)

Figure 5–10:   A successful Data Warehouse supports continuous user involvement and learning.

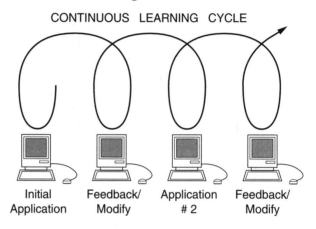

CONTINUOUS LEARNING CYCLE

| Initial Application | Feedback/ Modify | Application # 2 | Feedback/ Modify |

Question 17: What can the data warehouse become? What is the end game?

The data warehouse has the potential to fundamentally change how we think about and manage the business. One of the major barriers to effective management and execution is that, except in times of crisis, most organizations do not have agreement on the state of the organization (the data) and what to do about it (the linkage between actions and results). The act of creating a data warehouse generates the opportunity to get everyone on the same page, both in terms of definitions and how the business works. Dick Hackathorn, a noted data warehousing pioneer, discusses this in his August, 1995, Bolder Technology Report, where he notes in his data warehouse Insight #6 that

> The toughest part of reconciling inconsistent data is surfacing and reconciling the differing mental models of the business. When we talk about reconciling metadata, I bet that we don't appreciate the huge differences in the way people view the enterprise. For fun, ask several managers to define the important characteristics of your customer. This diversity is no wonder, given that we often

carve the enterprise into numerous pieces, each biased toward sub-optimizing.

In a recent conversation with Doug Neal, I was impressed with the importance of embedding data warehouse into mainstream management. As Doug stated, the data warehouse should be a management tool to achieve collaborative work. One should smash together those mental models to refine a common business model for setting goals and evaluating progress, with the data warehouse at the core. What a grand objective for the data warehouse!

An effective data warehouse can become the supporting structure for understanding potential, identifying opportunity, and managing the business. (See Figure 5–11.) It can become an active repository and source of dialog on how the business works, what its potential is, and what kind of commitments individuals and the organization can make.

Figure 5–11:   Data Warehouse Embedded into the Management System

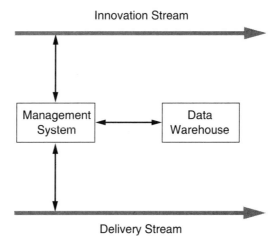

In the long run, the job of the Data Warehouse will be to support the management system that coordinates the two fundamental activities of the business: innovation and delivery.

Chapter 6

Data Warehousing: Putting It Altogether

Carol L. Burleson
David E. Tabler

Fellows,
The Data Warehousing Institute

Over the past few years, the world of data warehousing has shifted into high gear, providing companies and Information Technology (IT) organizations with new opportunities for survival in an increasingly competitive and downsized world. Companies are discovering that they can increase their competitive advantage by having access to better decision making information. IT organizations, on the other hand, are discovering that data warehousing provides an opportunity to position their resources to be more responsive and supportive of these changing business needs. It can be the classic "win, win" situation for both the company and IT as they pursue data warehousing opportunities. With the right partnership, data warehousing will be an integral part of your company's future for a very long time.

From a business perspective, a Data Warehouse (DW) provides the information intelligence necessary to target the resources and products of the company to its most valuable asset, its customer. The value to the business can be enormous and provide:

1. better decisions at reduced cost
2. greater targeting of markets, sales, and products
3. better service to the customer
4. better management of business resources
5. reengineered business operations
6. opportunities to flatten organizations

With rapidly changing markets, increased competition, and shorter product response times, companies are demanding the next generation of decision and information support systems to remain both focused and relevant in their markets. Data warehouses can provide a significant payback for companies who understand the power of information and for the IT organizations responsible for their deployment.

With all the promises and assurances associated with data warehousing, it would appear that both IT and business managers are responding with tepid optimism. After all, the IT industry is famous for hyping new technologies as the next wave of business solutions. But, past experience has shown that many IT-based business solutions have failed to provide companies with the capabilities required to support their fluid business operations. In many cases, companies have been left wondering about the benefits related to IT organizations, their growing costs, and increased resource demands. IT organizations have become increasingly skeptical of "the latest" methodologies, tools, and technologies "offering guaranteed solutions" to their less than desirable legacy system situations. But, as more and more data warehouses are successfully implemented, tepid optimism is giving way to a broad based enthusiasm for the concept and changing perspectives on the relative worth of IT organizations and investments.

How are IT managers responding to their company's requirement for Data Warehousing? A 1995 Gartner Group survey of Fortune 500 IT managers found that ninety percent of all organizations were planning to implement data warehouses within the next three years. From an IT investment perspective, the Gartner Group is projecting a five-fold increase in DW-related hardware and software purchases by 1999. Clearly, most IT managers are or will soon be focusing their investments and resources on their first DW project.

For many IT managers, the first project will be a very demanding one, for others it will be doomed to failure. Why is it that some projects are successful and others fail while using the same technologies and following the same development methodologies? Why does data warehousing require a fundamentally different approach to develop, deploy, and support? What are the keys to successful DW implementations and why do variations exist from project to project? How can you be successful when it is impossible to devise specific, detailed, long-term DW implementation strategies? "Putting it all together" will address those questions and provide strategies and approaches readers can use to be successful in their environment. Discussion topics will include:

1. Looking beyond your first DW project
2. The natural DW evolution process
3. Managing the DW evolution process
4. DW management framework
5. Building the DW support infrastructure
6. Strategies for sustaining business and user support

LOOK BEYOND YOUR FIRST DW PROJECT

It is very tempting for IT managers to focus solely on making their first DW project a success. After all, everyone wants their first try at something new to be a success. But your company's DW will not be, and should not be, a one time development effort. All companies will be demanding enterprise-wide DW capabilities to remain competitive. In reality, your DW will be a long term continuous effort that, for all practical terms, may never be finished. You will need to plan your IT strategies around being in the DW business for a very long time.

To be sure, the thirst for new DW capabilities will never be fully satisfied. Given the competitive nature of business today, success for the IT organization will be based on "what have you done for me lately?" That says that the IT leadership must have a game plan for how they will strategically expand the DW capabilities to continuously meet the most pressing business needs. Said differently, there is little benefit to your company if the first DW project cannot evolve into a corporate information support capability that meets an enterprise-wide set of business needs. Experience says that the company's long term DW successes will be based on how well the IT organization manages the *evolution* of the DW over an extended period of time.

THE NATURAL DATA WAREHOUSE EVOLUTION PHENOMENA

Something very different happens once your first DW project has been successfully deployed: A significant *minority* of your company's management and DW users want more data, and they want it now! Not all of the company's management and users mind you, that would be too easy. If experience and human nature are any indicators, the majority of your management and users will slowly embrace the DW at varying degrees during the first year, maybe two. For them, change comes slowly.

As Figure 6–1 depicts, business management and DW users are the ones that ultimately drive the IT organization to support a broad spectrum of users and an expanding set of DW capabilities. Those that readily accept the DW will soon want more data and ask the IT organization to quickly start enhancing the baseline system. The more data is added, the more users begin to see the possibilities for applying the DW to an expanded set of business problems. That, in turn, requires the IT organization to move out in another direction and add more data and tools. Finally, the more advanced DW users define a broader range of information needs and business requirements outside the original subject area. The IT organization must now move into a different business area and integrate more data into the DW. This effectively restarts a new development cycle.

In reality, the DW evolution phenomena is quite natural because most companies are in desperate need of an enterprise-wide decision support capability. But business management and DW user support can erode rapidly and threaten the viability of the DW if not properly supported. There are serious consequences for the IT organization that cannot support the spectrum of DW needs within the evolution process. The wide range of demands begins a chain reaction that most IT organizations are very much unprepared for: the requirement to actively support all phases of the DW evolution process at the same time. The IT organization must recognize the evolution process and prepare to manage its dynamics.

Figure 6–1: Continued DW Evolution

Customer Expectations	IS Organization
Accepting the System	* Original Baseline
	* Operating the new system * Performing system maintenance * Providing user support
Increasing Information Needs	* Baseline Enhancements
	* Adding data * Modifying queries and screens * "Public Library" releases
Changing the Requirements	* System Capabilities Expansion
	* Hardware * End User tools * Development tools
Seeing the Possibilities	* New Subject Areas
	* What's Next * Restart the process!

MANAGE THE DW EVOLUTION PROCESS

What is the DW evolution process? Fundamentally, it's a series of planned steps to continuously expand and migrate the DW in concert with the needs of the business. It is a process that *incrementally* implements your DW vision and direction over time and proactively guides the IT organization in making sound near-term project decisions within a "big picture" context. It is the hardest part of data warehousing! The evolution process is all about strategies for moving your company, its DW users and the IT organization into a DW environment that contributes to the bottom-line profitability of the business.

The evolution process has four phases that end up being executed concurrently. Each of the following phases must be supported by the IT organization and managed as an integrated set of DW requirements:

1. Supporting the current DW baseline—The IT organization must continue to provide the operational and customer support for the current DW baseline. To the business it means that the DW is being used to address today's business problems in a productive way. To the user it means that the DW is always available, supported, and loaded with the latest data. To the IT organization, it means providing the same level of operational support as other production systems but with the additional complexities of extensive data loading and validation. It also means providing a range of customer support services to a diverse group of users.

2. Enhance current baseline capabilities—As with any system, enhancements will be made to the current baseline. Some enhancements will be part of a planned phased approach to build the DW in manageable increments. Other enhancements will be identified as DW usage grows and the business and users see additional benefits to upgrading the current baseline of data, data access tools, and applications. For the IT organization, this means moving quickly to implement enhancements as a subset of the user base becomes proficient in using the DW.

3. Define new business requirements—The IT organization must be very selective of the next DW project so that it has the support of the business. This is a critical step in the evolution process. It is incumbent on the IT organization to proactively understand the major business issues facing the company and look for new and innovative data warehousing applications and/or possibilities. Some call it "reading the business" to make sure that DW investments are contributing to the company's bottom-line. The IT organization must shepherd a process that builds consensus among the key business areas, managers, and users. Each new project

must target a measurable business objective that everyone can understand, sign up for, and support. Follow-on marketing and selling is done to solidify support for the investment in new capabilities.

4. Implement new baseline—Based on the new business requirements, the IT organization would begin building the new DW baseline or manageable increments as appropriate. This would include the system life cycle steps of requirements analysis, design, development, testing, deployment, training, and support. New data, applications, tools, and customer support capabilities would be added to the DW.

Although it may appear that the evolution process is a sequential one, it is *not*. In fact, trying to make it a sequential one will certainly cause your DW efforts to fail because you will not be in a position to meet the spectrum of user's needs. An inherent part of data warehousing is being in each phase concurrently. It is a direct result of your company having pent-up demand for information, ever changing business needs, and a very diverse set of users across the company. This demand will require the IT organization to manage differently, be very flexible, and take a holistic view of their DW, its capabilities, and the possibilities it presents to their company. To the extent that the IT organization effectively manages the DW evolution process, they will be successful and so will the business!

DATA WAREHOUSE MANAGEMENT FRAMEWORK

As an integral part of your company's future, the DW will require a more fluid management approach than those used to manage traditional business systems. You will need to put in place a DW management framework that addresses today's baseline, tomorrow's enhancements, and future DW requirements—today. The purpose of the DW management framework is to set the strategic guidelines for making project investment decisions and consciously manage the DW evolution by prioritizing all DW efforts. Figure 6–2 presents the major framework components that must be managed.

Figure 6–2: Data Warehouse Management Framework

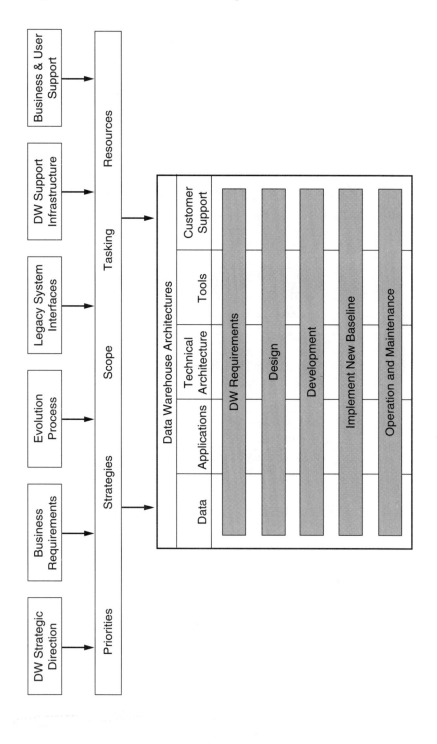

Why do you need a management framework? The dynamics of data warehousing are such that in the day to day world, it's hard to keep everything in perspective when being pulled in a thousand different directions. On the one hand, you want to move out smartly and add data that you feel will provide significant benefits for your company. But on the other hand, you are tied down dealing with the users who have not mastered the current DW baseline and the inevitable operation and maintenance problems that always seem to take up a significant amount of time. And of course, you will never have an unlimited amount of resources to use either. So you need a management framework to keep things in perspective in order to move your DW forward.

The framework must integrate the following to effectively manage your DW:

1. Architecture management—Inherent in the framework is the management of your DW by architectures. Architecture management provides the baseline from which to manage all DW changes throughout the evolution process. There are five architectures to be managed: data, applications, technical architecture, data access tools, and customer support. Each architecture manages important components of the DW throughout the system development life cycle, e.g., requirements, design, development, implementation, and support. All architectures are managed as a set to ensure complete integration across the DW product as it evolves. As importantly, they provide the required focus for aligning IT resources in the most productive way. Significant benefits accrue to the IT organization when architecture management is further extended to include legacy systems also. By doing so, greater integration is ensured with the very systems that feed your DW.

2. DW strategic direction—Your company will need a road map that defines what the DW will ultimately be. It should provide the vision and strategic direction that will guide the DW evolution process over time. It should also contain an enterprise level data model, diagrams, and other analysis products commonly

found in many Information Strategic Planning (ISP) methodologies. These products can be used as important tools to guide the DW evolution when making strategic, tactical, and operational decisions.

3. Business requirements—You will need to put in place a process for gathering and prioritizing DW requirements that are linked to a set of bona fide business needs. Ideally, the IT organization should be in a position to understand where the business is headed and what role the DW can play in achieving near- and long-term business objectives. Since the company operates within a dynamic business environment, the process should constantly read the company's business needs and adjust DW priorities and projects accordingly.

4. Manage the DW evolution process—As discussed earlier, the DW evolution process has four phases to be managed concurrently. This puts a significant strain on available IT resources. The input of strategic direction and business requirements are the critical links required to successfully drive the evolution process. They need to be integrated into the management process in order to keep the DW aligned to the company's business needs.

5. Manage the legacy system interface—Once your DW becomes operational, you are forever tied to the legacy system operational environment. You will need to put in place a process to tightly integrate the management of legacy systems with your DW. This includes both the operational aspects of the systems and any planned changes that may impact the source data feeding your DW. Failure to integrate legacy system management will result in chaos across the DW environment. Architecture management is one solution for this problem.

6. Manage the DW support infrastructure—The support infrastructure is the critical link to the company and the DW user. It is the principal vehicle for empowering the DW user. As such, it will require a significant amount of direction, coordination, and attention to ensure that it is doing the right things to make the DW users productive.

7. Manage business and user support—Managing busi-

ness and user support includes evolving the business management and DW users to make them more productive and supportive of what the DW can accomplish for the business. It means that the IT organization assumes responsibility for evolving the business and users in their usage of not only today's capabilities but tomorrow's as well.

As you can see, the DW management framework contains a variety of diverse yet related activities that must be managed to make your DW, company, and users successful. It is not an easy task. At a minimum, you will need to develop plans and strategies for all of the above. Maintaining tight integration across all of the framework components will be key to keeping your DW evolution effort moving along with your DW vision and requirements. It will always be a balance between moving forward, maintaining what you have, and keeping everyone's expectations in line with the resources available to the IT manager.

BUILDING THE DW SUPPORT INFRASTRUCTURE

The DW support infrastructure is the IT organization's lifeline to the DW user. It is the critical link that ultimately empowers the DW user to become proficient in using the full capabilities of the DW. User empowerment is the long-term goal of the DW support infrastructure. Its success will be measured by how effectively the company uses the DW and how much it contributes to better business decisions.

Traditional vs. DW Support Infrastructures

IT organizations must recognize that there are fundamental differences between a DW support infrastructure and those traditionally used to support transaction-oriented business systems. In a transaction-oriented business system, the system is targeted to a specific set of tasks and users, there are a finite number of application-based processes, completed transactions render predictable results, and the knowledge of data and technology required is limited. The user support can be specifically aligned to the system functions and implemented in a structured way. A DW support environment, by contrast, lacks predictability (or is predictably unpredictable). By design, the DW is used to meet a variety of business information needs (many discovered on the fly!), in a very unpredictable way, for a user base that spans the company. The results of a query are dependent on the question that was asked, the way it was formulated, and the range of data used. Knowledge of data and desktop tools are essential to effectively use the DW. The DW support infrastructure must be extremely flexible and highly skilled to meet a diversity of user and company needs.

Complicating the Support Equation: The DW User

One of the most important factors in developing your support strategy is assessing the overall ability of your users to use the DW. Their skills will dictate much of the support you will need to provide. If you step back for a moment and think about it, your DW will be supporting a variety of user types across the business, e.g., corporate staff, middle managers, sales representatives, and marketing forecasters. Those different user types will have a range of computer skills, e.g., novice, average computer literacy, or power users and a range of knowledge about the data in your DW, e.g., basic knowledge, specific business area knowledge, or broad corporate knowledge. Those user types will also need different types of data, e.g., transaction level, lightly summarized, or highly summarized, depending upon their styles for assimilating data into information. The number of possible combinations of user types, computer skills, data knowledge, and data types is the spectrum of users you must be able to support. Not an easy job!

Using Your Best People to Support the User

A critical success factor for your support infrastructure will be to put your best people out in front performing DW customer support functions. Experience shows that in the world of data warehousing, nothing less will do! It is only your best people that can teach, coach, and empower the DW user. It is only your best people who will be knowledgeable about the full DW capabilities and how they can be used to provide users and managers with the data they need. Obviously, this is a significant change from past system support strategies that provided user assistance or help desks with lesser skilled (and paid) staff. Using your best people is a prerequisite for both short and long term success and one that should not be short changed.

The IT manager must ensure that the support strategy can empower the broadest spectrum of user types identified. To do so means that the support services must be carefully targeted. Some of your users will need minimal training and support and catch on quickly, some will need additional help, and some will need a significant amount of help to become productive. Your strategy should include helping them all. There will also be those users that will never make the transition. They will become the first casualty of implementing the DW. Ultimately, your company must take some action to deal with these users. You must develop a strategy for dealing with the company's management in these situations.

Developing a Support Strategy

The specific DW support infrastructure requirements are driven by the capabilities of the initial DW implementation, the relative skills of the user population, the support and acceptance of the DW by the company's managers, the culture of the company, and cost. All play an important role in developing a concept of support for your DW. There are some basic support services that all IT organizations will need to provide. Figure 6–3 provides a generalized framework for DW support services. Given that no two companies are alike, the IT manager must develop a support strategy that is customized to its company's environment. In doing so, the following should be considered:

1. Application-driven tools—Your support staff will need to have expertise in all applications that are built to aid the user in accessing the DW. That expertise must include the system entry point, security controls, menus that link each individual application, and any data that the user may access. For example, if there are standard (canned) queries, reports, or download capabilities provided through applications, the support staff must fully understand the application logic, data accessed, and the intended results. If you

provide applications that access metadata or data dictionary information, the support staff must also have expertise in these DW capabilities.

2. Desktop tools—If you are deploying a desktop tool providing direct access to the DW, your support staff must not only understand the data but the full capabilities of the tool in developing queries and reports. Support is much more complex for desktop tools because the range of queries is endless and understanding the results requires a more detailed knowledge of the data and associated algorithms used. You must also understand more about the user's desktop environment and how the tool may compliment other desktop tools such as spreadsheets and graphics packages. If you provide the user with access to SQL, similar considerations apply to knowledge of the tool, data, and intended results.

3. Analysis support—Implicit in supporting application-driven and desktop tools is analysis support. DW users will need help in using both to meet their needs. Analysis support requires data analysts who understand the data inside and out. As importantly, they also must have a "business context" about the data, e.g., they can understand what the DW user is trying to ask from a business perspective and help them get the intended results. In some cases, the data analysts will develop the query for the DW user, in other cases the data analysts will "coach" the DW user in the development of their query. In either case, the long term goal is to empower the DW user to fully use the DW capabilities independent of the IT organization.

4. Training—Training support should be focused on teaching the DW users how to use the DW, its tools and its data. If you provide application-driven and/ or desktop tools, the DW users must be given enough training to become reasonably proficient at navigating the tools and data to get the results they are looking for. This may require either an intensive training session or a series of training classes to accomplish. Training for application-driven applications will have

an overall structure similar to the application itself. Desktop tool training is much more complex because you are trying to show the DW user the full range of capabilities (or possibilities) that the tool has.

Integrated into these classes is introductory training on the data itself. You will find that user knowledge of the data will be very limited, especially if your users are moving from a hard copy report environment. You may want to have follow-on classes that provide more insight into all data found in the DW. Lastly, there will be a need to have some workshops tailored to specific types of users or areas of business. These workshops would be more ad-hoc in nature emphasizing specific problem solving requirements while reinforcing the original training.

5. User assistance—First-line support should resolve system level problems and provide administrative assistance. It would be the place DW users contacted if they couldn't log on to the DW, wanted to become a DW user, or needed some generalized information about the DW. This would include system status, user ids, passwords, information about registering for training, and general desktop support. The skills of first line support would not include either specialized tool support nor data analysis support.

6. Customer information—Customer information provides the DW user with on-going information that documents baseline system functionality, available data, system enhancements, known problems and work-arounds, planned system maintenance, and emergency system problems. A major product of the support function would be the User's Manual and Data Dictionary. These would be periodically republished as new capabilities or data are added. On-going user information would be published on an as needed basis to give the status of new capabilities and problems, provide interim procedures for using new capabilities, and tips or tricks for getting at certain types of data. Newsletters and customer feedback workshops could also be a part of the information conduit to the DW user.

Figure 6–3: Data Warehouse Support Services

Applications	Tools	Analysis Support	Training	User Assistance	Customer Information

• Data
  – Definition
  – Design
  – Structure
 	
• Stnd. Queries
 	
• Reports
 	
• Ad-Hoc Queries
 	
• Downloads
	• Data
	  – Definition
	  – Design
	  – Structure
	
	• Ad-Hoc Reports
	
	• Ad-Hoc Queries
	
	• Downloads
		• Specialized Data Analysis
		
		• Custom Query Support
		
		• Future Req'mts
			• Standard Capabilities
			
			• Standard Applications
			
			• Standard Tools
			
			• Advanced Topics
			
			• Specialized Work Groups
			
			• One-on-One
				• System Status
				
				• General Information
				
				• General Assistance
				
				• Desktop Support
					• User Manuals
					
					• Daily Messages
					
					• Periodic System Enhancements, Updates Memo's
					
					• Marketing
					
					• Selling

In summary, the IT manager must build a support infrastructure that supports the DW from day one and constantly evolve its services as you evolve the DW. It is important to recognize that the support needs will change as the company and users mature in their use of the DW. System utilization statistics, user assistance calls, requests for additional training, and the frequency of requests for new capabilities can all provide an indication of how much the users have mastered. Knowing where your user is at all times is key to fine tuning your support capabilities!

SUSTAINING SUPPORT FOR THE DW

With all the competitive pressures on the business today, you would think that sustaining business and user support for the current and future DW capabilities would be a snap. But it isn't. In fact, it is one the hardest things for the IT organization to achieve. The reason is very simple: The implementation of your DW impacts the very people who originally supported the requirements for a DW. It also can affect those who did not. The impacts can cut both ways. There can be positive impacts that profoundly improve the way your company does business or reduces cost. There can also be negative impacts (real or perceived) that cause the users to resist using the DW. But as anxious as the business management and users are, many are not prepared to move from a hard copy, stovepipe information based environment to on-line, desk top access to integrated business data.

No matter what the impacts may be, they become something the IT organization must be prepared for and carefully manage to sustain continued acceptance and support. Change management within the company becomes an added IT responsibility and represents a significant paradigm shift for most IT organizations. Your success at sustaining business support for your DW is directly linked to your ability to manage the impacts on the company's managers, manage the impacts on the DW users and continually build the business case for future DW expansion.

Strategies for Sustaining Business Support

Sustaining business support for your DW begins with the initial deployment. After all, first impressions are lasting no matter the how good your DW really is. You will need to continually solidify the support of those business managers who have initially embraced the DW. Likewise, you need to convince, demonstrate, and persuade those business managers who have been less than supportive.

Your efforts should not just be limited to maintaining support for today's capabilities. The larger task for the IT organization is to continue marketing and selling future DW capabilities. Your management will want to understand what the "possibilities" are and how they and your company can benefit from it. Marketing the DW vision is something that must be done often enough that people understand it and remember.

Marketing and Selling Today's Capabilities

In many ways, marketing and selling today's DW capabilities is a very political effort. What needs to be managed most is the perceptions, opinions, and attitudes of those managers whose organizations will be most impacted by the DW. Fundamentally, it requires the IT organization to have more insight into the many uses of the DW within particular business areas. The IT organization needs to play an active role in showing business managers specific DW uses to meet today's information needs—today. After all, its use is really optional when it's first deployed. The "court of public opinion" is very powerful and, without careful management by the IT organization, can ultimately determine the DW's fate in the early stages of acceptance. Some key strategies for managing business acceptance:

1. DW leadership—One of the first priorities should be to find the right leader(s) to represent the DW to the business. The DW leadership can come from either inside or outside the IT organization. Regardless of the source, it should be someone who enjoys broad corporate respect and understands what potential and promise the DW holds in meeting today's business challenges. This person or persons should be someone who moves easily within the company's environment, has an established network of colleagues outside of the IT organization, speaks the language of the business, and has a working knowledge of what the DW can do for the business. The reason for this is simple—there needs to be someone who can champion the DW during the early stages of acceptance when resistance is very high and true believers are few. That someone must constantly monitor the on-going acceptance process and proactively work any real or perceived problems identified. As importantly, the DW leadership must continually market and sell the "business possibilities" your DW can support.

2. Understanding the political environment—As all IT organizations know, corporate politics plays an important role in the acceptance of any new product. In the world of data warehousing, politics are something that needs to be proactively managed. After all, for some managers, information is power and a DW can dramatically change the balance of power. At a more basic level, a DW changes who has access to data, the process for getting data, and the skills

required to access data. It can also fundamentally change the number and types of users involved in the information business and rearrange their jobs. The common theme is change when implementing your DW. To the extent that you impact an organization, you impact its managers. The DW leadership needs to be cognizant of the politics that may impact full acceptance of your DW. Keeping in front of organizational politics is key to sustaining acceptance.

3. Befriending major power brokers—No matter what the organization, there are a number of business managers who have more influence among their peers than others. There are also some managers who have more vision when it comes to using IT as an effective business tool. That being the case, is important to line up the support of as many of these managers as possible. You will need their support for two reasons: (1) to ride out any initial problems that may threaten the credibility of your DW; and (2) to further expand the DW. To be sure, there will be problems that must be addressed during the initial deployment phase, some may even undermine user and business support. You need to be sure that you have befriended those managers who recognize the DW's long term potential and who will not cut and run at the first sign of problems. Lining up support from key management within your company will ensure that minor problems are kept in perspective as your DW takes hold and becomes an integral information resource for your company.

4. Keeping support up, resistance down—As with any new IT product, your DW will be constantly evaluated in terms of accuracy, timeliness, ease of use, and business value. Its credibility is on the line every day. Unfortunately, managers are the first to hear of any problems, real or perceived, minor or major, some clearly stated or exaggerated. Ultimately, the managers are forming opinions based on user feedback. As we know, the tone of user feedback can significantly influence whether the opinions are favorable or unfavorable. Whatever the issues, the first step is to

respond quickly to fix any problems that arise. As importantly, the second step will be to manage whatever public opinion has formed to either reinforce support or minimize the damage. The "court of public opinion" is something that has a life of its own and is slow to change. It will be to your advantage to actively monitor the business manager's opinions in order to keep their DW support up and user resistance down.

Building Long Term Support

The process of building long term support is aimed at marketing and selling the business case for continued investment in your DW. This should be done by someone who has the trust and respect of your company's management. The following presents some strategies that can be used to ensure the support of key company management.

1. Support your current DW baseline. The first task of building long-term support centers on effectively supporting your current DW baseline every day. If you can't do that to the satisfaction of the company's management, you can't build the business case for future expansion. You also must reinforce the business benefits already realized with today's baseline. Future support will only exist when the company sees a solid track record of benefits from which to build on.

2. Seize "big bang, little effort" opportunities. One of the best ways to build long-term support is to implement some new information capabilities that the company has always wanted. The key is to jump on this type requirement, make it happen quickly and then demonstrate the new capabilities before they are asked for. This proactive approach will enhance the credibility of your DW and provide further evidence of its responsiveness in meeting a wide spectrum of business needs.

3. Implement major upgrades within 3 to 6 months. A long-standing complaint of IT organizations has been the length of time to deploy new systems. The lack of

flexibility in legacy systems has perpetuated the belief (mostly real) that any system upgrade will take at least a year, maybe two. Moving to a DW environment will allow you to rapidly upgrade your DW with new capabilities. You should put all major upgrades in a 3 to 6 month timebox and scope requirements accordingly. By doing so, you will be able to continuously provide new capabilities within an acceptable period of time.

4. Market and sell the DW vision. It is important to reinforce the vision of your DW among those managers who support the DW and those that don't. By doing so you can set expectations for the future, collect management feedback (pro or con) and provide a road map for evolving the initial DW capability into a broader corporate asset. The vision must be principally set in a business context and communicated accordingly. The overall benefits to the company should be emphasized, the role of technology should always be deemphasized.

Strategies for Sustaining DW User Support

By and large, the DW users are the group most impacted by the DW. Simply stated, the DW will change the way they do business every day. The degree to which the users embrace the DW is dependent on:

1. How much the business supports the DW
2. How well they understand what the DW can do for them
3. How well they accept what the system can do for them
4. How knowledgeable they are about the DW data and
5. How computer literate and skilled they are

For many users, the DW will become their principal source of business information. To the extent that the DW changes their existing processes and skills required to do their jobs, there will be impacts to the DW user. It is these very impacts that the IT organization must continually address with the DW support infrastructure. It is key in sustaining the user's acceptance of the DW as the preferred tool to do their job.

Continue Addressing the Basics

The IT organization must recognize that acceptance of the DW will progress unevenly across the spectrum of DW users. To the extent that this is true in your organization (and experience says it will be), it will drive your support infrastructure to continue supporting a broad range of user skills, e.g., novice to power user for months after initial deployment. You need to prepare for this requirement and plan your support workload accordingly.

Remember that use of the DW will require the users to learn more about the business and its processes. It requires the user to learn about data, its meaning and its relationships to other data. For those users dependent upon hard copy reports as a principal source of data, the change can be traumatic. For those users that have a sound understanding of data and it's role in business processes, the change will be easier. It means users must learn a new tool set for accessing the data. To the extent that the users are proficient at using desktop tools, the learning curve will be fast. Unfortunately, the opposite is also true. Lastly, it means that users must learn to ask their own business questions. The assumption of that responsibility is implicit in using the DW. Experience shows that most users are not ready to assume that responsibility.

Your DW support infrastructure should be geared toward continually helping the end user become productive. Resist pulling the support plug on basic support services until your are sure that most of your users have mastered the fundamentals. The key to making any changes is to monitor your users, know how they are progressing, and then devise support strategies that will further enhance their DW skills.

Actions to Increase User Acceptance and Usage

Once the initial set of DW users have been trained and are using your DW, there are many things the IT organization can do to further the initial levels of DW acceptance. The following are examples of proactive actions that will further DW usage:

1. Follow up with "just trained" users. Many users return to their offices and promptly lose the classroom basics they were taught. Following up with users in their offices reinforces the training and allows the IT support group to provide some DW consulting services targeted at the users individual needs. It also further establishes a working relationship with the IT support group.

2. Offer specialized workshops. In addition to general DW classes, it is important to provide specialized workshops for small groups of users with common information needs. The learning curve is very high using this format and the synergy among users produces additional ideas for using the full potential of the DW.

3. Demonstrate advanced capabilities. Not all users will easily take to using the full potential of the DW. Some will need to be shown what is possible. It is more effective to demonstrate these capabilities in the user's work space and on their own desktop device.

4. Build libraries of general purpose queries. Use this as a way to further build user reliance on the DW and demonstrate its broad capabilities. This is especially effective for those users who have not developed either the skills or confidence to begin developing their own queries. It will encourage many users to experiment and see what other opportunities exist.

5. Target your non-supporters. Every organization has users that are lukewarm in their support of the DW. Do some research and find out what their business information needs are. Demonstrate how the DW can satisfy their needs in ways that can make an immediate difference.

6. Anticipate emerging business needs. As new business requirements arise that can be satisfied by the DW, have your support staff be proactive in developing solutions. By doing so, the IT organization can further demonstrate the DW's broad business value and reduce the time and effort associated with each user reinventing the same wheel.

Using Metrics as Acceptance Indicators

IT organizations should develop a set of metrics to judge the user's progress in using the DW. These metrics can provide useful information in changing the DW support infrastructure areas of emphasis. Figure 6–4 provides examples of metrics that can demonstrate the changes and act as acceptance gauges.

Figure 6–4:   Gauging Data Warehouse Acceptance

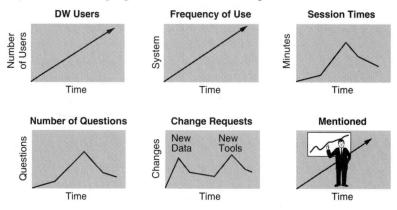

1. Number of active DW users—This metric is most useful after initial training is completed to see what users are going back to their offices and actually using the system. Growth of active users over time indicates that the DW is gaining some measure of acceptance. It also can provide insight into the quality of the initial training (or lack thereof).

2. Frequency of use—Frequency of use would indicate how many times users are actually logging on to the DW in some time period (weekly, monthly). Another dimension would be the time and day that the user is using the DW. This metric would show how often it is used and when. An increase in use would indicate that the users are frequently asking questions and provide system demand peaks.

3. Session times—Length of session times would indicate how much the DW has progressed in being a part of the user's job. Ideally, the frequency of use should be in short intervals. This would indicate that the users are asking questions and logging off to do other work.

4. Number/types of user questions—This metric can be used to judge where the user is in understanding the capabilities of your DW. If the questions are elementary in nature, it would indicate that some users have not progressed very far. If the questions are ones that explore current capabilities or ask for additional capabilities, then a portion of the users have moved past the initial stages of accepting the DW.

5. Types of change requests—An analysis of change requests can provide insight into how well users are doing in applying the DW to today's business needs. If the users are asking for system changes that expand the amount of data or functionality of the data access tools, it is a good indication that a number of users have moved past the initial stage of accepting the DW.

6. Hearing it mentioned—The last metric is called "hearing it mentioned." It is not one that you can gather hard data for and the number of occurrences are more an intuitive observation than anything else. Typically they occur in a business forum where some type of business information is either presented or needed. If you frequently hear users referring to your DW as their source of information, then you can take that as another indicator and endorsement of the DW as the official source of business information.

In summary, it's important to understand that the DW users will go through a life cycle of their own in accepting the DW. As we discussed earlier, there are different types of DW users with a range of computer skills and data needs. Although it may be convenient to treat the users as homogeneous groups, they are not. Therefore, the IT support infrastructure must be flexible enough to accommodate users across a spectrum of skills and knowledge levels. To sustain the users support, the IT organization must be skilled at recognizing how well the DW users are doing and adjust strategies and services accordingly. Be prepared to stick with your initial services longer than you feel should be necessary!

PUTTING IT ALL TOGETHER

Throughout this article we have tried to give you a sense of what lies ahead after implementing the first increment of your DW. For many, the first DW project would appear to be the hardest part of data warehousing. In reality it is not. For the IT organization, "putting it all together" will require a major paradigm shift from the way it manages, develops, and supports business systems today. (See Figure 6–5.) There are significant differences between the world of data warehousing and traditional business systems. Recognition of those differences are key to the successful management of the DW evolution process. As you continue evolving your DW, remember to:

1. Develop a strategic direction, make sure it is linked to the business and has broad support.
2. Recognize that your users will drive you to be in all stages of the evolution process, and proactively manage the evolution process and its impacts.
3. Put in place a DW management framework so you can evolve your DW and manage the many demands that will be placed upon your organization.
4. Put in place the right support infrastructure, understand how it can be used as a tool to evolve your business managers and users.
5. Build support from your company's business managers, ultimately they are the ones who can make or break your DW efforts.
6. Build support from your users, you must take an active role in their success.

In the final analysis, data warehousing is not about technology, it is about organizational change. The principal leadership role for evolving the DW will come from within the IT organization. The true challenge of data warehousing is in the management of its evolution. In many ways, data warehousing is like a triathlon: It requires multiple skills and it's a game of endurance!

Figure 6–5: NSWCDD Data Warehouse Implementation

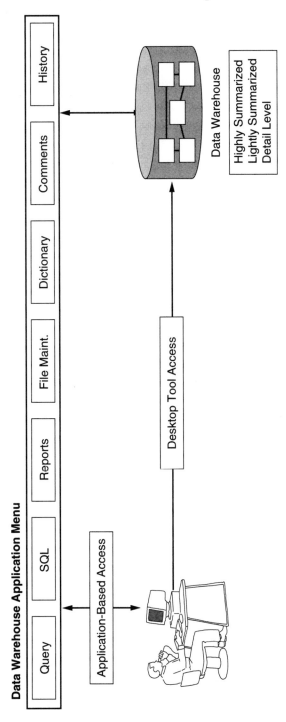

Chapter
7

Ten Mistakes to Avoid for Data Warehousing Managers

Ramon C. Barquin, Alan Paller,
and Herb Edelstein

The Data Warehousing Institute

INTRODUCTION

Database, data transfer, middleware, and hardware vendors are all touting the great benefits of data warehousing. Unfortunately, too few of them are pointing out the problems their users are having.

The staff of The Data Warehousing Institute has called upon experts across the industry and conducted meetings in several cities with active data warehousing project managers and IS executives to assist us in developing a compendium of the "ten mistakes to avoid for data warehousing managers." The mistakes are illuminated below.

This article originally appeared in the July 1995 issue of *Application Development Trends*.

1. Starting with the Wrong Sponsorship Chain

A data warehousing project without the right sponsorship chain is like an automobile with insufficient gasoline and oil and a linkage problem between the steering wheel and the wheels.

The right sponsorship chain includes two key individuals above the data warehousing manager.[1] At the top is an executive sponsor with a great deal of money to invest in effective use of information. Corporate presidents, vice presidents of marketing, and vice presidents of research and development often fit the bill. A good sponsor, however, is not the only person required in the reporting chain above the warehousing manager. When a data warehousing project craters[2], the cause can sometimes be traced to the lack of a key individual between the sponsor and the data warehousing manager. That person is often called the project "driver" because he or she keeps the project moving in the right direction and ensures the schedule is kept. A good driver is a business person with three essential characteristics: (1) he or she has already earned the respect of the other executives, (2) he or she has a healthy skepticism about technology, and (3) he or she is decisive but flexible.

Table 1 Shows the price paid when these sponsorship elements are missing.

---

[1] When we use the term 'data warehousing manager,' we mean the person who leads the data warehousing project. We are not presuming that a new organizational unit is being set up to manage data warehouses, although nearly thirty percent of active companies are creating a permanent or semi-permanent unit to plan, create, maintain, promote, and support the data warehouse.

[2] Data warehouses do not generally fail, if that word means to stop working. Rather, they lose their financial support, leading to little or no enhancement, longer and longer update cycles, and less and less user interest.

Table 7–1:

A. PROBLEM WITH THE SPONSORSHIP CHAIN B. PRICE PAID BY THE PROJECT
A. Sponsor is an IT executive rather than a business executive outside IT. B. Project is seen as a technology experiment rather than a strategic investment in the business.
A. Sponsor has a limited budget. B. Every unexpected technical challenge is a crisis as budget dollars are hard to get. Project gains reputation as 'problem-prone' and a 'budget buster.'
A. There is no driver; DW Manager reports directly to sponsor. B. No one on the project has authority to broker peace among competing data definitions. Sponsor soon tires of the data definition wars and withdraws support.
A. Driver has not earned the respect of peers at the executive level. B. Content of data warehouse is not trusted, in part, because no one can vouch for the validity of the definitions used.
A. Driver is excited, rather than skeptical, about technology. B. Project is viewed as a technical experiment (or toy); most business people avoid it.
A. Driver is indecisive or unwilling to shift quickly. B. Project slows, executive support dissolves, interest fades, users find alternative solutions.

2. Setting Expectations That You Cannot Meet and Frustrating Executives at the Moment of Truth

Every data warehousing project has at least two phases. Phase one is the selling phase in which you attempt to persuade people that by investing in your project they can expect to get wonderful access to the right data through simple, graphical delivery tools. Phase two is the struggle to meet the expectations you have raised in phase one. Sadly, it is not uncommon for overeager project managers to make claims that their data warehouse will give people throughout the enterprise easy access to all the information they need, when they need it, in the right format. Along with that promise (explicit or implied) comes a bill for one to seven million dollars. Business executives who hear those promises and see those budgets cannot help but have high expectations.

But, users do not get all the information they need. All data warehousing is, by necessity, domain specific, which means it focuses on a particular set of business information.[3] If a question asked by an executive requires information from outside the domain, the answer is often, "We haven't loaded that information, but we can, it will just cost (a bunch) and take (many) weeks." Executives feel enormous frustration when their expectations are dashed. They focus that frustration on the person who made the promises.

3. Engaging in Politically-Naïve Behavior (e.g., Saying, "This Will Help Managers Make Better Decisions")

A foolish error made by many data warehousing managers is promoting the value of their data warehouse with arguments to the effect of, "This will help managers make better decisions." When a self-respecting manager hears those words, the natural reaction is "This person thinks we have not been making good decisions and that his/her system is going to 'fix' us." From that point on, that manager is very, very hard to please.[4]

CIOs who have been in the industry for at least ten years get knowing smiles on their faces when they hear the words data warehousing. They know that the objective of data warehouses is the same one that fueled the fourth generation language boom of the late 1970s, and the Decision Support Systems (DSS)/Executive Information Systems (EIS) craze of the late 1980s—giving end-users better access to important information. Fourth generation languages have had a long

---

[3] This problem won't go away when you have enough storage and processing speed to 'load all the data.' All the data available for loading is simply the information generated by transaction processing systems. Those systems, however, are highly domain specific themselves, and leave out enormous amounts of important information that can be found in paper documents.

[4] A simple correction may suffice in cases where the data warehousing manager is trusted. The correction says, "help make better-informed decisions." However, when the data warehousing manager has not earned the respect and trust of the audience, even the term 'better-informed' can have implications that are insulting.

and prosperous life, but DSS/EIS had a quick rise and a quicker fall. Why? One possible answer is that Fourth Generation Languages (4GLs) were sold as tools to get data while DSS and EIS were promoted as change agents that would improve business and enable better management decisions. That positioning raised political issues that didn't have to be raised and made enemies out of potential supporters. On the other hand, few people are moved to fight the concept of a data warehouse when it is presented without fanfare as the place people can go to get the information they need.

4. Loading the Warehouse with Information Just "Because It Was Available"

Some inexperienced data warehousing managers send a list of tables and data elements to end users along with a request asking, "Which of these elements should be included in the warehouse?" Sometimes they ask for categories such as 'essential,' 'important,' and 'nice-to-have.' They get back long lists of marginally useful information that radically expand the data warehouse storage requirements and, more importantly, slow responsiveness. Extraneous data buries important information. Faced with the need to dig through long guides[5] to find the right field name, and having to deal with multiple versions of the same information, users quickly grow frustrated and may even give up entirely.

Extraneous data also leads to very large databases. One Chicago-area utility reported, for example, that their mainframe computing resources were being consumed to a greater and greater extent by analytical SAS programs. Loads were growing, so the company decided to move the data to a new machine where it would be kept for analytical purposes. The users demanded that every data item be downloaded and they wanted it updated every five minutes, but decided they could live with daily updates. Unfortunately, the relational

---

[5] Such guides are sometimes called meta data, in part because too many database experts have a self-destructive need to use jargon.

database (from the number two Relational Database Management Systems (RDBMS) vendor) did not load well in parallel, causing downloads to consume more than 22 hours per day. Worse still, the performance during the remaining two hours was, in a word, "AWFUL!"

5. Believing That Data Warehousing Database Design Is the Same as Transactional Database Design

Since the goals of transaction processing systems differ from the goals of data warehouses, the database designs must differ, as well. In transaction processing, the goal is speed to access and update a single record or a few records. Data warehousing is fundamentally different. The goal here is to access aggregates—sums, averages, trends, and more. Another difference between the two types of systems is the user. In transaction processing, a programmer develops a query that will be used tens of thousands of times. In Data warehousing, an end-user develops the query and may use it only one time. Data warehousing databases are often denormalized to make them easier to navigate for infrequent users. If instead, the transaction processing database (with as many as 250 or more normalized tables) is used for data warehousing, infrequent users have no idea where to find the information they need or how to ask for it. How are users supposed to pick the correct table name when 250 cryptic 8-character table names are arrayed in a table with only a few entries showing at any one time? With significant frustration, most likely.

An even more fundamental difference is in content. Where transactional systems usually contain only the basic data, in data warehousing users increasingly expect to find aggregates and time-series information already calculated for them and ready or immediate display. That's the impetus behind the multi-dimensional database market.

6. Choosing a Data Warehouse Manager Who Is Technology-Oriented Rather Than User-Oriented

"The biggest mistake I ever made was putting that propeller-head in as the manager of the project." Those are the exact words from the driver (the person between the executive sponsor and the data warehousing manager) at a large oil company. He had just finished explaining how the user-hostile project manager had made so many people angry that the entire project was in danger of being scrapped.

Do not let his words tar all technologists. Some make excellent project managers and can serve as effective data warehousing managers; however, many cannot. Most CIOs have already (mentally) separated their staffs into the people who can work with users and the people who need to be kept away from them. Keep the latter type far away from your project. Data warehousing is a service business—not a storage business—and making clients angry is a near perfect method of destroying a service business.

7. Focusing on Traditional Internal Record-Oriented Data and Ignoring the Potential Value of External Data and of Text, Images, and—Potentially—Sound and Video

In the early 1980s, a White House study attempted to learn how senior managers get business information. After interviewing the CEOs and two other levels of management in over 50 large companies, the White House analysts concluded that "the higher people are in the organization, the less value they place on internal data and the less time they spend using internal data." In fact, the study showed that the very highest executives rely on outside data (news, telephone calls from associates, etc.) for more than 95 percent of all the information they use.

Because of their focus on external sources of information, senior executives sometimes see data warehouses as irrelevant. It's not that they are uninterested in key operating indicators; they just don't have the time to bury themselves in the sort of detailed data a warehouse provides. A system that makes every piece of internal data available to senior management will likely be seen by top executives as only marginally useful. Without top management support, middle managers are less likely to continue supporting data warehouses. Therefore, it's imperative to extend the project focus to include external information.

In addition, consider expanding the forms of information available through the warehouse. Traditional record-oriented information transaction systems usually record the minimum possible amount of data to effect a business transaction. Frustrated users are starting to ask, "Where's the copy of the contract (image) that explains the information behind the data? And where's the ad (image) that ran in that magazine? Where's the tape (audio or video) of the key competitor at a recent conference talking about their business strategy? Where's the recent product launch (video)?" An old saying goes, "When the only tool you have is a hammer, every problem is a nail." When the only tool you have for data warehousing is a relational DBMS, you may be stuck delivering dull data. This is the age of television. Traditional alphanumeric data is two generations behind the current technology.[6]

8. Delivering Data With Overlapping and Confusing Definitions

The Achilles heel of data warehousing is the requirement to gain consensus on data definitions. Conflicting definitions each have champions, and they are not easily reconciled. Many of the most stubborn definitions have been constructed by managers to reflect data in a way that makes their department look effective. To the finance manager, sales means the net of revenue less returns. Sales to the distribution people is what needs to be delivered. Sales to the sales organization is the amount committed by clients. One organization reported twenty-seven different definitions of sales.

---

[6] A word of caution. It doesn't take a huge investment to get full text and images into your warehouse and there is little risk. But, unless you are already experienced in multi-media, you are probably better off waiting a year or two before moving ahead with audio and video.

Executives do not give up their definitions without a fight, and few data warehousing managers are in a position to bully executives into agreement. Solving this problem is one of the most important tasks of the data warehousing driver. (See mistake number 1 above). If it is not solved, users will not have confidence in the information they are getting. Worse, they may embarrass themselves by using the wrong data—in which case, they will inevitably blame the data warehouse.

Some data warehousing managers suggest that definitions are not a data warehousing problem, but a user problem. They try to deliver all the data, representing all the different definitions, along with lengthy on-line paper guides that try to explain each data element. Then they let the user decide which is appropriate. This generally does not work. A well-known tale from the early days of decision support describes a meeting in which the then-president of Boston's Shawmut Bank, after sitting through a strident argument about whose data was "right," told his senior managers, "If you people cannot agree on what data to use, I'll find people who can," and he stomped out of the room.

9. Believing the Performance, Capacity, and Scalability Promises

At a recent conference, CIOs from three companies—a manufacturer, a retailer, and a service company—described their data warehousing efforts. Although the three data warehouses were very different, they all ran into an identical problem. Within four months of getting started, each of the CIOs unexpectedly had to purchase at least one additional processor of a size equal to or larger than the largest computer that they had originally purchased for data warehousing. They simply ran out of power. Two of the three had failed to budget for the addition and found themselves with a serious problem. The third had budgeted for unforeseen difficulties and was able to adapt.

Bigger problems may lie in wait on the software side. Take Mervyn's data warehouse as an example. According to industry analyst Peter Kastner, Mervyn's chose Oracle Parallel

Server to get the power and speed to handle large (over 10 gigabytes) databases. Mervyn's dutifully indexed the huge files (not a quick job) and then set Parallel Server to work. Surprise! It didn't use the indices.

Problems with performance and scalability can also come from front-end applications. PowerBuilder applications at one retailer, for example, have recently improved to 3 to 4 second response time. That's right—improved to 3 to 4 seconds. Are users happy? Well, they are happier than they were with 7 second response time. The fix that speeded the queries from 7 to 4 is instructive. According to the Chief Information Officer (CIO), PowerBuilder moves modules in and out of memory frequently. In this retailer's facility a virus checker analyzed the modules for viruses every time they moved into memory. Disabling the corporate virus checking speeded the application (but it worries the manager). Even with this change, several users are asking to go back to the mainframe where they got better response time and could get their work done in less time.

An even more common capacity problem arises in networking. One company reported that they sized a network to support an image warehouse, but discovered that the network was soon overwhelmed. The surprise was that the images were not at fault. The problem turned out to be network traffic for data transfer between the end-user application and the databases of indices on the server. The images moved fast, but the process of finding the right one clogged the network. Network overloads are the single most common surprise in client/server systems in general and in data warehousing systems in particular.

10. Believing That Once the Data Warehouse Is Up and Running Your Problems Are Finished

Each happy user asks for new data and tells others about the "great new tool." And they too ask for more data to be added. And they, all of them, want it immediately. At the same time, each performance or delivery problem results in a high-pressure search for additional technology or a new process.

Thus, the data warehousing project team needs to maintain high energy over long periods of time. A common error is to place data warehousing in the hands of project-oriented people who believe that they will be able to set it up once and have it run itself.

Data warehouses need to be intensely nurtured for at least a year after their initial launch. Even after that, without a dynamic leader, they can easily lose their momentum and their sponsorship.

Data warehousing is a journey, not a destination.

11. Focusing on Ad Hoc Data Mining and Periodic Reporting, Instead of Alerts

11? Yes, you'll find eleven "mistakes" on our list. Believing there are only ten mistakes to avoid is also a mistake, so we've given you eleven to keep you on your toes.

This is a subtle error, but a very important one. Fixing it can transform a data warehousing manager from a data librarian into a hero.

The natural progression of information in a data warehouse is: (1) extract the data from legacy systems, clean it, and feed it to the warehouse, (2) support ad hoc reporting until you learn what people want, and then (3) convert the ad hoc reports into regularly scheduled reports. In other words, first data is fed to the system; then questions are asked and reports are generated on the fly. Finally, managers request those reports every morning, every "Monday," or every "month."

That's the natural progression, but it isn't the optimal progression. It ignores the fact that managers are busy and that reports are liabilities rather than assets unless the recipients have time to read the reports. Reports are like inventory; if they aren't used, they just generate costs.

Alert systems are a better approach and they can make a data warehouse mission-critical. Alert systems monitor the data flowing into the warehouse and inform all key people with a need to know as soon as a critical event takes place. Harris Semiconductor's industry-leading manufacturing alert server, for example, monitors patterns in semiconductor test data, and screams loudly (via e-mail) when wafer characteristics anywhere in the world (Malaysia, Singapore, or three U.S. sites) creep too far from the ideal.

Creating alert systems is a job that requires a data warehousing driver. The key to an effective alert system is infrequency. If alerts are sent too often, they become a burden rather than an asset. But to determine the contents and thresholds of that critical information, one must really understand what's going on in the mind of the business person. As one experienced driver said, "To make an alert system an integral part of the day to day business, you have to be there when they (senior management) talk about the competition and about the future and what's going to drive the business forward." Drivers with great ties to other senior managers are in the best position to do that job well.

Rethink the manager's need: Does he or she really want reports? Or would an alert system be better?

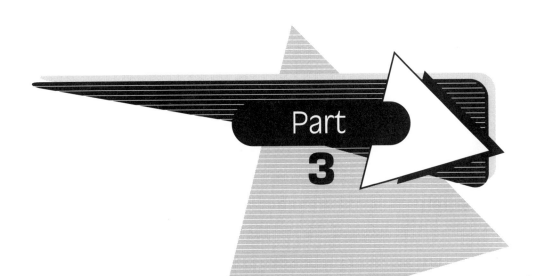

Part
3

DESIGNING THE
DATA WAREHOUSE

Data Warehousing Architectures

Pieter R. Mimno

Technology Insights, Inc.

STRATEGIC BUSINESS OBJECTIVES

Data warehousing is a powerful technology that is being used by many organizations to meet strategic business objectives. These objectives include improving services for customers and end users, reducing costs of business processing, getting products and services to market faster, meeting increased global competition, responding faster to competitive challenges, providing transparent access to data, and unlocking data trapped in host environments.

Access to data is a key issue. In a recent Gartner Group study, 73 percent of business managers said they could not access data in their own corporate databases. If managers cannot easily access corporate data and make business decisions, this is a serious problem that will have an impact on the business. Data warehousing provides a solution to this business problem.

In addition to improved data access, many organizations want to preserve their investment in host computer systems. They don't want to throw away mainframes or their investment in host computer systems. A common short-term strategy for these organizations is to augment existing legacy applications with application packages, such as human resources and financial applications packages, that run on high-speed servers. In addition, existing mainframe systems are being front-ended with client/server applications that support transparent access to data and implement new services that provide a competitive advantage for the organization.

Data warehousing supports a strategy to preserve the investment in legacy systems because in many data warehousing architectures mainframes stay in place. Data warehousing can be used to extract data from existing databases, clean it up, and reorganize the data to make it accessible and understandable to business analysts.

IMPLEMENTATION OPTIONS

There are a number of different architectural options that may be considered in moving to data warehousing. These include:

Rehosting mainframe applications

Using mainframes as servers in a two-tier architecture

Building a three-tier enterprise information architecture

Rehosting Mainframe Applications

Rehosting the mainframe means taking existing applications (which may be written in COBOL, PL/1, C, or FORTRAN) and moving them to much lower cost, microcomputer-based servers. The servers may run under UNIX, Windows NT, or OS/2. Rehosting tools include MicroFocus COBOL, Computer Associates CA-Realia, and UniKix from Integris. Tools such as MicroFocus COBOL emulate CICS, VSAM, IMS, and DB2, and run legacy applications without change on the new host processor. The operating environment on the new host processor may be DOS, Windows, OS/2, or UNIX.

Porting legacy code to low-cost servers is a proven, low-risk approach to reducing the cost of computing. Many organizations have reported a substantial reduction in the cost of running their legacy code after migrating to a server environment. There are few hidden costs since the code that is ported is not modified.

Rehosting mainframe applications is attractive for data warehousing environments because the existing legacy code and databases can be ported to lower cost platforms. However, rehosting does not address the strategic business problems faced by most organizations. These problems center on requirements to develop new applications and services much faster, provide transparent access to data, and deliver better services to customers and end users. Rehosting simply migrates legacy code to a less expensive platform. If the code was brittle and expensive to maintain on the old host machine, it will be just as costly to maintain on the new host computer. However, rehosting is an attractive way to reduce the cost of running legacy code and databases if it is likely they will be used for several more years.

Mainframe as a Server

Another architectural option for data warehousing is to use the mainframe as a server, as shown in Figure 8–1. This is a two-tier approach incorporating a front-end client component and a back-end server component that utilizes existing host computers as database servers. Front-end, LAN (Local Area Network)-based applications are built with tools such as Visual Basic, from Microsoft Corporation, PowerBuilder from Sybase/Powersoft Corporation, Delphi from Borland Corporation, or SQLWindows from Gupta Corporation. The function of the front-end applications is to hide the complexity of the existing mainframe systems. Mainframe applications that have been in use for 15 to 20 years often have extremely high rates of data redundancy. Organizations, such as insurance companies, that have built their insurance lines by buying other companies, gradually accumulate multiple computer systems, each of which may have redundant and incompatible data definitions. The redundancy and lack of consistent data definitions makes it difficult for business end users to access legacy data, and can impede the development of new front-end services.

Figure 8–1:   Two-Tier Data Warehousing Architecture

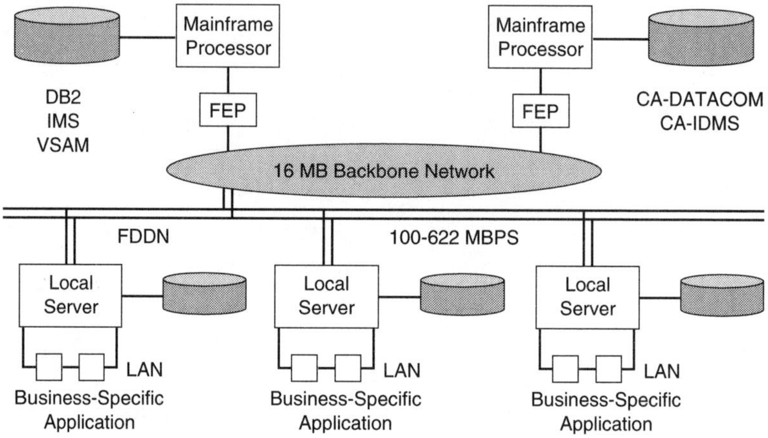

© Technology Insights, Inc.

One way to deal with this situation is to leave the legacy systems alone and build umbrella systems on the front end that provide easy access to data on the mainframes. Front-end applications built with client/server tools such as Visual Basic, PowerBuilder, Delphi, or SQLWindows, provide a user-friendly, graphical user interface and support front-end business-specific functions, such as order entry, customer service, or order tracking. The front-end applications provide transparent access to existing legacy databases, and hide the complexity and lack of consistency of the host databases from the end users.

The architecture illustrated in Figure 8–1 may be used to build a two-tier data warehouse that consists of front-end client components and back-end server components. The two-tier architecture is attractive because it utilizes existing legacy systems as database servers and requires minimal investment in additional hardware and software. However, the two-tier architecture is inherently not scalable and does not support large numbers of on-line end users. It encourages the development of "fat-client" front-end systems, in which excessive application processing is allocated to desktop workstations. As the number of end users increases, the data access requirements of the front-end applications imposes an increasingly heavy burden on the host computers. To support adequate response time, the processing and data access capability of the host computers must be increased, or they may be replaced with more efficient and less expensive multiprocessors.

Enterprise Information Architecture

An alternative architectural approach is use of a multi-tier enterprise information architecture, as shown in Figure 8–2. This flexible architecture supports a broad range of integrated services, in which the user interface, business processing functions, and database management functions are partitioned into separate processes that may be distributed across the information architecture.

Figure 8–2: Three-Tier Data Warehousing Architecture

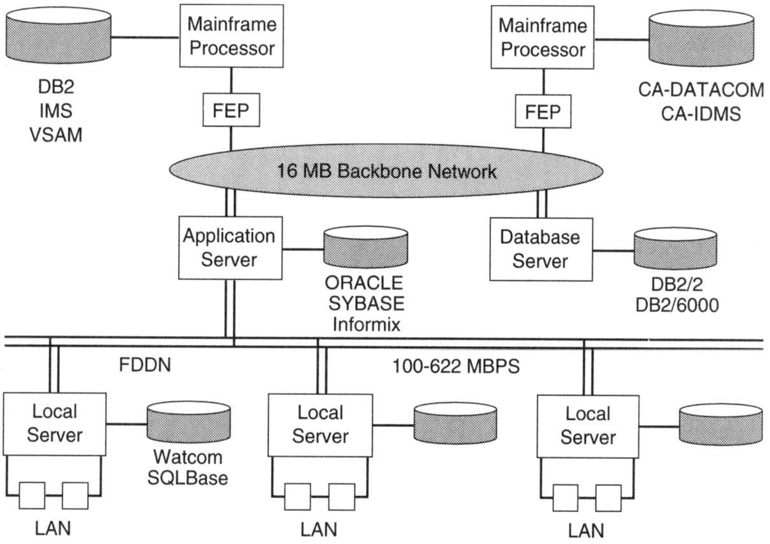

© Technology Insights, Inc.

The three-tier enterprise information architecture is widely used for data warehousing. Source data on host computers resides at Tier 3. Data and business rules that are shared across the organization, such as target databases for data warehouses, are stored on high-speed database servers at Tier 2. Graphically oriented end-user interfaces run on LAN-based PCs or workstations at Tier 1.

In a data warehousing environment, database servers and application servers at Tier 2 provide efficient, high-speed access to the shared data. Warehouse data are typically static in nature, i.e., non time-varying. The information is subject-oriented, integrated, historical in nature, and summarized or aggregated so that it is meaningful to business analysts. In contrast, time varying, operational data, such as on-line orders, prices, inventory levels, etc., typically are not stored in the data warehouse. As shown in Figure 8–2, operational data and the target database for a data warehouse are often stored on physically separate servers. Operational databases are optimized for high speed on-line transaction processing (OLTP). Data warehouse databases are optimized for high-speed on-line database queries and analysis.

Target databases for data warehouses are generally stored in relational form using conventional RDBMSs, such as Oracle, Sybase, Informix, or DB2/x. Applications that require analysis of large amounts of multi-dimensional data may utilize specialized on-line analytical processing (OLAP) databases, such as Essbase from Arbor Software Corp., Express from IRI Software (division of Oracle Corp.), OmniWarehouse from Praxis International, Inc., or Red Brick Warehouse from Red Brick Systems, Inc.

Front-end tools are used to support high-speed access and analysis of data in the target database. End-user access techniques may include relational queries, multi-dimensional views of relational data, custom-built user interfaces, or special-purpose DSS/EIS (Decision Support Systems/Executive Information Systems) user interfaces. A wide variety of tools are available to support these data access and analysis requirements.

It is important to recognize that there is no single "correct" data warehousing architecture. For some organizations, the two-tier approach is an attractive solution because it minimizes the cost and complexity of building data warehouses. For other organizations that require greater performance and scalability, the three-tier architecture may be more appropriate. In this architecture, data extracted from legacy systems is cleaned-up, transformed, and stored in high-speed database servers, which are used as the target database for front-end data access. Organizations that have more modest requirements, such as the need to build data warehouses for individual departments, may choose to build small data marts, which utilize a LAN-based architecture. In designing data warehouses, organizations should survey a range of alternative data warehousing architectures and select an architecture that meets their strategic business requirements.

COMPONENTS OF A DATA WAREHOUSE

As shown in Figure 8–3, components of a data warehouse include the following:

Source databases on host computers, such as on-line transaction processing (OLTP) operational data, batch operational data, and external data

Data extraction and transformation tools, used to extract data from source files, clean up the data, and reorganize it so that it is consistent and understandable by business end users

Data modeling tools used to prepare an information model of both the source database and target database for the data warehouse

Central repository used to store data models and metadata. Metadata describes the transformation between the source data and the target data in the data warehouse

Target database for the data warehouse

Front-end data access tools used by business professionals to support high-speed access and analysis of data in the target database

Source data for data warehouses is extracted from operational databases that may reside on multiple existing host computers. There may be a wide variety of source database managers, such as VSAM, IMS, RMS, DB2, etc. The data warehouse requires tools that extract data from existing host computers, clean it up, reorganize it, and load it into one or more data warehouse databases. Most vendors do not provide complete, integrated support for a data warehousing strategy. As a result, data warehouses are typically developed using products from multiple vendors.

Figure 8–3:   Components of Data Warehousing Architecture

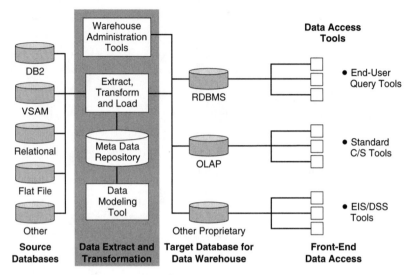

© Technology Insights, Inc.

THREE CRITICAL ISSUES IN THE DESIGN OF DATA WAREHOUSES

A solid architectural foundation must be defined for the data warehouse based on a clear understanding of the requirements to extract and transform source data, store the transformed data in the target database, and provide business analysts with transparent access to the target database. Specification of the data warehouse architecture requires resolution of three important issues:

1. Target database for data warehouse—Should the database for the data warehouse be supported by a conventional, relational DBMS (database management system), or a proprietary, multi-dimensional DBMS?

2. Data extraction technique—Should source data be extracted and managed for a data warehouse using the facilities of a standard relational DBMS, or through the use of specialized data extraction tools?

3. Front-end data access tools—Should data be accessed from the data warehouse using relational queries, multi-dimensional views of relational data, custom-built user interfaces, or special-purpose DSS/EIS user interfaces?

These critical issues in the design of data warehouses are discussed in more detail below.

Conventional RDBMS as Target Database

One of the first issues to be resolved in the design of data warehouses is selection of the target database. The issue is whether the target database for the data warehouse should be a conventional, relational database, or a proprietary, multi-dimensional database.

For many organizations, there is no strong operational requirement to use a proprietary, multi-dimensional, OLAP database to support data warehousing functions. In many cases, data warehouses can be built using conventional RDBMSs (relational database management system) and general-purpose data access tools already in use at the organization. All of the major RDBMSs provide uni-directional replication services and rapid response to queries from large numbers of concurrent on-line end users. They interface transparently with standard database query tools and client/server tools, using standard SQL interfaces. The latest releases of widely used RDBMSs are well suited to support complex query and analysis functions, and to serve as the database engine for both operational and data warehouse applications. To minimize cost and complexity, it is advantageous to consider the option of building data warehouses using conventional RDBMSs, rather than non-standard, proprietary databases and data access tools.

Vendors of high-end RDBMSs have enhanced their products to support the specialized requirements of data warehousing. Conventional RDBMS products that support data warehousing include CA-OpenIngres from Computer Associates, Data Warehouse from Information Builders, Informix OnLine from Informix, Oracle 7.x Symmetric Replication from

Oracle Corporation, Sybase Warehouse WORKS from Sybase Corporation, and Visual Warehouse from IBM.

Functionality added to conventional RDBMSs to support data warehousing includes data extraction and replication services, parallelization, query optimization, bit-mapped indexes, and major reductions in indexing, sorting, and loading times. High-end RDBMSs provide the ability to process all database functions in parallel, including query, index, load, backup, and recovery. Queries are controlled by a dynamic partitioning mechanism that enables queries to be handled by multiple processors in parallel. Dynamic partitioning of queries allows for automatic load balancing and avoids skewing of the processor workload. New, cost-based optimizers use statistics on table population, degree of data clustering, selectivity of columns, and other data, to optimize the performance of queries.

Recent releases of RDBMSs, such as Oracle 7.3 and the IQ Accelerator component of Sybase System 11, incorporate bit-mapped indexes and other advanced indexing capability. Bit-mapped indexes enable conventional RDBMSs to efficiently access low-cardinality data, which is characteristic of many multi-dimensional databases containing dimensions such as regions, married/unmarried, true/false, etc. Bit-mapped indexing extends conventional RDBMSs to support both traditional, high-cardinality database queries, as well as multi-dimensional queries, without resorting to proprietary multi-dimensional database engines. As a result of these improvements, relational database vendors are reporting a 10- to 100-fold increase in query performance in a data warehousing environment, relative to older versions of their products.

Proprietary Target Database

For some data warehousing applications, a clear business case can be made for the use of specialized, proprietary target databases. Proprietary databases will remain important for certain classes of decision-support applications, such as a business requirement to analyze large, multi-dimensional databases to uncover marketing trends and evaluate the effectiveness of sales promotions. For these applications, a proprietary database approach is justified due to its support for multi-dimensional OLAP processing, and tight integration between replication, data warehouse, and query functions.

A wide variety of proprietary data warehousing tools are available that are specifically designed to support the demanding requirements of decision-support applications. These tools include Essbase from Arbor Software Corp., Express from IRI Software (Division of Oracle Corp.), Omni-Warehouse and OmniReplicator from Praxis International, Inc., Red Brick Warehouse from Red Brick Systems, Inc., and SAS System from SAS Institute, Inc.

Vendors of proprietary data warehousing tools claim that conventional RDBMSs, such as Oracle, Sybase, Informix, and DB2/x, are not capable of providing high performance in a decision-support environment because they are optimized to support high speed, on-line transaction processing (OLTP) applications. In contrast, proprietary data warehousing tools incorporate a multi-platform engine specifically designed to provide rapid response to on-line queries. Features that support high performance include file segmentation and partitioning, stored procedures, custom data warehousing functions, support for iterative queries, and extensions to SQL for high-performance data warehousing.

Several proprietary data warehousing tools support multi-dimensional architecture features for on-line analytical processing (OLAP). Multi-dimensional database systems (MDBMS) are implemented through use of user-defined table groupings, nested tables, and advanced indexing options, such as Btrees, bit-maps, and list-derived functions. These so-called "post-relational" database capabilities include an iterative query enabler, and the ability to store large video images, audio, geographic information system data, and time-series files. These features support the analysis of multi-dimensional databases, drill-down for iterative queries and successive layers of detail, and trend analysis through time-series data presentation.

However, proprietary databases have significant limitations, including performance degradation as database size increases, slow loading rate, inability to incrementally load data into the database, and a proprietary approach. Specialized multi-dimensional databases are not compliant with SQL standards and do not integrate well with conventional RDBMSs. There is a danger that organizations could become dependent on a proprietary database solution.

The choice between a conventional RDBMS or a multi-dimensional DBMS for the target database is an important decision that effects many components of the data warehousing architecture. Proprietary databases for data warehousing appeal to many organizations due to their multi-dimensional architecture features, support for on-line analytical processing, speed of query processing, and implementation of data marts targeted to the needs of departments. However, vendors of conventional RDBMSs can make a good case that synchronous or asynchronous replication to heterogeneous target databases is supported by their products and is adequate for data warehousing. They can also demonstrate greatly improved performance for query processing, indexing, and database loads relative to previous versions of their products.

The latest versions of conventional RDBMSs are no longer optimized solely for OLTP applications. They now support high performance query processing and the ability to allow any data in the enterprise to be included in the query. To minimize cost and complexity, organizations should consider building data warehouses using conventional RDBMSs, rather than specialized, proprietary databases, unless a clear business case can be made for the use of a proprietary database.

Data Extraction and Management Tools

The second critical decision referred to above is whether conventional RDBMSs or specialized data extraction tools are required to extract data from source files and transform the data so that it is understandable by users of the data warehouse. Conventional RDBMSs, such as Oracle, Sybase, Informix, or DB2/x, address the data assembly, distribution, and access components of a data warehousing environment. They support multiple data replication models and can provide sophisticated database replication services across the enterprise in a data warehousing environment.

However, the replication techniques supported by conventional RDBMSs are not adequate if the source databases are logically inconsistent and require extensive reorganization and transformation to make the data understandable to business end users. Conventional RDBMSs support data extraction, replication, and some reorganization, aggregation, and summarization functions. However, they do not adequately address the transformation component, i.e., the requirement to extract source data automatically from host computers, resolve data inconsistencies, and aggregate, reorganize, and transform data prior to populating the data warehouse. Conventional RDBMSs selectively replicate, or copy, data from the source database to the target database. Replication is an acceptable mechanism for data warehousing if the source data is clean, well modeled, and contains unambiguous data definitions. Unfortunately, in the real world, source databases are often poorly modeled, contain redundant, conflicting data definitions, and are not easily understandable by business end users.

To create data that is meaningful to the end user, it is often necessary to augment the capability provided by conventional RDBMSs with specialized tools, called data extraction and transformation tools. These tools provide the ability to collect, convert, and modify operational data, and load the transformed data into data warehouses in support of decision making. Examples of data extraction and transformation tools include Extract from Evolutionary Technologies, Integrity Data Reengineering Tool from Vality Technology, Passport from Carleton Corporation, Platinum Warehouse from PLATINUM Technology, Inc., and Prism Warehouse Manager from Prism Solutions. Vendors of conventional RDBMSs have developed integrated interfaces with data extraction and transformation tools to extend the functionality of their database products.

Two major functions are supported by data extraction and transformation tools. First, the tools provide a graphical, point-and-click interface that allows IS analysts to identify source data to be extracted and define the transformation rules necessary to populate the target database with information that is meaningful to business end users. Transformation rules include the ability to match, merge, sort, apply rules, create new fields, select subsets of data, aggregate data, and convert operational data, resolving inconsistencies in syntax, data definitions, and formats among data in the same or different databases. Second, these on-line operations automatically create programs running on the mainframe that perform the extraction, cleanup, and reorganization of the data used to populate the data warehouse. At this stage, the user can also add global transformation logic to the extract program.

As part of these processes, the tools generate metadata that describe the format of the source data, the format of the target data, and the transformations that were applied to the source data to create the target data in the data warehouse. The metadata is stored in a centralized metadata repository that often includes plain-English definitions and descriptions of the data stored in the data warehouse, in a form that is easily accessible by business end users. The metadata is also used by database administrators to ensure that the operational data is logically consistent with the data in the data warehouse. Using the metadata, changes in the operational data are automatically mapped to required changes in the data warehouse. The metadata insulates the warehouse from changes in operational data structures.

The metadata repository may also contain an information model, generated by an upper-CASE tool, that defines how data structures are stored in the data warehouse. The model is essential to ensure that data structures in the data warehouse are logically consistent, and to prevent serious data access problems, such as semantic disintegrity. Data in the data warehouse is typically stored in relational form, although the information model may be deliberately denormalized to increase efficiency of database access. Representative upper-CASE tools used for data modeling include ERwin/ERX from Logic Works, Inc., Excelerator from INTER-SOLV, Inc., S-Designor from Powersoft/Sybase, SILVERRUN from Computer Systems Advisors, Inc., System Architect from Popkin Software Systems, Inc., System Engineer from

LBMS, and Visible Analyst Workbench from Visible Systems. Data models generated using these products may be imported into the metadata repository using standard Data Definition Language (DDL) interfaces.

Conventional RDBMSs support multiple replication modes and can provide sophisticated database replication services across the enterprise in a data warehousing environment. However, as discussed above, the replication techniques supported by conventional RDBMSs are not adequate if the source databases are logically inconsistent and require extensive reorganization and transformation to make the data understandable to business end users.

Specialized data extraction and transformation tools, such as Extract, Integrity, Passport, Platinum Warehouse, and Prism, extend the functionality of conventional RDBMS products by automating the extraction and transformation of data from legacy systems. As part of the transformation process, the tools generate a historical record of all changes and enhancements to the source data in the form of metadata. The combination of conventional RDBMSs and specialized extraction and transformation tools provides a highly effective mechanism to manage, access, and distribute data throughout an enterprise data warehouse environment.

Front-End Data Access Tools

The third critical question referred to above is: What kind of front-end tools are appropriate to access data in the data warehouse? Can you use general-purpose relational data access tools, or do you require special-purpose, multi-dimensional DSS/EIS tools?

A wide variety of alternative data access techniques are available, including relational queries, multi-dimensional views of relational data, special-purpose DSS/EIS user interfaces, and custom-built user interfaces developed with client/server tools. Each of these techniques is described briefly below.

Relational Query Tools

General-purpose relational query tools support requirements for highly user-friendly access to relational data. Additional requirements include the ability to specify queries, reports and graphical presentations without help from IS, support of industry-standard user interfaces, portability to all standard platforms, ability to access the native functionality of a wide range of databases, and support for multiple server platforms and RDBMSs. Representative relational end-user query tools include Esperant from Software AG, Power Objects from Oracle Corporation, Q+E from INTERSOLV, Inc., and SQR3 Workbench from MITI.

Multi-dimensional Views of Relational Data

An important new category of data access tools provides multi-dimensional views of relational data accessed from the data warehouse. The target database in the data warehouse is a conventional RDBMS. However, the end user is provided with the ability to analyze the relational data in multiple dimensions. The significance of these tools is that they support the ability to perform multi-dimensional data analysis without having to procure and support a proprietary, multi-dimensional target DBMS.

Tools in this category, such as BusinessObjects from Business Objects, Inc., FindOut! from Open Data Corp., and Forest & Trees from Trinzic (Division of Platinum Technology), provide a multi-dimensional view of relational data, but do not generate a local database on the client. Other tools, such as Brio Query from Brio Technology, Mercury from Business Objects, and PowerPlay from Cognos, extract subsets of relational data from the data warehouse and store them in local multi-dimensional structures called hypercubes. A more powerful category of tools utilizes a three-tier hardware/software architecture to perform multi-dimensional analysis against relational databases. These tools include Decision Support Suite from Information Advantage Inc., MetaCube from Stanford Technology Group (division of Informix Corporation),

ProdeaBeacon from Prodea Software Corp., and SAS/EIS from SAS Institute Inc.

DSS/EIS Tools

DSS/EIS products are more complex tools used for high-end multi-dimensional data analysis. Products in this category include Commander OLAP from Comshare, Inc., EXPRESS from Information Resources, Inc., (Div. of Oracle Corp.), and Lightship from Pilot Software, (Div. of Dun & Bradstreet). DSS/EIS applications include financial reporting and consolidation, line-of-business profit reporting, enterprise budgeting, and management reporting.

Client/Server Tools

General-purpose client/server tools may be used to build custom decision-support applications that meet the specific requirements of business end users. Applications generated with client/server tools can be designed to provide customized graphical user interfaces, specialized data manipulation and drill-down functions, and a wide range of custom reports. Front-end applications developed with client/server tools can support specialized functions that are not available in packaged DSS/EIS products.

Widely used, general-purpose client/server tools include CA-OpenROAD from Computer Associates International, Delphi from Borland International, PowerBuilder from Powersoft Corporation (division of Sybase), SQLWindows from Gupta Corporation, and Visual Basic from Microsoft Corporation. These products respond to the strategic requirements to provide transparent access to data, and build front-end decision-support applications rapidly, at low cost.

Applications built with general-purpose client/server tools support requirements for highly user-friendly graphical user interfaces, common look and feel across all GUIs, simplified database access, customizable on-line help, and extensibility to support a wide variety of multi-media applications.

The tools generate applications that can interface transparently with third-party products via DDE and OLE interfaces. This provides the capability to develop front-end applications that link transparently to spreadsheets, word processors, report writers, statistical packages, presentation graphics, bit-image processing, multi-media presentations, video conferencing, etc. It is recommended that IS development personnel become familiar with the hundreds of packages available from third-party vendors that can be used to extend the functionality of Delphi, PowerBuilder, SQLWindows, and Visual Basic applications. These packages include Visual Basic Extensions (VBXs), OLE Custom Controls (OCXs), and shrink-wrap products, such as spreadsheets, statistical packages, report writers, and word processors.

Due to their broad acceptance in the market and their range of strategic partners, client/server tools are highly recommended for the development of customized data access and decision-support applications. Vendors of client/server tools provide a family of products that support business end users, individual IS professionals, and teams of developers working in a collaborative development environment.

Selection of Data Access Tools

Selection of end-user data access tools should be driven by requirements for ease of use and robust functionality. Ease of use is based on the provision of a common set of features, such as point and click interfaces, multiple document interface (MDI) frames, icons, and help facilities, that shield the user from having to understand how to access the database or invoke component applications. Fortunately, most end-user query tools, DSS/EIS tools, and client/server tools support graphical user interfaces that provide intuitive access to product functionality.

Functional requirements drive the decision on whether to use a relational query tool, a DSS/EIS tool, or a general-purpose client/server tool. Packaged query products, such as relational query tools and DSS/EIS tools, are highly flexible. However, they may not support the specific requirements of end users for data access, manipulation, and presentation functions. If required functions are not supported by a packaged query tool, it may be necessary to develop a custom decision-support application that exactly matches the needs of the business, and can be enhanced rapidly to respond to changing functional requirements.

For many applications, a mix of data access tools may be required. Simple relational query tools, such as Esperant, Power Objects, or Q+E, are appropriate for use by business analysts to access data transparently, perform moderate data manipulation, and produce reports and graphs, without assistance from IS. More powerful query tools, such as Brio Query, BusinessObjects, Forest & Trees, PowerPlay, and ProdeaBeacon, support multi-dimensional analysis of relational data. DSS/EIS tools, such as Commander OLAP, EXPRESS, and Lightship, are used by financial specialists to analyze large amounts of historical data to uncover market trends. Finally, custom decision-support applications, supporting strategic business requirements, can be built using general-purpose client/server tools.

Chapter

9

Database Design for Data Warehouses: The Basic Requirements

Glen Livingston and Bob Rumsby

Red Brick Systems

INTRODUCTION

Many database designers would say that there are only three rules to designing a data warehouse: keep it simple, keep it simple, and keep it simple. Although data warehouses tend to grow rapidly, and the number of users rises dramatically, a good prototype design for any data warehouse application in any industry, from retail sales to telecommunications to healthcare, is always a very simple one. The simplicity principle is grounded in the concept that the database must be visualized as a schema that the real users, the business analysts, can understand. This principle is the focus of this discussion of effective database design for data warehouses, as are the complementary requirements of using clean, consistent data and designing for speed. The question of speed is a two-part issue: Designers must ensure that users can get quick responses to their queries and that administrators can expedite the loading of data from the source into the warehouse.

Before you consider these requirements in more detail, you need to be clear about the overall objective of designing a data warehouse: that is, to create a database schema optimized for decision support. There is a fundamental difference between databases designed for operational or on-line transaction processing (OLTP) systems and databases designed for decision-support systems (DSS). While OLTP systems sometimes provide the source data that feeds the data warehouse, they lack the architecture and the functionality required to perform efficient and accurate analyses and produce reliable reports that business analysts routinely require. As "data warehouse architect" Ralph Kimball describes it, a data warehouse is quiet, but an OLTP system "twinkles." In other words, the contents of a data warehouse are relatively stable business facts and figures, while the contents of an OLTP database change as each new transaction comes in. Accurate answers issue only from a warehouse database whose data is protected from change and whose integrity is rigorously maintained.

Given this essential distinction between a database designed to get raw data in versus one designed to get useful information out, this article discusses in some detail the four basic requirements of warehouse database design:

The schema must be simple

The data must be clean, consistent, and accurate

Query processing must be fast

It must be possible to load the data into the database fairly quickly

SIMPLICITY

Data warehouses must be designed for the benefit of their end users, not for the benefit of the designers themselves or the database administrators (DBAs) and Management Information Systems (MIS) personnel who maintain the warehouse environment. Traditionally, database schemas comprise complex interrelationships of tables with multiple, circular join paths between any two points in the model. Consequently, a query that joins two tables might be processed in different ways, depending on the path specified.

These kinds of schemas are hard enough for their creators to visualize, let alone for end users to recognize as a model of their business. For example, here is part of an OLTP schema designed for order entry.

Figure 9–1: OLTP Schema With Circular Join Paths

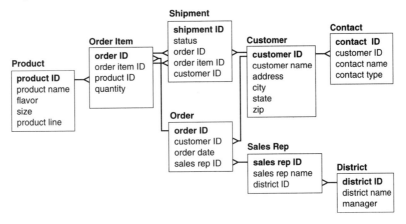

© 1996 Bob Rumsby

Schemas like those in Figure 9–1 are designed to facilitate updates to the data; each logical entity that might be updated has its own table so that each transaction has little or no "ripple" effect on the rest of the database. As a result, the schema (in its entirety) consists of dozens of tables, all connected by a maze of many-to-one relationships. Though efficient for transaction processing, these relationships tend not to be intuitive and can cause confusion when it comes to writing queries. Consider, for example, how you would use this schema to track which products have been shipped to a given customer. The Customer table has one-to-many relationships with both the Shipment table and the Order table, so at first glance it looks like you could use two different join paths to write the same query: Customer to Shipment to Order Item or Customer to Order to Order Item to Shipment. Users who take the second path may not realize that their queries will tell them what was ordered rather than what was shipped. This kind of ambiguity does not belong in a data warehousing schema; something simpler is needed if the business analyst is to make sense of the database, ask creative questions, and get the right answers back.

The business analyst is someone who knows the business inside out and wants to use that knowledge to drill down into the facts and figures stored in the warehouse to find trends and anomalies that can drive decision making: decisions about where the business should go, perhaps based on what products do well when and where, or the discovery that some sales strategies work well in some markets but not in others. Analysts are hired not for their knowledge of databases but for their knowledge of the business and how to analyze it to add value to the company's sales, marketing, distribution, and manufacturing strategies (to name a few). What these analysts most likely do not have skill or knowledge in is the advanced use of the Structured Query Language (SQL), how databases are put together and maintained, and what it takes to make the warehouse operational in the first place.

Most analysts use some sort of front-end querying tool, rather than raw SQL, to compose their queries, and ideally this tool allows them to access and use the database self-sufficiently. They shouldn't have to lean on the MIS department for ad hoc query-writing support or requests for reports. The SQL engine should reside in the database software, not inside the head of an MIS manager. This means that the schema underneath the query tool must be simple enough to facilitate direct database access.

To achieve such a schema, the database designer begins by evaluating the analysts' business requirements. During the long process of interviewing the users that should precede any database design, the designer must identify-in the users' vocabulary-all the essential characteristics, or "dimensions," of the business. The designer should look at the reports currently in use, study their headings and contents, and determine what needs to be preserved in the warehouse design. What are your typical report headers? What do you constrain on? What do you group by? These are standard questions that need to be asked before the correct set of dimensions can be mapped out. For example, in a sales and marketing environment, the design must reflect who the customers and products are, or in a health-care application, who the providers and patients are.

As the interviews move forward, the designer typically finds that the user community consists of many groups or departments. For example, a schema might need to combine information valuable for order tracking, sales analysis, and inventory management. If the design is simple and the relationships between the tables are easily understood, all the users, whether their interest lies in orders, sales, or inventories, will be able to pose their questions in the same way and get consistent answers back from the database. More advanced applications may participate in a network of data warehouses that cross enterprise boundaries, whereby data is shared between, say, retailers and their suppliers. A warehouse design that is kept simple is more likely to be flexible and manageable enough to accommodate the needs of all the user groups and to facilitate the batch updates required to synchronize the networked warehouses. What the designer needs to create is a picture of the warehouse database that the end users can readily understand-an intuitive data model based on the actual dimensions and terms of the business itself. The best way to visualize this model is in terms of a star schema. Star schemas have the advantage not only of being simple and intuitive; they also make good use of new, accelerated approaches to indexing and joining tables. The following sections describe the components of the star schema in some detail, and show how this kind of design can lead to considerable performance gains.

THE COMPONENTS OF THE STAR SCHEMA

The star schema articulates a design strategy that enforces clear and simple relationships between all the pieces of information stored in the database. A simple star consists of a group of tables that describe the dimensions of the business arranged logically around a huge central table that contains all the accumulated facts and figures of the business. The smaller, outer tables are the points of the star, the larger table the center from which the points radiate.

For example, Figure 9–2 shows a simple star designed for a consumer packaged goods (CPG) or retail organization:

You could use a schema like this to analyze sales activity over time, based on the performance of different products in different markets or regions during different time periods. This is a very basic application that might evolve into a much more complex schema according to the users' needs and the changing demands of the business. Your decision to use a star schema does not imply an alliance with a particular database software vendor; most warehouse database companies have adopted the term star schema and its methodology to some degree.

Figure 9–2: Simple Star Schema—One Fact Table, Three Dimension Tables

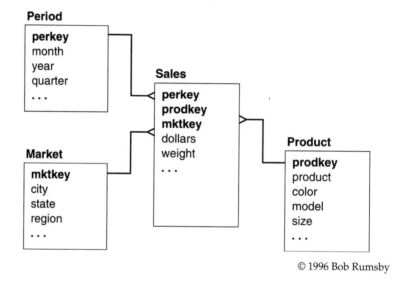

© 1996 Bob Rumsby

The Facts

The central table, by far the biggest-containing millions or hundreds of millions of rows, is known as the fact table. The contents of the fact table are the millions of "measured" values of the business, such as sales transactions or purchases, which are loaded in from operational systems or syndicated data sources. The fact table might account for as much as 95 percent of the disk space required to store the warehouse data, for despite its "skinnier," mostly numeric rows, the sheer number of records can dwarf the size of all the dimensions combined. When you are designing the specific columns and contents of fact tables, it's a good idea to keep the representation of the facts as narrow as possible, using the lowest possible number of bytes per row. Here are some examples of common fact tables:

Sales (daily, weekly, monthly, yearly)

Orders

Budget

Shipments

Accounts

Bookings

Purchases

Income

Policies

Claims

By themselves, raw facts might be meaningless, but analysts use them in conjunction with constraints on the dimensions to run standard calculations such as counts, sums, and averages: What were the total sales of a given product during the first two quarters of this year? or How many different products were sold in a given region last year? Such calculations can only work if the stored facts are truly additive. For example, to calculate a profit margin, you do the percentage (division) calculation at query time, based on sums of the quantities and the dollar amounts. If you were to store the margins themselves, as percentage values, summing them would return a meaningless number. There are ways to average an average (you can use weighted averages, for example) but to keep things simple, the database software should do the computations, not the analyst.

The facts stored in the warehouse must represent real values that the analysts need to track. For example, if they're interested in dollar amounts sold, the fact table should contain those measurements; if they're interested also in amounts sold by weight, the fact table ought to represent those additive values as well. By the same token, the granularity of the fact table data is critical; analysts might want to track sales or purchasing information in terms of monthly as well as daily sales, and orders by market or product line. Therefore, the schema might incorporate summary or aggregate data such as fact table roll-ups of sales dollars or costs, or dimension table roll-ups of products into product categories or customers into regional markets.

One approach to storing aggregates (using a family of fact tables) is discussed later in this article. The extent to which you use aggregations, and how you build them into the design, is a complex issue. Again, interview the users and study their existing reports to see what kind of summary data must be included. But before making extensive summary data available, remember that a high-performance database server can perform efficient aggregate calculations on the fly. Storing aggregates is a performance issue: How much do the users need them, and will query-processing performance stand up without them? Try loading the base data first, without aggregations, and see what the performance is like. Consider whether using aggregations is worth the maintenance effort and the extra disk space. If you decide to store aggregates, make sure they are additive, just like the base-level facts in your database (to keep the query-processing calculations simple).

The Dimensions

The contents of the dimension tables—the points of the star—are very much the "knowns" of the business: Each table has a fixed number of records, such as lists of products and services, the names of geographic regions and markets, and a host of other textual characteristics that describe-in a retail application, for example-what products are sold, what markets they are sold into, and what specific stores those markets comprise. These characteristics become the row headers of users' reports. Here are some examples of common dimension tables:

Time (or Period)

Market

Product (or Item)

Customer

Store

Vendor

Demographics

Promotions

Dimension tables tend to use character rather than numeric datatypes, so their rows are usually much wider, but they amount to a relatively small percentage of the disk space that the warehouse requires. Nonetheless, dimension tables contain an exhaustive list of columns, which must mimic both the analysts' vocabulary and the naming conventions required by business rules. Some "translation" of existing report headings might be required, so that when analysts look at a list of product codes, for example, they know exactly what those numbers represent.

Given these fundamentals of table design, the next requirement to consider is the condition of the data itself, and how the star schema enforces logical, reliable relationships between the tables.

Data You Can Trust

The DBA's nightmare is that two warehouse users will run identical queries and get two different answers back from the database. Getting consistent answers regardless of how a question is asked or who asks it is the second major requirement of the database design. At the outset, this requirement leans heavily on the source data and demands that it be "clean" before it enters a warehouse table. During loads, "dirty" data must be rejected, and once all the data has been loaded, its integrity must be maintained.

Data is typically loaded in batch format. Therefore, the designer—or someone in the MIS organization—must define what the data flows are in the business environment, and make sure that the data is quality-checked, or "blessed," before it is loaded in. In other words, a cleansing or transformation process is required. There are several software applications dedicated to this task, which involves checking large amounts of data for consistent format and updating records that do not "fit." For example, the data might be dirty because the OLTP system that collected it allowed manually entered universal product codes (UPCs), as well as automatically entered UPCs, to be logged for sales of certain products. So, in the process of designing a clean data warehouse, you might find yourself cleaning up the legacy systems that supply the source data as well. In any case, time has to be allowed for this critical and often protracted phase of the implementation. Once the data is in the warehouse, it is too late to manage its quality. As stated earlier, data warehouses must contain stable data; unlike OLTP systems, they do not accommodate extensive updates to individual records. Assuming that the loaded data is clean, how does the database enforce and maintain its integrity? The answer lies in the primary key foreign key references implicit in the star schema. To produce consistent answers to queries, the fact and dimension tables must intersect in consistent ways. Typically, fact tables are built with a multi-part primary key. This key consists of values that point to matching foreign key values in dimension tables, which typically have single-part primary keys. For example, if the Sales fact table has the key values Mktkey, Prodkey, and Perkey, the Market table will also have a Mktkey, the Product table a Prodkey, and the Period table a Perkey (as primary key columns). Figure 9–3 illustrates these relationships.

The point here is that every value in a foreign key column of a fact table must have a matching value in the primary key column of the referenced dimension table. This condition is known as referential integrity.

Referential integrity ties dimensions to facts. Say you discontinue some products, and drop their code names from the Product table, but forget to remove references to them from the Sales (fact) table. This violates referential integrity. In turn, if one user writes a query that sums sales dollars from the fact table while another user writes a query that runs the total by first listing all the products and their individual sales, the database will return two different answers although the question was essentially the same. Most organizations who are planning a data warehouse will say that they already have the referential integrity issue under control, but in practice database designers rarely see completely clean data sets.

Some organizations assume that referential integrity is handled by their operational systems, but this is not usually the case. In a point-of-sale situation, for example, transactions are often accepted without a legitimate UPC code or part number; the cashier simply substitutes a manual entry to simplify the process and close the transaction. This transaction carries the inconsistent code with it, so you cannot rely on operational systems or data sources to keep the data clean.

Figure 9–3:   Primary Key—Foreign Key Relationships

PERKEY	PRODKEY	MKTKEY	DOLLARS	⋯
101279	A66	3	199.95	
000119	G72	4	99.95	
112894	B10	8	219.95	

Sales Table

MKTKEY	CITY	STATE	REGION	⋯
3	SF	CA	WEST	
4	LA	CA	WEST	
8	SF	CA	WEST	

Market Table

PRODKEY	COLOR	MODEL	SIZE	⋯
A66	BLUE	AMERICAN	LARGE	
G72	BLUE	EUROPEAN	SMALL	
B10	RED	ALPINE	EXLG	

Product Table

PERKEY	MONTH	YEAR	QUARTER	⋯
101279	JAN	96	1	
000119	JAN	96	1	
112894	JAN	96	1	

Period Table

© 1996 Bob Rumsby

Another way to describe referential integrity is to say that it defines a reliable relationship between two tables and a means of joining those tables. Decision-support queries are join-intensive—that is, they rely heavily on joining the information from one table to the information from another table to find intersections or matching values. For example, some joins might be derived from the primary key foreign key relationships between the fact and dimension tables. If the UPC code in a product dimension table is joined to the UPC code in the fact table, and this is the only available path between these two columns, consistent query writing and consistent answers to queries are enforced. If "circular" or "cyclic" joins are possible, two departments could submit the same query via two different join paths and get different result sets back, as shown earlier in the discussion of OLTP schema design. Join paths do not have to be predefined, but the number of columns that can logically be joined should be somewhat constrained by the schema design so that users can see the relationships clearly; join paths should quickly become familiar and should be reusable in hundreds of different business questions. In many cases, a graphical user interface (GUI) will assume the task of supplying the explicit join specifications. This kind of client application will itself benefit from the built-in simplicity of the star schema, in terms of both interpreting the users' queries and presenting a comprehensible picture of the database that will encourage those users to ask more questions.

QUERY-PROCESSING SPEED

As far as business analysts are concerned, there's gold hidden inside warehouse data, but they often have to drill down to find it; they might start a session with a series of simple "browse" queries, but gradually zoom in on hidden trends by "slicing and dicing" the data in different ways. In other words, analysts must think quickly and creatively, and they need a stable, high-performance server that can expedite their queries and keep pace with their train of thought. If they have to wait too long-say, minutes instead of seconds-they might be distracted from the goal they had originally intended to pursue. Unless query-processing speed is built into the database design, creative thinking—and ultimately decision-making—will be much more difficult.

In general, query-processing speed is a function of the type and number of indexes built on different table columns. An index functions like a smaller version of the table it is built on, reducing wide column definitions for each row to much narrower, ordered sequences of rows that record the existence of a particular value or combination of values in the table. Just like a list of page references in a book's index, a database index provides direct access to the rows of interest without scanning the whole table.

Unlike OLTP databases, data warehouse databases use indexes extensively. To ensure that an optimal index is always available, you should create multiple indexes on most tables, especially the dimensions. In a retail schema, a dimension table might contain as many as a million UPCs, representing different products, and the number of base transactions against those products might rise into the hundreds of millions. To ensure fast access to this high volume of data, a good strategy would be to put indexes on every single column of each dimension table. Indexes on dimension table columns contain much narrower rows than the descriptive rows of the table itself; therefore, an indexed search for, say, all customers in a given city, is much faster than a full-table scan. If you index every column in the Customer table, not just the City column, all queries that constrain on that table will run faster.

Depending on the nature of the table data and the constraints that tend to recur in users' queries, you should experiment with different types of indexes on different dimensions. For example, bit-vector indexes are very efficient for highly analytical questions that involve multiple weakly selective constraints, such as queries that look for specific behavioral or demographic patterns. For example, a question such as, "What is the average checking account balance for single males who earn annual salaries over $75,000?" includes weakly selective constraints on the customer's sex and marital status, because the range of possible values for those dimensions (known as the "domain" of the column) consists of only two or three values. Such columns would definitely benefit from bit-vector indexing. But note that this query not only demands an ability to select out the single males; it also requests an analysis of the selected rows (an average). To get the best performance with a query like this, you would need to combine bit-vector indexing of the weak constraints (dimensions) with index structures that join the dimensions to the facts and take care of the analytical side of the query.

The star schema design is based on direct, logical paths between dimensions and facts; therefore, it lends itself to the use of advanced table-joining and indexing technologies that work together to join multiple tables in a single operation. The join processing is accelerated by specialized indexes built on multiple columns—typically, fact table columns that serve as foreign key references to the dimension table primary keys. Rather than index all the columns of a fact table, you can rely heavily on these primary key foreign key matches; when the server processes a query, the dimension table primary keys are concatenated, then matching rows in the fact table are quickly retrieved from the index without scanning the fact table itself. When you use this indexing technique, the database actually becomes more efficient as the SQL becomes more complex and as the number of joins increases. If you take a simple star schema, such as for a retail or consumer packaged goods (CPG) application, and expand it into a more complex schema suitable for, say, healthcare or insurance claims analysis, the database performance improves rather than deteriorates, and within multi-star schemas, both fact-to-fact and fact-to-dimension joins perform well. This approach to indexing both the fact table foreign keys and all of the dimension table columns improves performance for both browse queries that traverse large dimension tables and statistical calculations such as sums of sales dollars or market share percentages. By the way, indexing all the columns in the dimension tables does not, in the grand scheme of things, require a significant amount of disk space. Space is usually more of an issue for fact tables, since they typically contain the most rows.

You can increase the performance of data warehouse applications in other ways, such as by issuing queries that select from the smaller tables in the schema first and by making efficient use of aggregate data, but the fundamental gain in query performance derives from the schema design. The design should feature intuitive paths that join the dimensions to the facts, and the tables should use different types of indexes, based on the data distribution and datatype of each column and the kinds of queries that are most likely to be issued.

LOAD PROCESSING AND PERFORMANCE

Query-processing speed is a design measurement that concerns minutes versus seconds, or even seconds versus milliseconds. Analysts are crippled when a query that should only take 3 seconds actually takes 3 minutes. But perhaps an even more critical measurement of warehouse design is how long it takes to load the data from the source into the warehouse; in this case, it's a question of hours versus days. The DBA, and in turn the analysts, are crippled when an incremental nightly load of transaction data cannot be completed during the few hours when the warehouse database is offline. Loads of new data must happen quickly enough to allow the DBA to get the system back up by the time the first East-Coast analyst logs on in the morning.

Being able to load batch data efficiently inside this window of opportunity results from several aspects of good design that have already been discussed: the simplicity of the table structure, the cleanliness of the source data, referential integrity, and so on. In other words, loading speed is not so much a design requirement as a result of adherence to other basic principles of warehouse design—in particular, the principle of star schema style simplicity in data modeling.

If your schema involves aggregate data—which it almost invariably should—you will need to re-create or update aggregate summaries during the nightly loads, especially if there is correction data to be rolled into the base transactions in the fact table. To maintain discrete aggregate tables, or aggregate roll-ups inside your fact tables, you need to work from the base detail data, not from the existing data already stored in the warehouse. Again, because the warehouse functions as a repository of stable data, any updates or changes to its values need to be accomplished when it is offline and not accessible to the analysts. This is an important point to remember as far as speed is concerned because the loading window of opportunity gets smaller and smaller as other maintenance tasks enter the fray, and as the warehouse gets bigger.

The issue of loading source data also raises the question of how the database will store the data-whether the table or index data is stored in one piece or partitioned among multiple disk devices (or physical storage devices). Your approach to partitioning the data will in part be influenced by the functionality available in the database software you have chosen to use, but in all cases you have to keep the requirement of query-processing performance firmly in mind. Storing related data in one place tends to make query processing faster; however, the sheer size of a table might demand that its data be split up. Also, if users tend to constrain on certain portions of the data—such as specific time periods—keeping the "new" data in one segment and the "old" data in another might be a logical way to partition the database. This kind of partitioning could also be built into the schema design by creating separate tables for each year's data. During the early stages of designing a new database, keep the partitioning as simple as possible to expedite both the loading process and subsequent data access.

Variations on the Star

Warehouse design is an iterative process, with the simple star schema providing a foundation for expansion and experiment. The growing complexity of a warehouse schema can be tracked in terms of the number of stars it contains and how many dimension tables are built around each star, because the typical data warehouse—especially one used for complex business applications such as insurance, financial management, government, and healthcare—soon outgrows the simple star schema. In order to keep the design practical, you might make use of multi-fact stars and fact table families, as well as special kinds of dimension tables known as outboard tables.

Outboard tables

You might have a Product dimension table that contains some specialized information that not all users of that dimension are likely to constrain on or be interested in. If so, you might create an "outboard" or "outrigger" table that is linked to another "interior" dimension table via a foreign key reference. In this way, you can keep the design simple by isolating data that would otherwise overload the interior dimension. For example, you could split off information about a certain group of clients from a Customer table, or set up a demographics table that refers to a Market table.

Figure 9–4: A Demographics Outboard Table

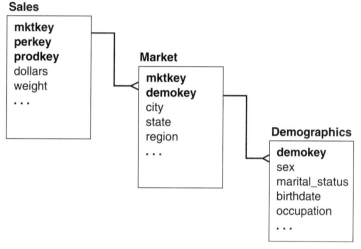

© 1996 Bob Rumsby

The advantages of the approach shown in Figure 9–4 are a reduction in size of the interior dimension, the avoidance of lots of repeated information in the interior dimension, and a cleaner, simpler picture of the model for users.

FACT TABLE FAMILIES

Data warehousing applications often form parts of a value chain across a large enterprise. A value chain is a set of linked business operations that reflect the flow of products or services through an organization—for example, from purchasing, through manufacturing and distribution, to retail sales. As goods move through the chain, different groups of analysts interested in different aspects of the business log into the same data warehouse, where they share some of the dimensions with other groups of users but access other dimensions and fact tables required for their own queries and reports.

This is one scenario that gives rise to a "family" of fact tables with a shared set of dimensions. A simple example is a retail application that provides three different sales fact tables—for daily, weekly, and monthly aggregations, or summaries, of the sales figures. One group of users might track sales data by month, but other groups by day or week. Figure 9–5 illustrates this scenario.

Figure 9–5:   A Fact Table Family for Aggregate Data

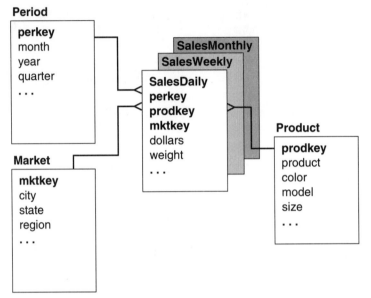

© 1996 Bob Rumsby

MULTI-STAR FACT TABLES

If any given combination of dimension table primary keys points to more than one row in the fact table, you have a multi-star schema. For example, a fact table might store sales data in weekly summaries; therefore, it would contain one row that represents weekly sales of each product in each market. To break out and track individual dollar amounts for the invoiced items that produce the weekly summary, you could create a more detailed fact table with an line item key as the primary key. This primary key would point to one row for each line item on each invoice, rather than one row for each week of invoices.

There are many other ways to build on the star schema (see Figure 9–6) that are outside the scope of this article, but these three variations are some of the most commonly used techniques for improving the efficiency and speed of the database. Nonetheless, the heart of the application is still the simple star.

Figure 9–6:   A Multi-Star Schema

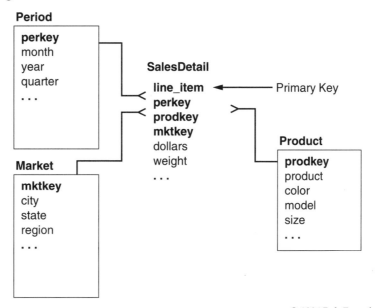

SUMMARY

This article discusses the business focus of data warehousing applications in terms of four basic design requirements: simplicity (though complex growth is anticipated), consistency and accuracy in the data (to avoid different answers to the same question), query-processing speed (so users can drill down and think creatively), and loading speed (to meet the nightly window and keep the database online). Some more advanced techniques for building complex star schemas are also briefly discussed: outboard tables, multi-star fact tables, and fact table families.

Successful designs model business needs. As a database designer, you need to service your customers, the business analysts; this means keeping the schema simple and understandable. Allow your first designs to be very basic, and let them evolve over time to meet the needs of different user groups accessing the same data warehouse. The design process is always iterative, so do something simple first to show proof of concepts and get feedback from the users on what works and what needs refinement. Throughout the process, make sure the database returns consistent, valuable information that helps analysts make good decisions.

Chapter

10

Choosing the Right OLAP Technology

Neil Raden

Archer Decision Systems

Though the volume of data captured and stored by organizations today would have been unthinkable five years ago, this trend shows no signs of abating. Yet despite this embarrassment of riches, organizations awash in data find themselves thirsting for information. Constrained in all of their initiatives by their ability to integrate and understand available, actionable business information, they turn to technology to solve the problem. Billions of dollars have been spent in the last decade on relational database systems, with the promise of improved access to data, but the promise has not been kept. Data is in a deep-freeze, impenetrable. As a result, the relatively obscure idea of data warehousing, percolating through the conventional wisdom since the eighties, has taken the spotlight as the "must-have" technology of the nineties. While data warehousing focuses on the gathering, cleansing, and storing of large volumes of information, the on-line analytical processing (OLAP) tools provide the means to manipulate and analyze the information. The synergy is clear: when married, data warehouses and OLAP provide a whole that is greater than the sum of the parts.

Data warehousing's provenance is rooted firmly in large-company information technology (IT) organizations and relational database concepts and methodologies. Ironically, its ultimate value is in enabling knowledge workers to manipulate the data to gain new insights, but the tools for this manipulation are distant cousins in the IT family tree. Much as anaerobic bacteria can thrive in an environment that is poisonous to most species, a separate class of technology tools emerged and flourished in the pre-warehouse information "deep-freeze," outside of the established IT channel. The early time-sharing and mainframe-based Decision Support Systems, conceived in the 70s, reached their zenith in the early eighties before being displaced by more "personal" tools, namely the PC-based spreadsheets and databases. Tools such as Comshare's System W, EPS Consultants' FCS, Execucom's IFPS, IBI's FOCUS and MDS' Express (now Oracle's Express OLAP) were deployed and used by accountants, actuaries, marketing researchers, financial analysts and other subject-matter oriented professionals, not programmers. They were the tools of choice of a new class of computer user: the "power" user. The descendants of these products today are OLAP tools.

USING DATA: A COGNITIVE VIEW

Data in an organization leads two lives. In its first incarnation, it is captured or created as part of the current process, that is, the ongoing activities of the organization. The chart in Figure 10–1 depicts a more or less typical arrangement of business functions. In each function, data is captured and stored at a low level, such as the items on a Purchase Order or Bill of Lading, an invoice or the FICA deductions for an employee in the current pay period. Data processing systems were developed over time to eliminate the human labor and/or error of the recording process, but the development was punctuated, leading to disparate approaches, lack of commonality, and redundancy in data standards. Nevertheless, each system was designed to serve its primary purpose: to keep a record of the minutiae.

This is the first life of data in an organization—an audit trail, an archive of small events, a listing of things, an official record. Organizations learned, eventually, that the data captured as part of these systems had value beyond its intended purpose.

Figure 10–1: Typical "Systems" Areas

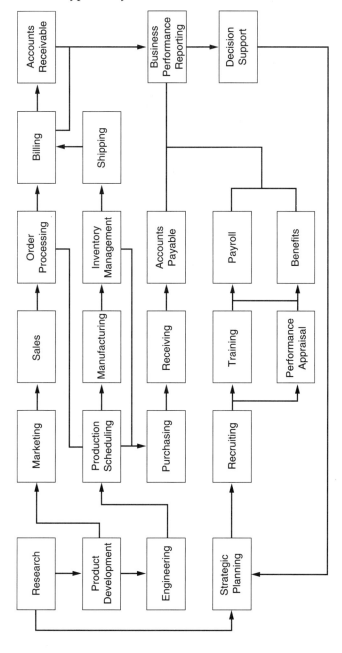

Shoshana Zuboff[1] named this phenomenon "informating" the process and used the example of a paper mill to illustrate the point, where process control instrumentation data was reused to find new and better ways to utilize resources. This is the second life of data in an organization. Other common examples are: analysis of the sales orders to find cross-selling opportunities, trend analysis (the operational systems typically carry only the most current data, an older information is archived "off-line"), or competitive analysis. In each case, data collected as part of an operational process was reused for analytical purposes distinct from the processes measured.

Since data serves two purposes, there is often a disconnect between the stewards of the operational systems and the "recyclers" of that data. Laboring under this bicameral mind, organizations are faced with a dilemma: Which is more important, the speed, accuracy, and availability of our operational systems or the ability to analyze that data? Of course, the answer is both and the premise that only one purpose can be efficiently addressed is a mistake. But it is also clear that the two approaches require different methodologies, tools, and even physical resources. OLAP technology is designed solely for the second life of data.

WHAT IS **OLAP?**

The term "OLAP" first burst onto the scene in 1992 in an article written by E.F. Codd.[2] Codd's 12 rules for OLAP (see Table 10–1) introduced the term into the collective consciousness, and it stuck. An interesting historical footnote is that one of the major OLAP players today, Arbor Software, at the time a small and obscure operation with its flagship product Ess-

---

[1] Zuboff, Shoshana (1988). *In the Age of the Smart Machine: The Future of Work and Power.* New York: Basic Books.

[2] Codd, E. F., Twelve Rules for On Line Analytical Processing, *Computerworld,* April 13, 1995.

base, received a perfect score from Codd for compliance with all 12 rules, a distinction bestowed on Arbor alone. What Computerworld failed to report was that Arbor commissioned the study by Codd, a clever marketing strategy that did a great deal to catapult the company onto everyone's short list. As a furor erupted, Computerworld issued a hasty mea culpa, but the die was cast. Essbase is now practically a household word.

Table 10–1: Codd's Twelve Rules for OLAP

1. Multi-dimensional Conceptual View
2. Transparency
3. Accessibility
4. Consistent Reporting Performance
5. Client-Server Architecture
6. Generic Dimensionality
7. Dynamic Sparse Matrix Handling
8. Multi-user Support
9. Unrestricted Cross-dimensional Operations
10. Intuitive Data Manipulation
11. Flexible Reporting
12. Unlimited Dimensions and Aggregation Levels

Fast, Heuristic Analysis

Though the impact of Codd's 12 rules is small compared to his impact on relational databases a decade earlier, and it is widely agreed that the 12 rules are too vague to be very useful, most of his analysis remains the definitive statement on the subject. There is still heated debate over the term, but this much is clear: OLAP always involves interactive querying of data, following a thread of analysis through multiple passes. One example is the display of summary data, followed by "drill-down" into successively lower levels of detail. It is often said that OLAP is "heuristic," meaning that an analytical session begins with a question, and each successive question is derived from the previous one. Ad hoc in the strictest sense, OLAP puts a great deal of stress on traditional data structures, including the relational model, the bedrock on which the data warehouse rests. Interactive, heuristic analysis requires exceptional performance, lest the train of thought is lost waiting for sluggish databases to respond.

Multi-dimensional

Underlying every OLAP tool is a conceptual data model often referred to as the Multidimensional Data Model. The process of transforming a business process into a multidimensional model is often called "dimensional modeling" or, alternatively, "multi-dimensional modeling" (MDM), the more common term. MDM is a technique for conceptualizing business models as a set of measures described by ordinary facets of business. It is particularly useful for sifting, summarizing, and arranging data to facilitate analysis. In contrast to the techniques for designing on-line transaction processing systems (OLTP), which rely on entities, relationships, functional decomposition, and state transition analysis, MDM uses constructs such as facts, dimensions, hierarchies, and sparsity. Multidimensional models are designed around numeric data, such as values, counts, weights, and occurrences. Though a typical OLTP problem statement might be, "Model the order fulfillment process," a MDM problem statement is, "What is my profitability by customer over time, by organization?"

Sparse Matrix

Codd used the phrase "dynamic sparse matrix" in his 12 rules, and every OLAP vendor talks about sparsity, but what does it mean? Let's look at a simplified version of a multidimensional model. Suppose we are a retailer and that we wanted to track the daily sales of all products in all stores for 3 years, especially watching for the effects of promotions on sales. Further, let us suppose that the "dimensions" of our problem looked like those in Table 10–2:

If we were to put this information into a spreadsheet, a little quick arithmetic shows that we would need 1,156,320,000,000,000 cells! That's over 1,000 trillion, a pretty large number. Clearly, there needs to be some scheme to deal with this much information. The good news is that the number of valid combinations of these dimensions is vastly smaller, and we need not concern ourselves with the total problem space. The quick arithmetic using this notion of "sparsity" is shown in Table 10–3.

Table 10–2

Dimension	# of "Base" Elements
Stores	1,200
Promotions	2,200
Products	40,000
Time	1,095
Measures	10

Table 10–3

Store dimension: 1200 stores reporting sales every day
Product dimension: 40,000 total products, but only 4,000 that sell on an average day
Promotion dimension: A product sold on a given day in a given store can only be part of a single promotion
Time and Measures Dimensions: No help here, every day and every fact is represented

Total cells = 1200* 4000* 1* 1095* 10 = 52,560,000,000

That's 20,000 times smaller than the first calculation, and though 52 billion is still a pretty large number, at 4 to 8 bytes per number, 200 to 400 gigabytes is certainly within the realm of the possible with some tools. Keep in mind that our model is large and fine grained. Tracking the sales of individual products across 1,200 stores daily is not for the faint of heart and much good analysis is accomplished on a vastly smaller scale. The point of the example is to illustrate the value of handling sparsity. Multidimensional models are always sparse and a tool that cannot deal with it is useless.

Manual Manipulation

The visualization of multidimensional data is typically a cross-tabular report, and tools provide the ability to pivot the axes of the cross-tabulation, as well as expand and refine the domain of analysis ("slice and dice"). In Figure 10–2, a simple five-dimensional model is shown.[3] Three of the dimensions appear in the cross-tabulation: Department, as the rows, and Time and Measure as the columns. The other dimensions are Store and Scenario (scenario meaning "actual," "plan," "updated forecast," etc.), here represented as drop-down buttons, currently set to All Stores and Scenario–Actual. Two items are worthy of note. First, it is common, but not necessarily given, that OLAP tools allow for the stacked display of dimensions as is the case here with Time and Measure. Some tools limit the number of dimensions in the grid to only two; others may allow the stacking only in rows or only in columns. For the greatest degree of flexibility, choose tools that place no limitations on this feature. Second, the Measure dimension is a special case. Some tools refer to it as a dimension, others simply as the "measures," "facts" or "metrics."

Figure 10–2: Typical OLAP Cross-Tab Report

Stores	Scenario
All	**Actual**

	1994		1995		% Change	
	Sales	Margin %	Sales	Margin %	Sales	Margin %
Clothing	234,670	27.2	381,102	21.5	62.4	(21.0)
Housewares	62,508	33.8	66,005	31.1	5.6	(8.0)
Automotive	375,098	22.4	325,402	27.2	(13.2)	21.4
All Other	202,388	21.3	306,677	21.7	50.7	1.9

An analyst might examine this report and notice that sales in the automotive department have decreased 13.2%, yet Margin % has actually increased 21.4%. Since this is an anomalous situation, the analyst may wish to see more detailed facts, prompting a drill-down operation on the "automotive" row to reveal its next level of detail, as in Figure 10–3.

---

[3] We've taken some liberties here for the sake of simplicity. It is rather unlikely that an organization would capture scenario views (actual, budget, forecast, etc.) at the level of detail shown here, that is, departments in a store.

Figure 10–3: Drill-Down Report

	1994		1995		% Change	
	Sales	Margin %	Sales	Margin %	Sales	Margin %
Clothing	234,670	27.2	381,102	21.5	62.4	(21.0)
Housewares	62,508	33.8	66,005	31.1	5.6	(8.0)
Automotive	375,098	22.4	325,402	27.2	(13.2)	21.4
Repair	195,051	14.2	180,786	15.0	(7.3)	5.6
Accessories	116,280	43.9	122,545	47.5	5.3	8.2
Audio	63,767	8.2	22,071	14.2	(65.4)	7.3
All Other	202,788	21.3	305,677	21.7	50.3	1.9

All   Actual (dimension selectors above table)

One of the more colorful terms to describe OLAP operations is the "slice and dice." Slicing the data refers to zeroing in on a column or columns (or row or rows), eliminating the rest of the display. Figure 10–4 is a slice of Figure 10–2, where the analysis is focused to the single column that represents 1995 Sales.

Figure 10–4: "Slice" Report

Stores: All	Scenario: Actual
	1995
	Sales
Clothing	381,102
Housewares	66,005
Automotive	325,402
All Other	305,677

Another common OLAP operation is the "pivot," which involves either switching the arrangement of the dimensions in the grid, or adding more of the dimensions to the grid. In Figure 10–5, the Scenario dimension is dragged into the grid below the Measures dimension, providing a cross-tab of 1995 Sales, across all Scenarios (Actual, Plan, Variance, and Variance %). The astute reader will note that we skipped a step, namely, dragging the Scenario dimension would probably result in a single column report with Scenario = Actual, until it was exploded with a "drill-down" operation.

Figure 10–5: "Pivot" Report

Stores				
All				

	1995			
	Sales			
	Actual	Plan	Variance	%
Clothing	381,102	350,000	31,102	8.9
Housewares	66,005	69,000	(2,995)	(4.3)
Automotive	325,402	300,000	25,402	8.5
All Other	305,677	350,000	(44,322)	(12.7)

Other Types of Manipulation

In the examples above, the manipulations were purely mechanical. Transformation of the display was initiated by human intervention, probably through the use of a pointing device (mouse) and/or a series of choices from lists. There are two other types of manipulation in OLAP, though many of the tools available now do not support them. The first is agent-based manipulation, which implies that some form of intelligent agent can be dispatched. This can take many different forms, such as alert reporting, time-based reporting, or exception reporting, to name a few.

In alert reporting, an analyst may specify that the system should perform some analysis and notify her only when certain conditions occur, such as daily sales reports are completed or the monthly books are closed. Time-based reporting is similar, but is based on the calendar and clock rather than the occurrence of an event. Exception reporting is a highly focused analysis that alerts the analyst only when certain boundary conditions are exceeded, such as sales reported above or below predefined thresholds, or when inventory levels fall below a certain level. The value in agent-based manipulation is its time-savings potential, particularly the time of expensive resources like analysts. An important point to keep in mind, though, is that deriving the benefit requires more than providing the tool. Unless an effort is made to ensure that analysts make the most of these capabilities, many of them will continue to rely on manual methods.

Both mechanical- and agent-based manipulations are highly personal, that is, they are either driven or directed by individuals and the results of the manipulation are directed to the same individual. Work group-based manipulations connect the manipulations across a group of people. For example, after an analyst finishes a series of mechanical manipulations, he may wish to distribute not the results of the manipulation, but the actual steps, in a way that the process can be reproduced or modified by other members. This is an excellent mechanism for improving the "numeracy"[4] of an organization. Distributing a finished report to colleagues may tell part of the story, but having them actually be able to retrace your steps through the data and watching the emerging trends or patterns in exactly the same way as the author can be much more illuminating. The cumulative effect of this process, as each modified analysis is distributed across the group, can be a powerful tool in a learning organization.

Narrow versus Wide OLAP

All of these manipulations described so far are read-only. That is, they start with a set of data and perform operations on it. This is the accepted definition for OLAP, but it leaves much to be desired. In our practice, we refer to this activity as "narrow

---

[4] Numeracy is akin to literacy. When people have the opportunity to actually work with the numbers, rather than just look at them, they gain a comprehension that transcends mere measures, but rather develop an intuitive feel for how the numbers, and the underlying real-world events they describe, relate to the business.

OLAP" and distinguish it from "broad OLAP" (or just OLAP), which includes the following characteristics:

- generating (synthesizing) information as well as using it, and storing this additional information by updating the data source

- modeling capabilities, including a calculation engine for deriving results and creating aggregations, consolidations, and complex calculations

- forecasting, trend analysis, and other complex models, such as optimization, statistical analysis, or other "esoteric" functions

Arguments about what OLAP is are mostly valueless. What is important is understanding your own requirements and searching for the best fit. "OLAP" was coined by an industry expert, subsidized by a software vendor, and thus is like so many other terms in the industry, invented by vendors to put a straight jacket on the real world so that it matches the features of the product they are selling this week. OLAP, analysis, decision support—whatever you want to call it—should be the sweet spot of your IT investment, the place where creativity, competence, and quality are most evident. This is not the place for worrying about dogma.

TYPES OF **OLAP** TOOLS

Multidimensional Databases (MOLAP)

The so-called "merchant" databases (Oracle, Informix, Sybase, Ingres, DB2), though very different products from one another, are all similar in that they share a common model (the relational model) and all speak a mostly common language (SQL). It is an entirely different situation for the multidimensional database (MDD). The concept of a multidimensional database is actually rather simple. Rather than storing information as records, and records in tables, MDDs (logically) store data in arrays. Unfortunately, there is not much else that the different flavors of MDDs have in common. Each product is substantially different from any other. For example:

- unlike the relational model, there is no agreed-upon multidimensional model·

- MDDs have no standard access method (such as SQL) or APIs (Application Programming Interfaces)

- each product could realistically be put in its own category

- The products range from narrow to broad in addressing the aspects of decision support

At the low end, there are single-user or small-scale LAN-based tools for viewing multidimensional data. The functionality and usability of these tools is actually quite high, but they are limited in scale and lack broad OLAP features. Tools in this category include PowerPlay from Cognos, PaBLO from Andyne, and the soon-to-be-released Mercury from Business Objects. All of these tools are designed to work with their own proprietary data structure (often incorrectly referred to as the "cube"). All of them use the somewhat simpler arrangement called a symmetric hypercube, which is described in more detail below, but essentially limits the model to one n-dimensional shape. Considering the sparsity of multidimensional models, this one-size-fits-all can collapse if the models are large and sparsity isn't handled cleanly. Generally, these tools are considered more "personal," meaning that the size of the database is measured in megabytes, not gigabytes. They are read-only and provide very limited functionality for complex calculations, drilling, and any form of manipulation other than mechanical.

At the high end, tools like Acumate ES from Kenan, Express from Oracle, Gentium from Planning Sciences, SAS, and Holos from Holistic Systems are so broad in their functionality, that to label them multidimensional databases is to do them a disservice. In fact, each of these tools could realistically define a separate category, so diverse are their features and architectures. Each tool provides a complete development environment, with its own flavor of a 4GL (fourth generation language), statistical, time series, financial, and user-written functions, multi-tier architectures, graphing and charting, and some more esoteric features, such as text databases, agent architectures, EIS development, and integration with workgroup tools. Though each product incorporates its own multidimensional database, use of it is optional, since all of these products are capable, to varying degrees, of utilizing the relational databases as their storage medium. Generally, this arrangement adds some overhead, and hence some processing time, by requiring the execution of SQL and subsequent transformation of the result set(s) into memory-resident multidimensional structures. However, since both the relational database and the tool itself are processing on high-end UNIX servers, this arrangement can be very effective and fast.

The pure multidimensional database engines are represented by Essbase from Arbor, LightShip Server from D&B/Pilot, and TM/1 from Sinper. Though these tools lack 4GLs and full development environments, they are in most cases much more sophisticated databases than the integral databases of the high-end MDD tools mentioned above. They also possess many of the statistical, financial, and time-series functions, though each product has some limitations. Some of them have their own Application Programming Interfaces (APIs) allowing them to be "opened up" to front-end development in tools like Visual Basic, PowerBuilder, etc. Because of its API and efforts to position itself as a database, Essbase is far ahead of the others in partnering with other software vendors to extend its functionality, including all of the low-end MDD tools.

Concentrating on just the multidimensional database capabilities of all of the products, there are two prevailing approaches to multidimensionality. The first, the hypercube, is exemplified by Essbase. In the hypercube model, symmetry is the paradigm. The "cube" in hypercube is actually a little misleading, since "cube" implies that each side is of equal length, which is rarely the case in these applications. The term hypercube is meant to describe an object of three or more dimensions with flat sides and each dimension at right angles to all of the others. For those without training in formal mathematics and physics, this example can be a little startling, but try this approach. Figure 10–6 depicts the 5-dimensional model described earlier, composed of a three-dimensional cube, sparsely populated with small, dense two dimensional squares. In fact, Essbase uses a scheme like this to conceptualize its storage arrangement. What happens, in effect, is that the coordinates of the sparse dimensions (Store, Product, and Promotion) are taken and stored as an index, and the uniformly sized dense squares (Measure, Time) are lined up in storage, one after another. This way, when a given Store/Product/Promotion combination is meaningless, no storage space is taken. The logic behind this is that a single occurrence in one of the dense dimensions generally implies occurrences in most of them. For example, if actual Sales are recorded on a given day for a Product in a Store, chances are that will also be recorded for that combination on most days. Granted, this view leaves a little to be desired and is far from rigorous, but it does have simplicity. If the time dimension were weeks, or even months, the "dense" squares would be very dense, indeed.

Figure 10–6: Sparse Hypercube

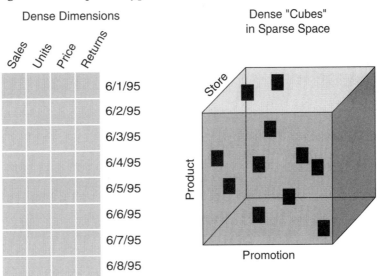

Designing a hypercube model is a top-down process, with three major steps. First, you decide what aspect or process of the business you will capture in the model, such as sales activity or claims processing. Next, identify the values that you want to capture, such as sales amounts or elements of costs. This information is almost always numeric. Last, identify the granularity of the data, that is, the lowest level of detail at which you will capture it. These elements are the dimensions. Common dimensions are measure, time, scenario, geography, product, and customer. For example, a single cell in a cube could refer to the budgeted $ Sales in January of this year, in the Northeast, of blue hair dye to K-mart.

MDDs are capable of providing stunning query performance, which is mostly a function of anticipating the manner in which data will be accessed. Because information in a MDD is stored in much coarser grain than a relational database, the index is much smaller and is usually resident in memory. Once the in-memory index is scanned (in a blink of the eye), a few pages are drawn from the database. Some tools are even designed to cache these pages in shared memory, further enhancing performance. Provided the application designer made the right assumptions about usage patterns, this scheme works pretty well.

Another interesting aspect of MDDs is that information is stored in arrays. This means that values in the arrays can be updated without affecting the index. This is the reason that MDDs are so nicely suited for read-write applications. Unfortunately, many of them are pretty primitive in the way they handle multiple writers. Essbase in the exception in this case. A drawback to this "positional" architecture is that even minor changes in the dimensional structure require a complete reorganization of the database.

Another drawback in the hypercube model is that every value shares the same dimensionality. In the above example, we may use allowance % by customer, and it is redundant to store it repeatedly by geography (for example, the allowance % for K-mart is invariant across geography). Some hypercube products have techniques to get around this inconvenience, but the other multidimensional alternative, multicubes, uses a more elegant solution. Though implementations vary across products, multicubes dimension each variable separately and deal internally with the consequences. The downside is that these approaches are less straightforward and carry steeper learning curves. Conclusion: If your problem can be handled with a hypercube, you may be better off with one.

Relational OLAP (ROLAP) Tools

Though the name "Relational/OLAP" or, alternatively, "OLAP-on-Relational" is recently coined, the concept is not new. Pioneered by Metaphor, the concept of providing multi-dimensional analysis from relational databases is more than a decade old. The next-generation tools that trace their lineage from Metaphor include AXSYS Suite (Information Advantage), Microstrategy's suite of DSS products, MetaCube (Stanford Technology Group/Informix), and Prodea Beacon (Platinum).[5] Just like the MDDs, this is a rapidly evolving market, and all four of these products had their first production releases in the last year or two. The field will get more crowded, both from new entrants and from vertical expansion of existing vendors in other categories. Express, with improved SQL drill-through to relational databases, will slip into this group also. One could argue that, among its other capabilities, Holos provided Relational/OLAP capabilities since 1988, or that Red Brick Warehouse, with any front-end that can produce or pass through RISQL (Red Brick's extensions to SQL), is a Relational/OLAP tool.

I consider a product a Relational/OLAP tool only if it can meet the following criteria:

- has a powerful SQL-generator, capable of creating multi-pass selects and/or correlated subqueries; powerful enough to create non-trivial ranking, comparison, and %-to-class calculations

- generates SQL optimized for the target database, including SQL extensions

- provides a mechanism to describe the model through metadata and uses the metadata in real-time to construct queries

---

[5] Red Brick Warehouse, from Red Brick Systems, though not really an OLAP tool, was founded by Ralph Kimball, one of the founders of Metaphor. Red Brick is a relational database, but it is designed and optimized for dimensional modeling delivering what is essentially OLAP.

- includes a mechanism to at least advise on the construction of summary tables for performance, preferably with the ability to monitor usage
- ability to partition the application between clients, servers, and a middle tier for managing threads to the database

Based on these criteria, there are only four products that come close. Information Advantage is a powerful tool, but its SQL generation capabilities are limited. In place of a robust SQL engine, IA offers a very powerful three-tier architecture, with a middle tier designed to compensate for the inherent weaknesses in SQL as an analytical tool. These features combined more than make up the difference, but one wonders how this will play out as the database vendors themselves add more OLAP functionality to their core products (see DOLAP below). Microstrategy comes closest to meeting all of the criteria, but its aggregate manager is very rudimentary. Prodea is similar in many ways to Information Advantage and MetaCube has perhaps the best aggregate advisor of the lot, but no middle tier to speak of unless and until Network OLE is a reality. Its SQL engine is similar to IA: somewhat basic, with an application-based analytical engine.

Hybrid Tools

Database OLAP (DOLAP)

With Oracle's acquisition of Express and Informix's acquisition of MetaCube, it is clear that the relational database vendors intend to offer ROLAP capability within their engines, a development named DOLAP by the industry analysts, for Database/OLAP. One can only speculate what the form of such an offering might be, but it is clear that the first glimpses will appear in 1996. Since the lingua franca of RDBs is SQL, the limitations are inherent, and a simple "bolt-on" product will offer little to compete with the ROLAPs. The best guess is that the SQL-92 specification includes some extensions to the SQL language (in fact, Red Brick implemented these extensions a few years ago, its RISQL, for "Intelligent Red Brick SQL") to facilitate ranking and tertile operations, and this would be the likely first step, along with a metamodel specification for building OLAP analysis, generating SQL tuned for the database. Though this may pose a threat to the ROLAP vendors, simple market economics should prevail: data warehousing is the hottest sector in databases, the ROLAP vendors are generating a tremendous amount of business based on their understanding and reputation in data warehousing, and the RDB vendors are the ultimate beneficiaries of this process. It's doubtful that Oracle, for example, will want to kill the goose that laid the golden egg.

HOW TO CHOOSE

When we conduct an evaluation for our clients, we separate the criteria into five major categories: Functionality, Fit, Performance, Scalability and Future. It is difficult to assign a hierarchy to these criteria, but one thing is clear: Functionality, though a critical and visible item, is transitory at best. First, features and functions of these products are changing rapidly. Second, the stated requirements of your clients at the beginning of a project rarely endure. Rather, what is frequently cited the "must have" feature is only that issue that is causing the most pain at that point in time. If one thing is certain in data warehousing it is that requirements change and flexibility is the coin of the realm. Performance is a deal-breaker, therefore it is more of a restraint than a constraint. Fit, Scalability and Future are the most important issues.

Functionality

Matching your requirements to the functionality of an offering is an elusive prospect at best (see Table 10–4). If you listen carefully, you can almost hear the cells dividing in some of these products, they are evolving so fast! In addition, every day brings more press releases of vendors partnering with each other, linking their products to provide more end-to-end functionality. In this atmosphere, it is often easier to start by identifying the show-stoppers and working backwards. Here are a few that point to MDD as your solution:

Table 10–4

Choose Multidimensional Database for:	Choose Relational/OLAP Solutions for:
Bounded dimensionally	Fluid dimensionality
Cross-dimensional calculations	Multidimensional view of a data warehouse
Row level calculations	Scale – very large database, many users
Read-write applications	Rapidly changing dimensions
Rules-rich applications	Data-rich applications
Data marts	Data warehouses

- Updating the database—If your application calls for updating the database interactively, Relational/OLAP is out of the question for now. First, the RDB schema used to get adequate performance, the so-called star schema, are remarkably inept for incremental update, because their indexes are based on a "quiet" database. Second, the SQL code generators are designed to generate only SELECT statements at this point.

- Built-in features—Most MDDs engines (Essbase in particular), as well as the high-end tools like Holos, Gentium, and Acumate, have extensive libraries of financial functions, including currency conversion, depreciation, interest, and Internal Rate of Return. Relational/OLAP tools have just begun this process and are far behind. Other tools have quite sophisticated time intelligence, LightShip Server in particular.

- Cross-dimensional calculations—The phrase is a mouthful, but some examples include cost allocations and intercompany eliminations. Relational/OLAP is showing some signs of life here, especially DSS/Agent, so look closely for innovations. At the present, Relational/OLAP can't handle it.

- Row-level calculations—Only rocket scientists can perform calculations down a result set in SQL, as opposed to across the columns. Simple metrics, like "margin = sales – cost of goods sold" can be performed in SQL by transposing the rows to columns, but there is a practical limit to the number of columns that can be handled with ease, even with multiple pass SELECTS. For applications that are like spreadsheets, such as an Income Statement, MDDs will be superior.

- Rules rich—Relational/OLAP is not designed for modeling; most MDDs are. Acumate ES, Essbase, Express, Gentium, and Holos have rich features for modeling, including the ability to develop UDFs (user-defined functions), extending the capabilities of the product to suit your needs.

MDDs are subject to a few show stoppers, too. Here are some indications that a Relational/OLAP solution may be best:

- Data warehouse—Data warehouses and relational databases are inseparable. If your requirement is to do OLAP analysis from a data warehouse, Relational/OLAP is a natural; MDD doesn't make sense. However, subsetting the data warehouse into smaller, manageable pieces, often referred to as data marting, is an area where MDDs hold some promise.

- Rapidly changing dimensions—Good examples of this situation are product codes that can be superseded at any time or customers who merge, change ownership, or go bankrupt. At the detail level, this poses no threat to a MDD, but if the database carries historical data, the aggregations have to be run back to "the beginning of time." If this happens often enough, a MDD is the wrong choice.

- Fluid Dimensionality—MDDs excel when the dimensionality of a problem is neatly bounded and mostly static. Changes in the dimensional structure require a physical reorganization of the database, which is time consuming. Certain applications are too fluid for this, and the on-the-fly dimensional view of a Relational/OLAP tool is the only appropriate choice.

- Data rich applications—In general, MDDs are designed to exploit the relationships between dimensional elements through their powerful calculation engines. Those applications with massive amounts of data (10s, 100s or 1000s of gigabytes) and relatively simple relationships are best left to the relational bases, for now.

Fit

Decision support doesn't happen in a vacuum. Unless the suite of tools can be rationalized in the computing environment of your organization, it will be very risky. The goodness-of-fit is dependent on a number of factors, such as:

- Development—Some tools require a fairly steep learning curve, particularly those at the high-end with the broadest functionality. Is your organization supportive of another sub-specialty, particularly if it is not similar to other initiatives? The 4GL languages of these tools are quite idiosyncratic, and the skills do not transfer well.

- Fat client/thin client—What is your existing IT architecture? Are you committed to providing state-of-the-art workstations to your OLAP audience, and the network bandwidth to serve it? If not, consider products that operate with a "thin client" and place a heavier burden on the server. Information Advantage, Holos, and Essbase all operate efficiently on midrange PC equipment. DSS/Agent, provided it can rely on DSS/Server, can as well. MetaCube and TM/1 are more client-heavy, as are Express and Gentium.

- Network impact—Closely related, but not identical to the issue immediately above, is the impact placed on the network. Clearly, pure ad hoc query tools without governors are the worst. Following closely behind are tools that assemble a multidimensional model in client workstation memory, like the low-end tools and, to some extent, MetaCube. Information Advantage will create local print files and spreadsheet extracts on the server and broadcast them across the WAN, a less than optimal situation.

- The Internet—Will you want to provide access to your

data through a Web Browser? Some products are already promoting their Web versions, notably Information Advantage and Microstrategy, but expect everyone to at least announce products in 1996. Look closely, many of them will do it with mirrors!

- Connectedness—MetaCube, for example, is completely OLE2 compliant. If your computing environment is committed to this form of distributed objects, MetaCube will make sense, but unless and until Network OLE is a reality, it is decidedly two-tier. Information Advantage, on the other hand, is the polar opposite and has a more UNIX/CORBA flavor. Does your organization have a history with MDDs, perhaps from prehistoric times with products like System W from Comshare or Express (same product, to a certain extent, has been around since the 70s)? Or is your organization committed to relational databases? Missionary work is probably not in your job description.

Performance

Comparisons of speed between MDD and Relational/OLAP are misleading. MDD advocates crow that there is no comparison between the almost instantaneous response in MDDs, as opposed to the often sluggish performance of a RDB. There are plenty of MDD applications in production with pretty poor performance, particularly at the high end occupied by Express and Holos. Consider this:

- The "comparisons" generally pit a standard On Line Transaction Processing (OLTP) design to a MDD optimized for OLAP analysis. Tuning a RDB with a "pure" star schema design, with precalculated and aggregated tables, along with a SQL generator that knows how to take advantage of them, is going to perform similarly to a MDD. If the database supports parallel query and advanced indexing (meaning almost anything other than B-trees) and the query optimizer understands star schema, the comparison will be even more dramatic.

- The two approaches occupy separate application spaces that should rarely overlap. For that reason, speed comparisons are not terribly useful. Multidimensional databases designed for lower levels of scalability (in terms of both size and number of users), are much more useful for read/write applications and handle row-oriented functions more fluidly. This is changing, though, as the ROLAPs improve their analytical calculation engines.

- MDDs have more subtle performance limitations. Queries that cross all arrays, as opposed to reporting from a handful of them, are similar in response time to full table scans in an RDB. Updating the MDD can take an excessive amount of time, and cannot be improved with parallelism, as the products are not yet designed to benefit from it in any meaningful way.

Scalability

Since Relational/OLAP tools rely on the RDB for servicing their queries, scalability is usually a function of the underlying database. There are some subtleties here, though. Without a middle tier to manage the interaction between client and server, it is possible to overwhelm the database server with the volume of separate processes. Advanced Relational/OLAP tools provide a middle tier to "multiplex" the clients into a smaller number of active processes on the server. This technique can even serve to maximize the use of caching and shared memory by sharing processes.

The actual size of the database is critical. Though many OLAP servers can scale up to multi-gigabyte size, careful analysis of "boundary conditions" (those situations that represent discontinuous reliability or worse, catastrophic failure) is necessary. For example, what factors determine when an index can no longer fit in memory? Will the system be able to update the database in its bulk load mode within the update window each night or each month?

RDBs can handle much larger databases and take advantage of more powerful server architectures, but this is a distinct advantage for Relational/OLAP TODAY. In 1996, it will start to dissipate. Here is the key point: RDBs have no advantage over MDDs architecturally for exploiting SMP and MPP, they've just been doing it longer (and not much longer). MDDs will catch up quickly, even though the vendors are surprised by their own success and never dreamed they would be entering the 100GB+ space so soon. With the acquisition of Express by Oracle and MetaCube by Informix in 1995, expect the line between ROLAP, MOLAP, and DOLAP to blur.

Future

Keep in mind that whatever tool(s) you select, you will have to live with your choice for a while. In that sense, it is just as important to evaluate the vendor as it is to evaluate the product. Will the vendor be able to keep up? What is the overall quality of the product? Is the vendor closely tied to a standard that is at variance with your direction? What kind of partner are you looking for? These are certainly "soft" issues, but important ones.

SUMMARY

Many factors muddy the water. We are doing things in our practice in Relational/OLAP that would be extremely difficult in MDD, such as comparable sales reporting or "on promotion" analysis. These applications are certainly multidimensional, but they require the power of an enterprise data management system. Likewise, we've used MDD for applications that would have been impossible in Relational/OLAP, like financial modeling. Here's another thing to consider: Vendors are linking their products at a dizzying pace. You can no longer think about the features of a product in isolation, you must consider its "extended value chain" and how it is complemented by its partners. For example, none of the Relational/OLAP tools can stand on their own, they require a RDB. If you consider DSS/Agent or MetaCube or IA, you have to look at in concert with Oracle/Sybase/Informix or even Red Brick. Red Brick is the same, it lacks a front end; so does Essbase. For example, Cognos' PowerPlay may be a poor choice in a given situation because it lacks the capability to store vast amounts of data and support dozens of simultaneous clients. Essbase may fail the evaluation because the look and feel of its supplied front-end (spreadsheet add-in) is unacceptable for the intended purpose. But the combination of the two products (and they do work very well together) could be a perfect fit.

On the other hand, certain other tools are less cooperative and either offer no API or a limited one, like Express, Holos, or Gentium. Here the analysis is a little easier, because the products are more-or-less self-contained and you can decide if it has what you need. The problem is that a perfect fit still may require a substantial amount of missionary work. Corporate IT loves standards, but real-life problem-solvers loathe them. It wasn't very long ago that relational databases were considered toys, not ready for the corporate big-time. The so-called post-relational databases are in the same position now, but the situation won't endure. MDDs are enjoying a huge increase in interest and sales, despite their non-standardness. Once the RDBs incorporate MDD technology into their products (Informix and Oracle are already doing it), the approach will be in the mainstream. What isn't clear is where that leaves the MOLAP and ROLAP vendors.

One thing is sure: Vendors in both categories, multidimensional databases and ROLAP, are highly creative, capable, and competitive. This subject area is finally getting the attention it deserves. With the exception of Express, now owned by Oracle, and Cognos, all of these companies are relatively small. But many of them are experiencing spectacular growth. This will attract more attention, capital, and competition. All of us will benefit from it.

Metadata Repositories: The Key to Unlocking Information in Data Warehouses

Duane Hufford

American Management Systems

INTRODUCTION

Managing data and supporting customers for a data warehouse requires a variety of metadata: data about the customer views of data; the suppliers of that data; processes used to extract, validate, load, and archive the data; and rules for synchronizing the data. A variety of commercial tools are now on the market that address themselves to one or perhaps several data warehouse componentry requirements, and each tool usually comes with a capability to capture and use metadata. Similar sets of metadata are used for a variety of functions such as helping end users to find and access data from the data warehouse, transforming data extracted from source systems into a format suitable for the data warehouse, or measuring the quality of data populated into the data warehouse.

In general, the value of metadata stems from its ability to be used as a standard description for a wide variety of data structures. All software programs need to operate at some level from a fixed set of inputs and outputs. From the perspective of a commercial tool vendor, if the tool they sell cannot know in advance what the user's database will look like, then the tool must process the database based on a standard description of that database. This standard description is captured in metadata.

None of the various data warehouse tools currently on the market represent a complete hardware vendor independent solution, and at this stage it appears that the large majority of vendors believe that they are still better off using proprietary rather than open metadata repositories for their product offerings. To protect investments made in capturing metadata to support the warehouse solution appropriate for today, the wise architects will make use of open repositories— even if it means double entry into a closed repository for one or more vendor tools. The metadata repository will allow these organizations to more easily migrate to other commercial tools that will emerge, and to experience the benefits of being able to adopt plug-and-play tactics with open data warehouse componentry sooner.

This report describes metadata for managing the data warehouse, and as a design paradigm for establishing the flexibility to incrementally expand the subject area scope of data captured in the data warehouse. Several point of departure metadata models are presented to allow the presentation to go into a level of detail that design practitioners will find useful and thought provoking, but at the same time provide material understandable and interesting to those whose prior exposure to metadata may be at a higher level.

METADATA: WHAT IT IS AND WHY THE SURGE IN INTEREST CONCERNING ITS ROLE IN DATA WAREHOUSES

Metadata describe the data and the environment in which the data are managed. This definition is often compressed to three words—"data about data." But this is a trite definition that still needs to be more fully developed. The best way to fully understand metadata is to look at some examples and compare them to actual values of data.

Consider an example of metadata in Figure 11–1 describing what is in a file or table named Customer. Metadata are the values for the characteristics labeled as Logical Name, Definition, and Physical Name of the File/Table, as well as the information provided on each attribute appearing in the table (e.g., Customer Identifier and Customer Description). From this example, we can make several observations about the potential uses of metadata in a data warehouse environment:

- Some of the metadata support "user oriented" functions. For example the definition of a customer and the definition of each attribute in the customer table (e.g., Customer Identifier and Customer Description). This type of metadata can help a user discover what data are in the data warehouse.

Figure 11–1: Examples of Metadata—Descriptions of 'Data Places'

File/Table	Logical Name	Customer
	Definition	Organization or person that purchases goods or services
	Physical Name	TDW.CSTMR
	Record Edit Proc Name	VALCSTMR

Attribute	Logical Name	Customer Description
Attribute	Logical Name	Customer Identifier
	Definition	Unique identifier assigned for each customer
	Physical Name	CSTMR_ID
	Type Code	Character
	Length	9
	Null Rule	Not null
	Field Edit Proc Name	VALCS D

- Other items of metadata have a technical or "system administration" orientation. For example, the record edit and the field edit procedure names (i.e., Record Edit Proc Name and Field edit Proc Name). A generic extract program could, for each field to be imported into the data warehouse, investigate the validity of the field using the field edit procedure identified in this metadata item and perform consistency checks across fields using the record edit procedure. It could do this using either an interpretive approach or a compile and run approach. Using an interpretive approach, the name is read from the dictionary at execution time. With a "compiled" approach—the metadata are used to generate a COBOL program. This is what Evolutionary Technology, PRISM, and Carleton do in their commercial products. The compile approach delivers better run-time performance at some cost in terms of flexibility. The compiled code runs faster because it does not perform interpretation to look things up in the dictionary, but flexibility suffers because every time you make a change you have to regenerate and recompile the code.

- Some of the metadata are useful to both the users and the warehouse technical support staff—for example, the physical names for the tables and columns in the data warehouse.

If we think of metadata as descriptions of 'data places,' then data become facts in the data places. Figure 11–2 shows some facts about customers in the customer table within the two fields named Customer Identifier and Customer Description, described by the attribute metadata in Figure 11–1.

Figure 11–2: Example of Metadata Versus Data—Facts in Data Places

TDW.CSTMR

CSTMR_ID	CSTMR_DSCRPTN
126784532	Joe's Auto Parts Store
893564201	Sam Smitty Stevens
673249012	Nathen Averdone
675849302	Don Littlemore
453627189	Dan Nathen
768594030	Louis Knewus

Traditionally, we have used metadata to support system developers. The system developer was the customer of the vendor's tools, and the tools focused on capabilities such as:

- documenting the logical and physical design of a database

- generating the database definition language for creating the database (e.g., SQL create table and create index statements)

- mapping database structures to on-line data maintenance and browse/report screens
- generating on-line data maintenance and report applications

We used data dictionaries for standardizing data structures and for assisting with database and system configuration management tasks.

The data warehouse's use of metadata involves the data warehouse administrator and the end-user as customers of the metadata. People are looking for tools that include capabilities to:

- map source system data to data warehouse tables
- generate data extract, transform, and load procedures for import jobs
- schedule and monitor import jobs
- help users discover what data are in the data warehouse
- help users structure queries to access data they need

Today, metadata repositories house rules for converting data to standard structures and validating data against data quality characteristics. We also use metadata repositories to support end user access to data in the data warehouse. Demands for these capabilities have spawned more sophisticated tools, addressing a larger scope of metadata. This trend for addressing a progressively larger scope of metadata is likely continue.

If we look at the data management landscape in the 1970s through 1980s, and compare it to what we see in the 1990s, we find metadata are being put to a wider use for the same reasons that data warehouses are now being developed by larger and larger numbers of organizations. The comparison in Figure 11–3 illustrates differences in the data processing environment, the perspectives data managers and system developers adopted while resolving data access and data integration issues, and the customer market for metadata.

In the 1970s and 1980s, the focus of data integration efforts was to reduce the development and maintenance costs for management information systems (MIS). At that time managers did not have tools that they could use to go after data on their own terms. The issue of the day was simply getting geographically dispersed offices connected to the mainframe so that standard reports could be pulled rather than pushed.

In the 1990s, data management and system development organizations are experiencing a very new set of demands and pressures from the businesses they service. End users want to be empowered to put the data collected by transaction systems to new uses. These decision makers and managers want to know what data are available and subtleties between systems that govern how the data should be used (i.e., they want to put the data to new uses, but they do not want to misuse the data).

Figure 11–3:   Changing Technology and Business Environment: New Customers of Data Are Also Customers of Metadata

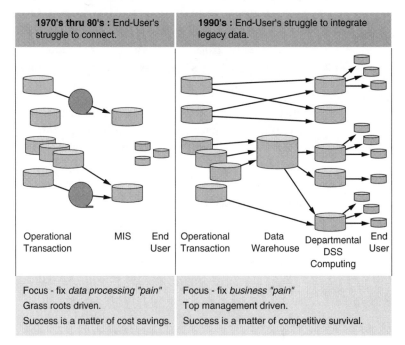

1970's thru 80's : End-User's struggle to connect.	**1990's :** End-User's struggle to integrate legacy data.
Operational Transaction MIS End User	Operational Transaction Data Warehouse Departmental DSS Computing End User
Focus - fix *data processing "pain"* Grass roots driven. Success is a matter of cost savings.	Focus - fix *business "pain"* Top management driven. Success is a matter of competitive survival.

METADATA MODELS SUPPORTING DATA WAREHOUSE OPERATIONS

In this report we will describe metadata models for supporting five categories of data warehouse management functions:

- describing what is in the data warehouse

- specifying what comes into and out of the data warehouse

- scheduling extracts based on a business events schedule

- documenting and monitoring data synchronization requirements

- measuring data quality

Read more about each of these topics in Sections A through D below.

The Basics: Describing What is In the Data Warehouse

Those familiar with metadata can probably look over the model shown in Figure 11–4 fairly quickly and understand it. But let's briefly look at what this information gives us and use this first model to become familiar with the syntax and semantics of the IDEF1X modeling method used to represent each of the models presented in this paper.

Figure 11–4: Metadata Model Describing What is in the Data Warehouse

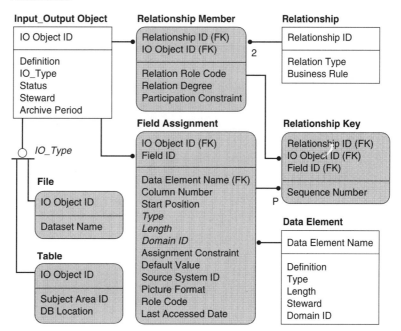

Figure 11–5 provides a quick reference for the IDEF1X syntax. Most data modelers will find that there is not too much of a difference between IDEF1X and other data modeling approaches they may already be using. The primary features of the syntax relate to the relational model for representing data and data relationships. These include:

Figure 11–5: IDEF1X Data Modeling Semantics and Syntax

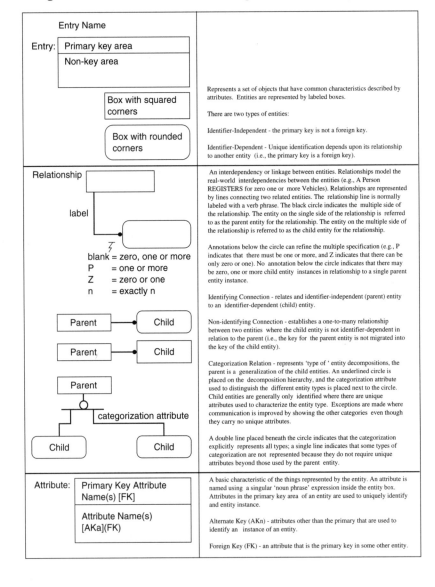

- Entities—Represented by square or rounded boxes. The square boxes represent independent entities that pose keys that are assigned independently of the existence of any other entities. The rounded boxes represent dependent entities that pose keys that inherit their values from values assigned to the keys of another entity. Entities are labeled with a noun phrase above the box.

- Attributes—Represented by noun phrase labels inside an entity box. A horizontal line is drawn across the entity box to separate the primary key attributes from other attributes. Primary key attributes appear above the horizontal lines while all other attributes appear below the horizontal line. Other distinctive roles assigned to attributes are indicated by parenthetical postscripts:

  - (AKn) identifies an alternate key
  - (FK) identifies a foreign key

- Relationships—Represented by solid or dashed lines connecting pairs of entities. A one-to-many cardinality is specified by the dot or circle on the many side of the relationship. For each related pair of entities, the entity on the "one" side of a one-to-many relation assumes the role of a "parent" while the other (i.e., the entity on the "many" side) assumes the role of a "child." The solid lines represent identifying relationships (i.e., relationships providing a basis for the child to inherit the key values from the parent). The dashed lines represent non-identifying relations where part or all of the foreign key supporting the child's relationship to the parent are not part of the primary key for the child entity.

There are other syntax elements to the IDEF1X language, but those described above should be sufficient to understand the models presented in this paper.

The model in Figure 11–4 has been simplified to facilitate understanding by taking liberties to not fully address associations that may occur among columns of data. Also omitted are administration attributes for version control and change control management of the metadata. The models presented in this paper are designed to draw attention to metadata requirements for supporting day-to-day data warehouse operations. Adding information to address design configuration management into the model would certainly ensure that we would all get lost in the details.

This model follows through on the Entity, Attribute, Relationship paradigm as follows:

- Input_Output object—Roughly correlates to an entity in a data model
- Data element—Roughly correlates to an attribute in a data model
- Relationship—Roughly correlates to a relationship in a data model

In much the way an entity relationship diagram helps designers organize and understand data requirements for a system, the information in this model can be used to help users discover and understand what data are in the data warehouse. The paragraphs that follow describe the metadata appearing in Figure 11–4 and suggest how they can be used to support data warehouse operations, progressing through the model one entity at a time:

- Input_Output object—Describes objects supporting data warehouse input output operations. Specific examples include files for importing data into the data warehouse, or tables in the data warehouse that a user would access. The Input_Output_Type attribute is used to distinguish between these two types of uses (e.g., "file" or "table"). It is easy to anticipate that there are attributes that only apply to the file or table use, and the related entity subtypes of File and Table are used to accommodate these unique properties. One attribute of the Input_Output Object worth calling attention to is the Archive Period and Archive Event for a table. The archive period represents the minimum period of time that we would expect data for a specific table to reside in the data warehouse before they are considered obsolete and archived. The Archive Event specifies when the table is processed to copy obsolete data to the archive medium.

- Relationship—Defines an association among two entities in relationship with one another. As depicted in this model, however, the relationship is modeled as an independent entity keyed by a Relationship ID. Consider this an unintelligible key, such as a sequential number simply used to identify each relationship. The Relationship Type attribute allows each relationship to be categorized based on its purpose (e.g., connective one-to-many, a many-to-many resolved as two one-to-many relations, or a one-to-one relationship that categorizes a generic entity into a subtype). The Business Rule is usually a verb phrase text expression to describe the business context of the relationship.

- Data element—Describes the basic units of fact accessible as columns from the database. These days some of the columns represent binary large objects that convey substantial amounts of text, graphics, and voice. Information captured about data elements typically includes a Name, Definition, Type (e.g., character, date, integer, decimal), length, and steward (i.e., an organization responsible for the care and upkeep of the data element's representation and certifying its appropriateness for different uses). The Domain ID is a label for a specification of allowable values a data element can take on. For instance, the domain for gender code might be specified as "male," "female," "unspecified," or "unknown". The data model for a domain specification itself can be quite complex because there are a number of types (e.g., a range, an enumeration of allowable values, a function (e.g., for determining allowable values for a date), or reference table look-ups), and there are domain interdependencies (e.g., domain subsets and domain collisions) that often need to be accommodated. For our purposes, consider the Domain ID as a pointer to a reference table of allowable values or to a specification of maximum and minimum values.

- Relationship member—Describes each entity's participation in a specific relationship in terms of a Role Code (i.e., parent or child), Relation Degree (e.g., one or many), Participation Constraint (e.g., mandatory or optional).

- Field Assignment—Specifies properties of a data element relevant to its assignment as a field to a specific Input_Output Object. Some attributes already represented in the data element entity cascade over to the Field Assignment entity because, in the world of mortal databases, a data element's properties may take on interesting and sometimes subtle contextual changes for some of these assignments. The same data element may take on different role names (accidentally or on-purpose) when put into different tables or files. Regrettably, its type and length may also be different if we have to implement a change in phases. The domain of values appropriate within the context of a data element's assignment to a table or file may represent a subdomain of the total domain for that data element when considered outside the context of the field assignment. Other attributes characterizing the nature of the data element's assignment to the table or file include Assignment Constraint (i.e., "optional" or "mandatory"), Default Value, Source System ID, Picture Format, and Role Code (e.g., "primary key," "foreign key," "non-key"). The Last Accessed Date is introduced as a field whose value could be periodically refreshed by software evaluating a log of queries that have been run against the data warehouse.

- Relation key—Describes the implementation of a relationship among two entities by correlating the key fields of one table or file with the key fields of the second table or file based on the sequence of each key field in the composite key.

The metadata depicted in Figure 11–4 describes what is in the data warehouse, and how these data are related. This set of metadata provides a foundation for helping the user locate data, and can also be used to run some basic objective edits against the data. There are several user interface dialogs possible for helping people locate data in the data warehouse with this data. One, for example, would be to present a list of tables in the warehouse, allow the user to select one or more tables from which the data are needed, let them select attributes, and specify what relationships will be used to join the tables. Tools are actually starting to emerge on the commercial market that hide the structure of the database from the user and allow the user to simply specify what data elements they want. Examples include Business Objects sold by Business Object Inc. and a product called English Wizard sold by Linguistics Inc.

The types of objective edits that can be performed with this metadata for measuring data quality include format checks against the picture format, validation of a field against its associated allowable values, and verification that referential integrity constraints documented by the relationships metadata are actually supported by the data.

The relationship construct depicted in Figure 11–4 is abstract enough to allow n-ary relationships, and this makes it difficult to understand without viewing an instance diagram such as the two part example shown in Figure 11–6. An entity relationship describing the relationship between employees and skills shown at the top of the figure is documented in the relationship entity instance diagram shown at the bottom. This example does not show all metadata but communicates how the data model works.

Figure 11–6: Example Relationship Metadata

Employee		Employee Skill		Skill
Social Security	12	Social Security Number (FK) Skill Code (FK)	13	Skill Code
	Has		Possessed By	

Input_Output Object	Relationship Member		Relationship
IO_Object ID	Relationship ID	IO_Object ID	Relationship ID
Employee	12	Employee	12
Employee Skill	12	Employee Skill	13
Skill	13	Employee Skill	
	13	Skill	

2

Relationship

	Relationship ID	IO_Object ID	Field ID*
	12	Employee	Social Security Number
P	12	Employee Skill	Social Security Number
	13	Skill	Skill Code
	13	Employee Skill	Skill Code

The three tables at the top of Figure 11–6 represent a resolution to a many-to-many relationship between Employee and Skill using two one-to-many relationships: 1) relationship 12—An Employee has zero, one, or many Skills and 2) relationship 13—a Skill is possessed by zero, one or many Employees.

In the lower part of the figure, this many-to-many relationship is documented as follows:

- Input_Output object—Documents three tables: Employee, Employee Skill, and Skill

- Relationship—Documents two relationships: 12 and 13.

- Relationship member—Has 2 table entries for each relationship: Relationship 12 associates the Employee table with the Employee Skill table and relationship 13 associates the Skill table with the Employee Skill table.

- Relationship key—Correlated fields used in each table to support the relationship: The field Social Security Number supports relationship 12 (i.e., the association between the Employee Skill and Skill tables) and the field Skill Code supports relationship 13 (i.e., the association between the Skill and Employee Skill tables).

A very generalized user interface can be developed from this metadata for navigating through the data warehouse catalog using relationship information. A user could request a list of tables, select one of the tables, and obtain a list or star diagram of the related tables. The steps to select a table and list or diagram related tables can be repeated as often as needed in order to explore the database structure and find the data needed. Furthermore, capabilities could be included for presenting descriptive information about a specific table and listing fields assigned to a specific table. Using metadata as the input/output parameters for governing this type of software provides a framework for easily accommodating data warehouse growth because new tables can be added to the data warehouse without changing the software. Configuration management activities are reduced to tasks for updating the contents of the metadata.

Describing What Comes Into and Out of the Data Warehouse

Let's expand our understanding of data warehouse metadata. Let's take a closer look at those inconspicuous arrows that move data from a source database to a target database. They are a lot more complicated than you would infer from many presentations comparing the merits of data warehousing to other alternatives for enterprise-wide or interorganizational data sharing. Yet, you can expect the arrows to consume approximately 80 percent of the work effort for designing and developing a data warehouse.

Two complexity issues concerning data extracts dominate the metadata design requirements for documenting what comes into and out of the data warehouse. The first item of complexity concerns the relationships among extract jobs. Completing a single extract job may involve any number of processing steps, and the individual steps may involve intervention responsibilities of a number of different organizations.

Figure 11–7: Example Job Steps for a Data Warehouse Import

As suggested in the example shown in Figure 11–7, completing an import job may involve performing the following processes:

- extract data of interest to the decision support system customer community from the internal or external source systems

- filter out instances that are not needed (e.g., data that have not changed since the last extract)

- validate the data to measure its quality from the perspective of downstream DSS uses

- merge the data with other extracts

- aggregate summary level data

- load the new data into the destination (e.g., the data warehouse)

- archive any data that become obsolete in light of the refreshment represented by these newly loaded data

The second item of complexity has to do with the mapping of source tables and attributes to target tables and attributes illustrated in Figure 11–8.

Figure 11–8:   Example Implication of a Many-to-Many Mapping Between Source Input Objects and Data Warehouse Objects on an Import Job

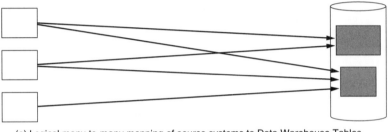

(a) Logical many-to-many mapping of source systems to Data Warehouse Tables

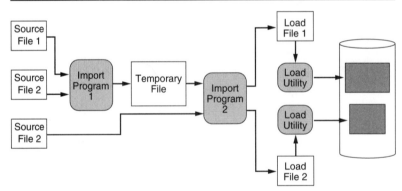

(b) Breakout of programs and temporary files to implement the many-to-many transfer using a commercial product

As is shown in Figure 11–8, the relationship for many extract jobs is many-to-many. Vendors of data extract management tools such as PRISM Data Warehouse Manager, Carleton Passport, and the Extract Tool Suite have developed metadata for extracts that can be used to generate COBOL source code. There are constraints to the complexity that a generalized program can support. To process a many-to-many mapping using a commercial product, you normally must specify metadata to merge several files into a temporary file for subsequent splitting by a downstream program. This source code can be compiled and used for importing data into or exporting data out of the data warehouse.

In short, one extract job has many job steps, and source tables map to target tables as a many-to-many relationship. Understanding these constraints is critical for understanding the metadata for describing an extract job shown in Figure 11–9.

Figure 11–9: Metadata Describing Data Warehouse Inputs and Outputs

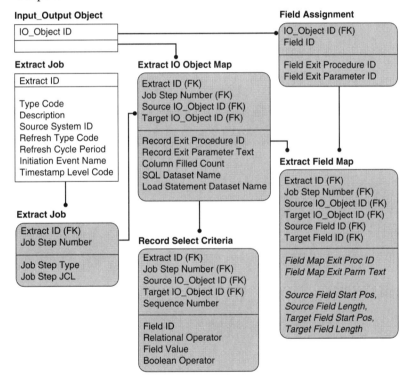

The one-to-many relationship between Extract Job and Extract Job Itinerary supports the rule that one extract job has many job steps. The many-to-many mapping of source tables to target tables is supported by including both the Source Input_Output Object and Target Input_Output Object as part of the key for the Extract Input_Output Map and as part of the Record Select Criteria. Support for this many-to-many mapping rule extends all the way down to the attribute level by appending the Source Field ID and the Target Field ID to this key for the Extract Field Map.

A quick review of some of the attributes shown in Figure 11–9 will illustrate how metadata models provide a useful framework for organizing requirements related to managing data warehouse operations. Keeping in mind that these are point of departure models that can be extended to support a variety of special types of data warehouse processing, the paragraphs below summarize the nature of requirements supported by attributes identified in each entity.

- Extract job—Describes each extract job, and identifies the source system for each extract. Each extract is assigned a Refresh Type Code indicating how snapshots of data are managed in the data warehouse. There are four basic approaches:

  - Wholesale replace—A single version of data extracted at a specific point in time is stored in the data warehouse. Each import completely replaces data previously imported.

  - Wholesale append—Multiple versions of data are stored in the data warehouse, and each version represents all instances of data extracted at a specific point in time. When the maximum number of versions to be retained is reached, the oldest version of data is archived with each new version of data imported.

  - Update replace—A single version of data extracted at a specific point in time is stored in the data warehouse. An initial copy of data is loaded into the data warehouse, and each import thereafter cascades only the add, change, and delete transactions that have been applied to the supplier system subsequent to the previous import. The results of these transactions are reflected in each refreshment of the data warehouse

  - Update append—Multiple versions of data are stored in the data warehouse. An initial copy of data is loaded into the data warehouse, and each import thereafter cascades only the add, change, and delete transactions that have been applied to the supplier system subsequent to the previous import. The results of these transactions are reflected in each subsequent refreshment of the data warehouse.

Closely associated with the Refresh Type Code is the Refresh Cycle Period, which specifies the approximate time interval between two executions of a particular extract. Some organizations prefer to completely refresh all the data in the warehouse with each extract (e.g., manage using wholesale replace or wholesale append) and as a result view the data as having a periodicity rather than the extract. This is because under wholesale refresh practices, the data inherit the refresh cycle based on executions of the extract job. It becomes evident, however, when an append update approach is used, that data are decoupled from the concept of periodicity. Much like ocean waves, extract jobs have a periodicity, while data instances are like sand on the beach. We can observe that each time a wave strikes the beach, some sand are deposited, while other sand are removed, and some sand remain through the arrival of many waves. Each time an extract is processed, some data are refreshed, some data are archived, and other data remain unchanged—possibly through many extracts.

The Initiation Event represents an occurrence in the business environment to which the system responds by initiating the extract process. Data are either pulled or pushed from the system identified by the Source System ID. The Timestamp Level Code specifies whether data timestamping is to be monitored at the table level, a partition level, or the record instance level. Table level timestamping is appropriate for replacement refresh approaches (i.e., wholesale replace or update replace) so long as the organization considers the data to simply represent a single point in time view of the data. Partition or record instance level timestamps are appropriate for append refresh approaches (i.e., wholesale append and update append), especially when a single table in the warehouse is designed to store all snapshots of the data. The timestamp then represents an effective date for the data that gets appended to the primary key for the record.

- Extract job itinerary—Specifies the job's steps that collectively constitute a specific extract procedure to include Job Step Type (e.g., data extract, transformation, validation, aggregation, and load steps) and the Job Step JCL (e.g., the job control language dataset used to initiate a specific extract job step).

- Extract table map—Correlates input files/tables to output files/tables for each extract job step. This entity introduces two important types of attributes providing a framework for accommodating special processing requirements of particular extract jobs. The first represents procedure input dataset names for special types of extract jobs (e.g., SQL Dataset Name for extract job steps and Load Statement Dataset Name for load job steps). The second represents exit procedure related attributes (e.g., Record Exit Procedure ID and Record Exit Parameter Text). These attributes allow a generalized program to invoke the services of specialized subroutines to handle complex transformation or validation requirements.

- Extract attribute map—Correlates source field storage areas to target field storage areas. Once again, the exit procedure related attributes are introduced at the attribute level to allow a generalized program to support specialized processing that may be required for some attributes during extract processing. Similar attributes also appear in the Field Assignment entities.

- Record select criteria—Provides a mechanism for specifying rules for filtering out instances of data at any step of the extract process. An example rule based on the last update date or create date for a record might be expressed as follows:

LAST_UPDATE_DATE > '1995-11-01' or

CREATE_DATE > '1995-11-01'

In the Record Select Criteria entity shown in Figure 11–9, each rule identifies a field, a relational operator (e.g., <, =, or >), and a field value for determining whether or not a record is selected for downstream processing. The Boolean Operator (e.g., AND, OR) specifies how two or more select criteria are considered together in determining whether or not a record is qualified. The rule described for the example using last update date or create date would be described in the Record Select Criteria Entity as follows in Table 11–1:

Table 11–1

Field ID	Relational Operator	Field Value	Boolean Operator
LAST_UPDATE_DATE	>	'1995-11-01'	OR
CREATE_DATE	>	'1995-11-01'	END

The metadata presented in the model shown in Figure 11–9 can be used to generate COBOL source code for an extract job to import data into or export data out of the data warehouse. With a little inference logic and rules constraining how extract programs are structured, a source code generation program could perform the following work for each extract job:

- Identify the source and target tables for the import job step using the Extract IO_Object Map metadata

- Generate a paragraph of source code to select a subset of data in the source using the Record Select Criteria

- Generate move statements to transfer data from a source table format to a target table format based on the Extract Field Map metadata

- Provide field level exits for performing special transformations or validations against fields involved in the extract job step

- Provide record level exits for validating records before they are saved for use in downstream processing

This metadata can be used for more than supporting data warehouse efforts. It can support any data conversion effort (e.g., interface software for commercial applications, or system migration projects). What this metadata cannot do is schedule extracts—a topic we introduce and describe in the next section.

Extract Schedule Based On a Business Events Schedule

The data warehouse directory should be used to schedule data extracts and to improve corporate awareness of subtle differences in context for similar data provided by different source systems in response to different events in the business environment. To better understand the data extract scheduling, consider an example. Let's assume that a corporation is interested in synchronizing data spanning two functions. One function is responsible for developing the corporation's budget. The other function must schedule and resource new product developments. A time-leveled entity relationship diagram in Figure 11–10 shows two groupings of data:

- Budget—Identifying dollars required to pay for various types of projects in the corporation. The Budget data includes the Budget Master and the Budget Detail tables.

- Project schedule—Identifying the milestones and planned configurations of products to be delivered by various divisions in the corporation. The Project data includes the Project Description, Project Milestones, and Project Resource tables.

For the purposes of this discussion, we do not need to know the details of the database table structures; we are more interested in scheduling extracts for these two groups of related data when the processes to maintain these separate groups are unsynchronized.

Figure 11–10:   Relationship Between Budget and Project Schedule

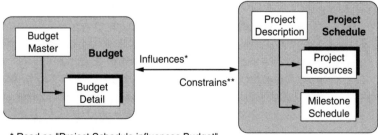

* Read as "Project Schedule influences Budget"
** Read as "Budget constrains Project Schedule"

Assume that a separate system maintains data for each of these entities:

- BUD is the source system for the budget data
- PROJ is the source system for the project data

Figure 11–11 depicts a schedule for extracts from these two systems. Timing for these data extracts are driven by different requirements. Data from BUD is published in response to major budgeting events, while data from PROJ is published monthly. The arrowed line going out of the PROJ publication schedule at the end of September indicates how these systems formalize the relationship "Project Schedule influences Budget" identified in Figure 11–10. Every October, the status of current projects is reviewed as input for formulating the next year's budget. This scheduling introduces you to the concept that events in the business environment serve as catalysts for source systems to send data extracts to the data warehouse, or for the data warehouse to pull data from the source systems. The system responds to the event by initiating an extract procedure. But let's proceed further to investigate the issue of data synchronization.

Figure 11–11: Example Extract Schedules for Two Source Systems

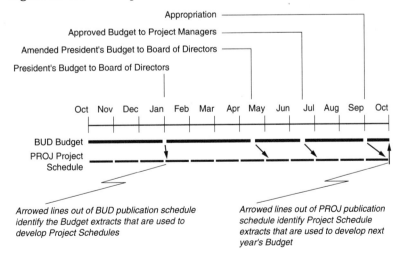

Arrowed lines out of BUD publication schedule identify the Budget extracts that are used to develop Project Schedules

Arrowed lines out of PROJ publication schedule identify Project Schedule extracts that are used to develop next year's Budget

The arrowed lines going out of the BUD publication schedules indicates how these systems formalize the relationship "Budget Constrains Project Schedule" shown in Figure 11–10.

When the Budget information is published, project managers review the information and attempt to make their projected resourcing and scheduling conform to moneys available. This takes some time to accomplish, and the time lapse creates a synchronization problem; simply getting the latest data published for the budget and the project data will result in an unsynchronized view of the data.

Consider, for example, a query that gathered the latest data from both systems in the second week of May as shown in Figure 11–12. Pulling the latest data from both systems merges an April publication of the budget with project data aligned to the budget presented to the board by the president in January. Users must realize that a synchronized view of the "Budget Constrains Project Schedule" relationship is generally obtained by merging the previous snapshot of the budget with the most recent snapshot of the project schedule. Synchronizing the data gets more complicated when adding more entities and source system import schedules.

Figure 11–12: Example Query Timing on Data Extracts That Would Not Produce a Synchronized Set of Data

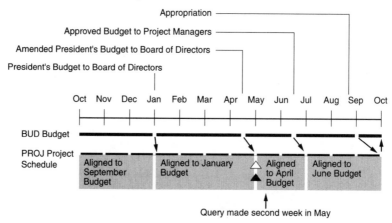

The data model depicted in Figure 13 provides a framework for tracking three general categories of information for scheduling extracts:

- Event related entities—Comprising entities on the left side of the model (i.e., Event, Event Dependency, Event Calendar, and Extract Schedule).

- Extracts that respond to events—Comprising entities arranged in a vertical column down the middle of the model (i.e., Extract Job, Extract Job Itinerary, and Extract Audit).

- Timestamp related entities—Comprising entities on the right side of the model (i.e., Input_Object, Field Assignment, Timestamp Audit, and Timestamp Label). If timestamps are applied to data imported into the data warehouse for each import, these timestamps help align snapshots of data into synchronized sets for specific user views.

Figure 11–13: Metadata Describing When Extract Jobs Are Scheduled and Run

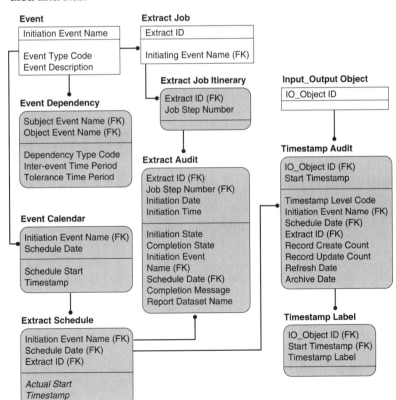

The following paragraphs summarize the meaning and use of the metadata represented by the entities depicted in this model.

- Events—Relate back to the Extract Job. Events are observable happenings in the corporation's environment that cause data to be processed. Extract Jobs are initiated in response to events in the business environment (e.g., start of month, end of month, or signing of the budget). Some are periodic, some are scheduled, and some hit us by surprise. If we know about their nature in advance, we can document their dependencies and schedule them. Otherwise we may find ourselves responding to unknown or uncoordinated events with little more than a three day planning horizon.

- Event dependency—Correlates related events and describes time interval rules for characterizing these dependencies. One event may precede a different event by an average Inter-event Time Period, plus or minus a Tolerance Time Period. A periodic event such as "end of month" or "start of quarter" may also be characterized as being recursively related to itself (e.g., end of month occurs every 30 days plus or minus 2 days).

- Event calendar—Specifies the schedule dates for events to occur. Events may need to be manually scheduled (e.g., submittal of the president's budget) or they may occur on a predictable calendar cycle (e.g., the 2nd Tuesday of each month). The data warehouse directory should allow users to define events, specify how they are to be scheduled (i.e., manually or automatically based on the system clock), and enter estimated dates for manually scheduled events.

- Extract schedule—Records instances of extracts that must be initiated in response to scheduled events and provides a logical place for capturing the actual timestamp to be associated with data imported for a specific extract.

- Extract audit—Records when each extract job is run and associates the run with the initiation event and any extract scheduling done. Extract Audits can be maintained for both import and export jobs. Knowing when each export extract is run allows you to monitor data access patterns based on field mappings for each extract. Background jobs periodically evaluating export audits could derive a last access date for each field involved in an export job and subsequently update the Last Accessed Date in the Field Assignment table.

- Timestamp audit—Associates timestamps appearing in data records of each table with specific extract jobs and table refresh statistics. Timestamp audit records can be processed with comparisons to the system clock to determine when there are records that need to be archived and purged to support policy specific by the archive Period attribute in the Input_Output Object table.

- Timestamp label—Associates logical labels with specific timestamp dates. Sometimes the users do not want to remember specific timestamp dates. They just want to extract saying "Most Recent" or "June" or "June through July." The Timestamp Label table supports this type of timestamp specification using a subselect statement (e.g., start timestamp in (SELECT start timestamp from Timestamp Label table where Timestamp Label = "June").

Time can be a significant element for relating data across functional boundaries of a corporation. The entities and attributes shown in Figure 11–13 provide users, who know the dependencies among unsynchronized processing within the organization, information needed to develop synchronized views of the data. But, additional information is needed to help the unenlightened user; synchronization rules are needed to identify how data with one timestamp should be related to data with a different timestamp to obtain a synchronized view of data from an unsynchronized set of processes. In situations involving large numbers of tables in the data warehouse and many different events governing the extract schedule, this additional information describing how the data are synchronized may be required to help users avoid misusing or misinterpreting information they derive from the data. Data synchronization rules can be documented through two additional categories of metadata shown in Figure 11–14: (1) Synchronization View and (2) Synchronization Instance.

Figure 11–14: Metadata for Documenting Data Synchronization Requirements

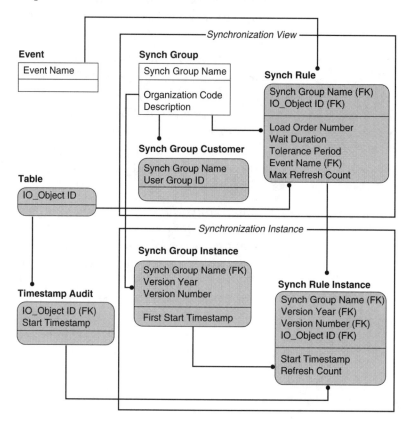

- Synchronization view—Identifies the timing rules for synchronizing the data to support different users. Synchronization views can be defined by specifying a name and description for a particular functional view and the list of tables included in this view. Each table identified as participating in the view should be characterized by the event populating the table and its sequence within the group of events for populating the tables (e.g., a Load Order Number). It may also be important to document the approximate time interval passing between the occurrence of one event and the next (e.g., a Wait Duration and Tolerance Period). This time interval helps discriminate between intervening occurrences of any particular event that may be insignificant for delivering the related data.

- Synchronization instance—Provides data for tracking the formation of synchronized sets of data from various systems as events actually occur. Synchronization Instances correlate timestamps for data imported into tables participating within a Synchronization Instance based on events occurring as recorded for the Synchronization View. When all import requirements for a Synchronization View have been satisfied, the data warehouse directory could alert users of the Synchronization View that their data are ready for exporting out of the data warehouse.

Measuring Data Quality

The data warehouse prepositions data extracted from source transaction systems for new uses in DSS applications. These new uses put new data quality demands on the data that were not foreseen or tended to in the transaction systems. If we are not careful about measuring data quality in terms of characteristics required by the DSS applications, strategic decisions may be made based on "bad" data. In an environment of constrained resources, data quality assurance practices for the data warehouse should focus on high-risk elements that are likely to cause costly problems. As procedures are adopted to systematically mitigate the risks associated with one set of elements, the focus shifts to another set of elements.

As a first step to data quality assurance, data quality expectations should be defined to support the business goals and then the risks identified for failing to achieve these expectations. For example, if the goal of the business is to improve market presence by better understanding customer behavior, the data quality expectations should focus on what data are needed to support the DSS application and the quality characteristics associated with these data.

Figure 11–15 describes a set of commonly referenced data quality characteristics and identifies useful metrics for measuring the actual quality achieved. Instead of defining metrics for all the data required against this entire set of characteristics, identify the important characteristics of specific elements that cause the "at risk" situation. Then, define metrics for important characteristics of only the high-risk elements.

This approach aligns the risk analysis with the business goals of the application putting the data to a new use. For example, if the goal is to improve market presence by better understanding customer behavior, the metrics should be developed for one, two, or three high risk characteristics for achieving this goal (e.g., matching keys for data from disparate systems providing customer and products data or improving the timeliness for capturing data needed to evaluate the impact of different marketing strategies). If, in contrast, the DSS application's objective is to optimize shipping and handling operations for product delivery, the completeness of weight and dimension data for delivered products becomes very important.

Figure 11–15: Commonly Used Set of Data Quality Characteristics

Data Quality Characteristic	Descriptions	Example Metric
Accuracy	Degree of agreement with what is correct.	Percent correct.
Completeness	Degree of required data with entered values.	Percent complete.
Consistency	Agreement or logical coherence/ freedom from contradiction.	Percent matching value conditions satisfied.
Relatability	Logical coherence that permits rational correlation with other similar or like data.	Percent of referential integrity rules supported.
Timeliness	Provided at the time required or specified.	Percent of data available within a threshold time frame.
Uniqueness	Constrains the data values to a set of distinct entries.	Percent of records with uniqueness violations.
Validity	Conformance of data values to edits for acceptability.	Percent of the data having values that fall within their respective domains of allowable values.

Data quality is inherently a characteristic of the relationship between the facts being gathered and their intended use. Aligning the risk analysis with the business goals of the application provides a logical lead for completing three other important tasks for data quality assurance:

- Verify, Validate, and Certify (VV&C) the appropriateness of the data to new uses proposed by a DSS application

- Measure the quality of high-risk data required to support the DSS application in terms of the important characteristics

- Initiate projects to fix known data quality problems as close to the source of data entry as possible

When metrics are established to measure and report on the data's quality, an issue always surfaces concerning the proper disposition of data that fail to pass (e.g., should we not allow bad data into the data warehouse). Again, it's important to stress that individual choices concerning whether the quality is "good enough" depend on the intended use. For example, one application may be very interested in the weight of products being distributed, and if weight is not filled in, the application cannot use the data. However, another application may only be interested in the number of products sold and really does not care about the missing weight values. For this reason, the model we propose in Figure 11–16 is based on the assumption that the important task is to measure the data quality and alert the users when data quality is below the tolerance levels they have established for their particular applications. The informed user can then to decide how best to respond.

In the model presented in Figure 11–16, the Target Quality Characteristic and Actual Quality Characteristic entities provide a framework for capturing expected and actual quality metrics relevant to each field registered for a DSS application recorded in the Functional Use entity. The User Representative VV&C entity documents any quality issues concerning validation, verification, and certification. A functional user representative (e.g., the data representation steward) should periodically review the sources of data fields used in the warehouse to certify them for the uses registered—noting any constraints on this certification. This is an opportunity to pursue issues concerning quality characteristics (e.g., accuracy and timeliness) that are important for each application.

Figure 11–16: Metadata Describing Data Quality Characteristics

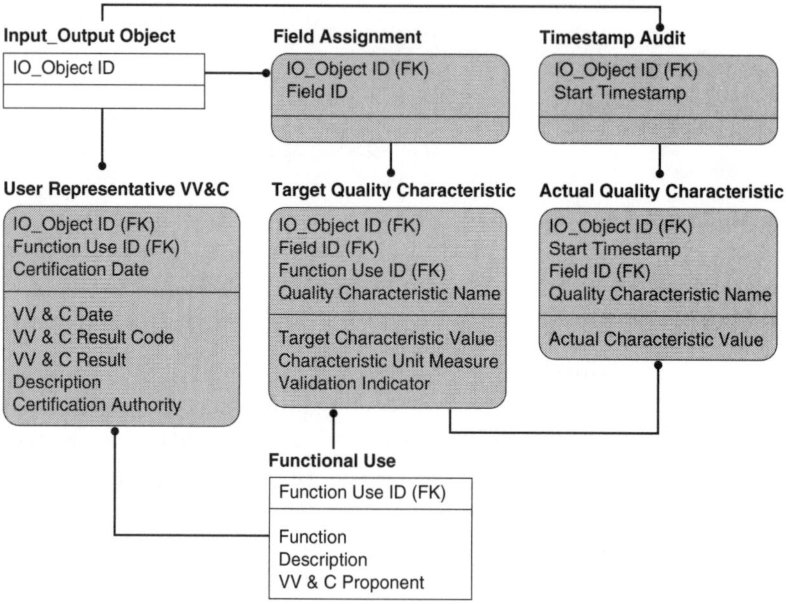

The platform a data warehouse architecture provides for resolving discrepancies across multiple extracts represents a major benefit for enterprise data management. Requirements for discrepancy resolution often have their roots in emotional incidents where several divergent answers are developed to the same question with supposedly the same data. To allow discrepancy resolution to work, the data warehouse must capture detailed information on the results of data warehouse administrative activities. Figure 11–17 proposes one practical approach for using administrative fields at the record level to summarize the current status of the record's data and to support probes into quality assurance or discrepancy resolution issues.

The fields introduced include:

- Start timestamp—Appended to the primary key for each table to allow multiple point in time snapshots of data to exist in a data warehouse table.

Figure 11–17: Administrative Data to Provide Record Level Visibility for Extract Events and Data Quality

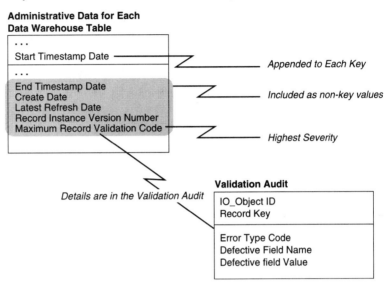

- End timestamp—To allow users to easily determine the time frame over which a specific record is considered active.

- Create date—Specifying the date a particular record was created.

- Latest refresh date—Specifying the most recent date a particular record was updated with new field values from an import.

- Record instance version number—Providing a count of the number of times a particular record has been refreshed after its initial create date.

- Maximum record validation code—Capturing the highest severity code that a record experienced in validations run against the data.

If these fields are specified as a part of every table in the data warehouse, they can be used as an index into a Validation Audit for probing deeply into observations concerning the data quality characteristics and the discrepancies in answers developed by two or more organizations to a single question when the answers are supposedly based on the same data.

The data provides a quick resolution to three common sources of discrepancy:

- Inconsistent time frames—If two or more organizations pull the "latest data" from the data warehouse, but on different dates, the Start Timestamp, End Timestamp, Create Date, and Latest Refresh Date will all provide insights into whether or not the data are actually the same across the dates in question.

- Inconsistent select criteria—If two or more organizations use different select criteria, the equivalency of these select criteria can be tested using a query designed to retrieve any records selected by one query that would not be included in the result sets of the other query.

- Inappropriate use of data—If one or more organizations uses 'bad' data, the effects of that data can be investigated by probing the validation audit for the data values (or a sample of data values) found to be in error.

CONCLUDING THOUGHTS

The potential applications of metadata to managing a data warehouse are perhaps more numerous and promising than any other category of system formalized to date. In this report we have discussed five applications for metadata in data warehouses:

- Data discovery—Helping users find and access data in the data warehouse using metadata describing the data warehouse structure and contents.

- Data extract management—Posturing the data warehouse architecture to easily accommodate new data suppliers and customers (e.g., organizations with new DSS applications).

- Data extract scheduling—Coordinating the dates for extracts based on the schedules for business events to which systems respond by making data available to the data warehouse.

- Data synchronization—Tracking when data have been imported into the data warehouse, and capturing documentation on the rules for obtaining synchronized views of data from unsynchronized source processes.

- Data quality assurance—Measuring and reporting on the quality of data imported into the data warehouse in relation to specific uses registered by various DSS applications extracting data from the data warehouse.

The customers and stake holders of this metadata include system designers and end users of DSS applications using data pre-positioned from transaction systems by the data warehouse.

All software programs need to operate at some level from a fixed set of inputs and outputs. Commercial vendors of data warehouse tools—such as PRISM Warehouse Manager, Carleton Passport, and Extract Tool Suit—have found metadata can effectively be used as the fixed set of inputs and outputs for processing a wide variety of data structures. Information system shops can leverage metadata in similar ways and are likely to find it profitable to build metadata governed componentry to address data warehouse management requirements not currently supported by commercial tools. The implication is that in-house solutions can be developed reasonably if done right. This author recommends that a commercial repository tool be assigned the task of metadata maintenance for future versions of the data warehouse, and that extracts from this repository tool be used to populate an operational repository for the data warehouse. The operational repository can be used to address capabilities not currently covered by commercial tools.

Several trends in data sharing requirements suggest that the metadata requirements for data warehouses are going to continue to grow. These trends are succinctly represented in four observations:

- Practices for handling traditional text and numeric data are expanding to address multi-media types of data

- Disciplines and practices for deploying the data warehouse to support data sharing within a single enterprise are being extended to address requirements to share data across multiple organizations (e.g., in conjunction with Electronic Data Interchange (EDI) initiatives)

- Information flow controls to preposition new data into the data warehouse from the source system are now being extended to allow formal feedback to the source systems (e.g., Pyramid technologies 'Smart Data Warehouse' initiative).

- Data warehouse tools that offer proprietary repositories in order to capture and hold market share in the current customer base for data warehouse componentry are starting to adopt open standards for exchanging metadata (e.g., CASE Data Interchange Format (CDIF)).

For these trends to continue successfully, data warehouse tools and practices must also change to adopt metadata representation standards developed under sponsorship of the American National Standards Institute (ANSI). An initiative to develop standards for integrating or interfacing commercial vendor data warehouse tools must consider the use of two types of metadata standards: 1) exchange standards (e.g., CDIF) and 2) metadata representation standards. Requirements for metadata representation standards can be easily overlooked in the rush to establish a common interchange standard, but a brief consideration of representation issues that accompany any attempt to exchange metadata should adequately motivate this second requirement.

Consider, for example, what happens if there is an agreed upon interchange standard adopted, but the following conditions prevail:

- The maximum lengths of names for data elements used in one tool are longer than the maximum lengths for names used in a second tool. Data element names transferred from one tool to another may get clipped.

- Two types of metadata related through a one-to-many relationship in one tool may be related through a resolved many-to-many relationship in a second tool. The issue emerges for determining how to transfer relationship artifacts developed under the many-to-many schema into the tool supporting a one-to-many schema.

- Two tools capture the same metadata using different representation, naming, or coding conventions. An issue emerges concerning what representation should be adopted as a standard.

Metadata representation standards assure that a consistent, sharable set of data are described and named in a predictable and repeatable fashion. National and international efforts are underway to produce this metadata standardization. The ISO/IEC JTC 1 Subcommittee 14, Data Element Principles, has developed a six-part standard (ISO N 11179) addressing the rules, principles and guidelines for classification, attribution, definition, naming, standardization, and registration of data elements:

- "Classification" of the components of data elements into a taxonomic structure facilitates the selection of appropriate components for particular elements.

- "Definition" standards describe rules and guidelines for specifying well-formed data element definitions.

- "Naming" standards use the classification prescription to discipline the way data elements are named and defined.

- "Attribution" guidelines provide standardized attributes, some with sample values, as a base set of information to be recorded about each data element. Sets of complete and discrete data elements can be developed into coherent descriptions of subject areas they characterize.

- "Standardization" guidelines provide concepts and rules appropriate for assembling structured set of procedures for developing a set of standard data element representations that mirror the discipline of the data elements.

- "Registration" of standard data elements provides a facility for sharing the benefits of standardization among organizations.

The U.S. Technical Assistance Group to SC 14, ANSI Committee X3L8, Data Representation, supplied five of the six editors involved with the ISO standard. X3L8 has now begun an independent effort to develop a Metamodel for the Management of Sharable Data, which attempts to model the components of standard data elements and describe the relationships and dependencies among these components. Other new efforts are concerned with data element concepts and data value domains.

These standards represent the results of significant work and thought by experienced data management practitioners. They are particularly appropriate for data warehouse projects, because data formally separated from the legacy environment and pre-positioned in a data warehouse for new uses in DSS applications need to be legible to designers of the data warehouse and the user community. The designers need metadata representation standards to ensure that the metadata can be exchanged without corruption across different commercial data warehouse tools. The user community—representing customers putting data extracted from the data warehouse to new uses—need representation standards to facilitate discovery and effective use of the data stored in the data warehouse.

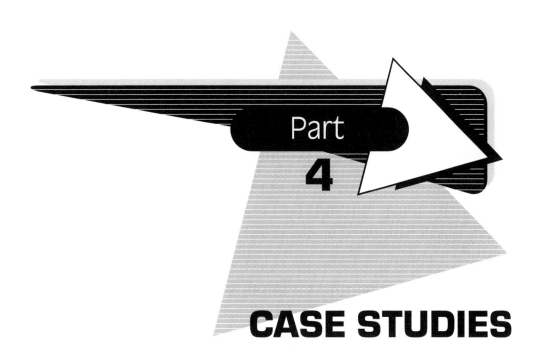

Part
4

CASE STUDIES

Chapter 12

Data Warehousing at NSWCDD: A Case Study

Carol Burleson and David Tabler

Fellows, The Data Warehousing Institute

The Naval Surface Warfare Center, Dahlgren Division (NSWCDD), is a research and development organization specializing in surface warfare for the Navy. The business environment at NSWCDD is comparable to that of other major businesses throughout the country. NSWCDD is impacted by external influences that ultimately drive business decisions and the allocation of resources within the division. Department of Defense (DOD) downsizing initiatives have resulted in a reduction of resources and, like all major businesses, our corporate thrusts are concentrated on gaining competitive advantages and developing new methods and techniques to accomplish more with less. The ability to market and sell existing R&D products and evolve new products are critical to the survival of the Division. As reductions occur, the pressure to reduce "overhead" costs while improving the quality of business and information services has driven the Information Systems organization to change the way they design, develop, deliver, and support information products and services.

NSWCDD is organized into major technical departments and business support organizations. The technical departments are comprised of major program support areas and research and development components that specialize in various aspects of work related to the technical mission of the Division. Technical programs have external sponsors that provide funding for the work being performed within each technical program and department. The business support organizations specialize in providing business support products and services to the technical components. Finance, Procurement, Personnel, and Information Systems are considered business support functions and are funded through Division "overhead" funds.

THE **NSWCDD** DATA WAREHOUSE

The NSWCDD Data Warehouse (*"Corporate Database"*) has been in production since July, 1992. It currently supports 700 users physically located at three primary locations: Dahlgren, Virginia; Panama City, Florida; and White Oak, Maryland. Major data entities currently maintained within the data warehouse include: (1)Sponsors (customers), (2) Funds (money), (3) Programs (work), (4) Costs (labor & non-labor), (5) Organizations, (6) Employees, (7) Procurement, (8) Supplies, and (9) Workload Plans. History data is maintained as appropriate for all major entity types. The data warehouse runs on a UNIX server utilizing the Oracle DBMS. This architecture includes multiple "shared" UNIX clients that can be accessed by users of the data warehouse. These clients provide "application driven" access to the data warehouse through canned queries and standard reports. Oracle development tools are used to support this application driven approach. Additionally, the following special customer support features are also provided through the data warehouse application: (1) an on-line Data Dictionary; (2) a Product Library providing user information on standard reports, canned queries, and SQL user scripts; (3) an ad-hoc data query access through SQL; (4) data download capabilities for integration with any end user tool, application, or system; and

(5) on-line end-user feedback mechanisms for articulating requirements, problems, and requests for special assistance.

Direct access to the data warehouse is also available through the utilization of DataPrism and BrioQuery products provided by Brio Technology. The Brio tools allow any user to bypass the standard application and enter directly into the data warehouse. This capability is provided to support requirements for advanced data retrieval and analysis capabilities and to ensure complete flexibility to the end user in the usage of the data warehouse. The data warehouse is available 24 hours a day, 7 days per week except during weekly data updates and for required maintenance.

WHY DATA WAREHOUSING?

In late 1990, the Information Systems organization found themselves in the final phase of an enterprise-wide information strategic planning (ISP) process. Utilizing a popular information engineering (IE) methodology, the IS organization was hopeful that the strategic planning process would offer strategies that would help them improve the quality of products and services being provided and help identify the most critical business needs of the enterprise. An additional goal of the organization was to repair the reputation they had acquired over time as an expensive, unresponsive organization providing very little corporate benefit.

Like most IS organizations, inflexible legacy business systems and antiquated IS methods and techniques were being utilized to provide corporate business information. The stovepipe nature of the information being produced, hard copy information delivery mechanisms being utilized, cost associated with maintaining legacy systems, and the inability to meet the changing and demanding information requirements of the organization were major contributors to the less than popular reputation of the IS organization. Corporate attempts to "fix" the IS problem had resulted in several major reorganizations of IS resources and had impacted the overall morale, well-being, and stability of the organization. The IE approach to systems development offered the IS organization an opportunity to develop a strategic direction for information technology, identify and focus on critical information needs, and rekindle the spirit of the IS organization.

As the IS organization wrapped up their strategic planning process, they set their sights on "phase 2" of the methodology: Business Area Analysis. However, after carefully considering the proposed "next steps," it was realized by IS management that the IE methodology being utilized neglected to provide solutions for enterprise-wide integrated management and decision support information desperately needed throughout the organization. In a meeting with the IE methodology company to discuss this obvious oversight, IS management was advised to "follow the methodology" and make improvements to their legacy system environment. The methodology consultants suggested that the IE approach would build an improved business system foundation that could then be utilized to provide improved management information. They concluded their advice by saying that any attempt to provide integrated management information, decision support, or other data warehousing type capabilities would be considered "high risk" without first improving the source systems environment containing the required data.

IS management was not surprised by the advice given to them by the IE consultants. After all, it was the era of information engineering and data warehousing was a little known and seldom practiced concept. Legacy systems supporting most major businesses needed to be modernized and re-engineered and information engineering methodologies were the "hot ticket item" for accomplishing legacy system improvements. However, the IE approach to "rejuvenated legacy systems" required a substantial amount of time, money, and resources and did not address the need for enterprise-wide integrated management information, decision support capabilities, and executive information!

In spite of the warnings, IS management literally became zealots in their conviction that by extracting data from legacy systems, defining, transforming and integrating the data across business areas, and providing the data in a timely and flexible way, they could provide tremendous business benefit to the enterprise. As a result of their convictions, they had little difficulty deciding to "assume the risk" of providing enterprise-wide data from their legacy systems. Three major goals were immediately identified as "drivers" for the initial data warehouse project: (1) reduce costs and increase efficiency of the data gathering and analysis process throughout the enterprise; (2) reduce the internal IS costs associated with delivering information; and (3) help NSWCDD become more competitive through improved information.

DEVELOPING THE CONCEPT

Planning for a data warehouse project in 1991 was a very difficult task! Data Warehousing was not a well-advertised concept and supporting methodologies, tools, and techniques for implementing data warehouse technologies were not readily available. In fact, it was not clearly evident to the IS organization that they were actually embarking on "data warehousing" until a chance meeting with Bill Inmon. During a social event while attending an IS conference, managers of the IS organization had a conversation with *Bill*. It was during this conversation they described their recent experience with IE and their decision to deviate from the methodology in order to extract source data into a database that would provide integrated data access throughout the enterprise. It was not until the next day that the IS managers realized they had discussed their plans with the now famous "father of data warehousing"! This chance encounter with Bill Inmon had a very motivating impact on the IS organization and increased their confidence in their ability to make a positive impact on their organization. Bill Inmon eventually spent 3 days with the IS organization, validating their proposed approach and providing technical insight into the concepts and techniques associated with data warehousing.

The IS organization had to literally develop a methodology in order to venture into data warehousing. Their IE experience and the products produced during their strategic planning efforts proved to be invaluable assets during the early phases of planning for and designing the data warehouse. Products produced during the ISP process were immediately reevaluated by the IS organization for their potential effectiveness and value to the data warehouse effort. Utilizing some unique analysis techniques and many of the matrixes and models produced during the ISP process, the following critical information requirements were identified: (a) data entities supporting corporate information requirements; (b) data relationships between the identified entities; (c) user types requiring access to corporate information; (d) specific organizational requirements for corporate information; and (e) information pertaining to the source legacy systems containing the corporate data.

After considerable analysis, a high level data warehouse concept began to emerge. It was decided to evolve the data warehouse over time utilizing a phased development approach. A time line of 9 months was established for the first increment of the data warehouse with additional increments occurring in 3 to 6 month intervals (time box development). Existing IS resources would be used for the data warehouse project by freezing activity on all legacy systems being maintained and development cost would be held to a minimum by using existing hardware, software, and development tools. A corporate steering committee would be established to validate system concepts, identify system requirements, gain corporate support for the initiative, and to establish initial data priorities. Instead of producing a "detailed" 5 year plan, it was decided that the data warehouse would need to be driven by unpredictable business requirements that would "naturally evolve" the data warehouse over time.

Building Management Support

The data warehouse project was named "Corporate Database" and the IS organization immediately began to develop strategies for gaining management support. Ultimately their marketing strategy was very simple; focus on the business need that had been identified and potential business benefits to be gained by developing the Corporate Database. Up until this point, most of the IS focus had been on legacy systems and satisfying business support requirements associated with these systems. Corporate Database would be designed to support corporate information requirements, therefore shifting the IS focus, and customer base, away from specific business support units and more towards corporate enterprise-wide information requirements. This was a very powerful customer base that had basically been neglected from an information systems perspective for many years. The need for corporate information was tremendous and therefore, support for the Corporate Database concept was very strong and enthusiastic. Resistance to the effort was centered primarily within business support organizations who feared that their internal operational requirements would be neglected and that they would loose ownership and control of data being extracted from the operational systems. However, due to the overwhelming need for timely, integrated corporate information, support for the Corporate Database concept became a logical conclusion for most of the enterprise.

The real issue for the IS organization was how to overcome the skepticism associated with their ability to actually accomplish the Corporate Database effort. Years of dedicating money and resources to legacy system efforts had resulted in high IS costs with very little "corporate" benefits. Legacy computing platforms were expensive to maintain and modifications to supporting applications were time consuming due to the technologies utilized for these systems. It was easy for corporate management to understand the business need for Corporate Database, but their concerns centered on how long it would take and how much it would cost to actually implement the system. This skepticism added additional pressures to the task of developing Corporate Database, however; the IS organization knew that only time and a successful implementation could eliminate these corporate concerns.

THE TEAM APPROACH

Three teams were initially assembled to support the data warehouse effort: a corporate steering committee, a user group, and the IS team. The Corporate Steering Committee was assembled to validate concepts and provide high level system requirements. The committee consisted of 10 senior level members who represented each major user type requiring access to corporate information: technical program managers, line managers, department staff and administrative support personnel, corporate analysts, and functional experts. In addition, members of the IS organization acted as facilitators for the steering committee helping to extract, model and document system requirements. The committee identified a set of high level requirements that were converted into system requirements by the IS organization. These requirements specified the types of system capabilities desired, system availability and performance requirements, and support structures that would be required for the data warehouse. From a data perspective, the steering committee indicated that they wanted all the data currently being provided from legacy systems, all of the data they always wanted from legacy systems but could never get, and flexibility to ensure that IS would be able to respond to their future data requirements and changing business demands as they occurred. They wanted the data to be integrated across different business areas and they wanted it at detailed and summary levels. The steering committee unanimously agreed that financial data was the number one priority and should be provided in the first increment of the data warehouse.

Throughout the early development of the initial data warehouse capabilities, the IS organization worked very closely with the steering committee in order to validate systems requirements and capabilities, provide project status and feedback, and ensure continued support for the project. This committee was a very valuable asset to the IS organization and provided tremendous creditability to the overall data warehouse effort. Once the Corporate Database project evolved into the design phase, the steering committee requested that a user group be formed to help identify "detailed" requirements and specifications for canned queries and reports.

The user group consisted of approximately 25 users from throughout the enterprise who specialized in gathering and using corporate information. In addition to identifying detailed requirements, this working level group helped identify "data usage" requirements, which became a driver for the physical database design. The user committee had difficulty describing exactly how they wanted to "view" canned information. The antiquated information methods they were accustom to prevented them from envisioning the possibilities of the data warehouse. Most of the data provided by the legacy systems was transition level reports providing piecemeal views of information. Data integration, summarization, and drill down analysis were very new concepts for the users.

After spending considerable time with the user group, the IS organization discovered a major impact associated with deploying enterprise-wide data warehousing capabilities: not only would they need to evolve the data warehouse over time but they would also need to help evolve the data warehouse users! It became obvious that if the data warehouse was going to change the way information was utilized, it would be critical for the IS organization to show the possibilities to the users and to help them identify new ways to use data differently. This was indeed a major discovery and not a role the IS organization felt immediately comfortable with, however; it continues to be a major role and requirement for the IS organization today.

The IS team consisted of data analysts, database administrators, developers, technical architecture specialists, and product and customer support personnel. Project leadership was initially assigned to a senior developer and the team consisted of approximately 10 full time employees at any given time although membership varied depending of what phase of the development cycle the project was in. Technical guidance and leadership was provided by IS management. For a variety of reasons, the IS team approach to data warehousing ultimately turned out to be unsuccessful. IS management realized that many of the management issues related to developing the system were less technical in nature and more culturally oriented. In addition, having a specifically dedicated team for Corporate Database was creating a split within the IS organization. Therefore, the dedicated IS team was eliminated, project management and leadership was assumed by IS management, and a concept of "management by architectures" was initiated within the IS organization. IS resources were divided into 5 architectural components; data, applications, technical architecture, data access tools, and customer support. Each component was assigned responsibility for specific life cycle functions (e.g., requirements, design, development, implementation, and support) across all business and information systems (e.g., legacy and data warehouse). This management approach has resulted in a greater integration of IS resources and has provided greater flexibility for utilizing resources across all product lines.

Most of the skills required to support the data warehouse effort were new to the IS team and as the effort progressed it was realized that many new skills not traditionally thought of as IS skills would be required. New methodologies had to be developed "on the fly" to support the effort and old development techniques related to database design, and development soon became obsolete. This was a difficult transition and learning experience for the IS team, however; the initial increment of the data warehouse was delivered on time and was a tremendous success!

DEVELOPING INITIAL CAPABILITIES

As the technical architecture personnel examined the system requirements, they determined that client/server capabilities would be required to support the ad-hoc and canned requirements for data warehouse access. They also determined that a "pure" client/server approach would not be the best implementation strategy for the Corporate Database. Requirements indicated a definite need for an application driven approach to the data warehouse in order to satisfy the requirements for standard "canned" capabilities. The state of the desk top computing environment at NSWCDD was one that was not standardized and would require considerable modifications in order to support an enterprise-wide deployment of a "standard" desk top data warehouse application. Another complicating factor resided with the knowledge and skills of the proposed user base. It was felt that many users would not be prepared to move from a hard copy, stovepipe information

based environment to on-line, ad-hoc desktop access to integrated business data.

Figure 12–1: NSWCDD Data Warehouse Implementation

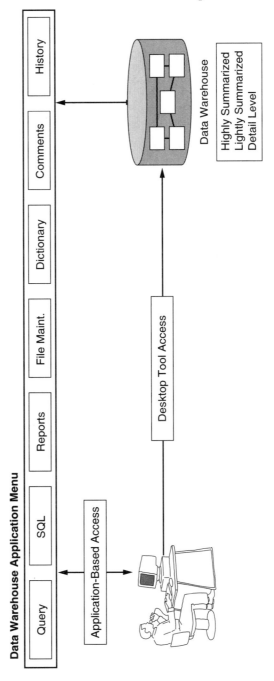

From a technical perspective, client/server technologies were just beginning to be discussed and the tools and support mechanisms for this technology were immature at best. Ultimately, the team decided to develop a "three-tier approach" that would utilize a combination of application clients that would support the standard data warehouse application and to also support direct desk top access to the server for users not requiring the application driven approach. These were very advanced technical concepts for early 1990, and the technical architecture personnel did a fantastic job of assembling the required hardware and putting a system concept into operation that is still utilized today due to its inherent support of the varied system access requirements. The flexibility of the three-tier technical architecture, the ability to support a spectrum of users with different skills and abilities, and its dependability over time have been key contributors to successful data warehousing at NSWCDD. Figure 12–1 is a representation of the NSWCDD Data Warehouse implementation.

After developing the technical architecture concept, the IS team went into full scale development. Data analysis efforts focused on identifying target financial data for the initial population of the data warehouse. Entity models produced during the strategic planning process provided road maps for identifying the types of financial data required. Legacy system analysis identified the source for the required data and data extract, conversion, and load specifications were developed. Existing reports provided a foundation for data display requirements and the user group provided additional insight into the deficiencies of data currently being provided and the types of data structures and data integration that would be required to handle summarized and drill down data analysis capabilities. All data extracted for the data warehouse was normalized into detailed data warehouse tables to ensure that all data was captured at its lowest level of detail. This would allow for flexibility in presenting different user views of data and changing business requirements once the data warehouse became operational. Once the detailed data schemas were designed, denormalized schemas were developed to support usability requirements and advanced data analysis requirements.

The need for an on-line data dictionary was identified as a critical end user requirement. Data being loaded into the data warehouse was not exact replicas of the data existing in the legacy systems. Therefore, the end-user would need to understand the data as well as conversion routines or algorithms used to produce the data. Data analysis activities within the IS organization were being supported by the KnowledgeWare CASE tool. It was decided to extract data from the KnowledgeWare tool and make it assessable through relational tables that could be integrated into the standard data warehouse application or the desk top access tools. The data dictionary development effort was another key to the success of the data warehouse.

The initial user base for the data warehouse was estimated to be approximately 400 users and it was predicted to expand to 1,000 users as additional business data and capabilities were integrated into the data warehouse. The IS organization decided to develop an on-line communication capability for users accessing the data warehouse to enter comments, problems, or requests for additional data and capabilities. This capability reduced the demand on the IS organization to respond to general user questions and comments on a daily bases. An existing user assistance hot line capability was also integrated into the data warehouse support infrastructure for users requiring immediate assistance.

The User Group helped to identify requirements for standard forms, menus, and reports to be provided through the application driven approach into the data warehouse. Developers utilized the standard Oracle tool set for developing these capabilities. Due to the inability for many users to realize the potential of the data warehouse, IS decided to develop some initial "baseline" forms and menus and then evolve these capabilities over time based on user feedback. It was at this point that the IS organization made a major decision relating to the data warehouse and the types of capabilities that would be provided. For the past 20 years users had complained that the reports from legacy systems did not satisfy their information requirements. However, when designing reports for the data warehouse, they requested the exact same reports being produced from the legacy systems. The

IS organization made the decision to delay providing standard reports from the data warehouse until users became familiar with its capabilities and potential. This was a very political decision (not warmly received by some users) and had to be managed carefully by IS management to prevent negative impacts.

Due to the complexities associated with extracting data from legacy source files and transforming the data into usable data warehouse structures, data validation was considered to be a critical task during the development of Corporate Database. Fortunately for the IS organization, many years of supporting legacy systems had given them experience with data validation and elaborate criteria was developed for each extract, conversion, and load process. Data validity has become a critical component of Corporate Database and some additional benefits related to legacy systems and end user support have been accomplished as a result of this effort. The quality of legacy system data has improved over time because the validation process identifies "problems" with the data that can be undetected by the legacy systems due to the lack of edits and validations within these systems. In addition, processing errors that can be very common within the legacy system environment are now immediately detected through the Corporate Database validation process. This has resulted in timely reruns within the legacy systems environment and has prevented complex problem solving activities commonly associated with analyzing legacy system problems.

Another benefit of the validation process has been the ability for IS personnel to quickly respond to end users having difficulties utilizing the Corporate Database. The first time an unexpected answer is derived by a user, the natural response is for the user to question the validity of the data within Corporate Database. Many phone calls have been received informing IS that the data within Corporate Database is "incorrect" due to answers the user has obtained from ad-hoc queries of the data. It is imperative for the IS organization to respond immediately to these situations because this type of "rumor" can instantly kill support for the system. As a result of the elaborate validation process, the IS organization is confident that the data within Corporate Database is correct and instead of spending valuable time "checking the system," they can focus on the query criteria used by the user to produce the questionable results. The ability to immediately focus on the business question being asked by the user has resulted in the timely resolution to most data problems.

Hands-on user training was provided to over 400 users from all across the enterprise. Training focused on the data within the data warehouse, integration between data, and possibilities for utilizing the data. Data analysts from the IS organization were utilized as trainers for the data warehouse effort due to their knowledge of the data and their ability to demonstrate possibilities associated with utilizing the data warehouse capabilities. Training sessions were followed up by advanced training sessions, special SQL training for end users, and focused workshops addressing specific business needs. Training is another key to successful data warehouse implementations.

DATA WAREHOUSING IMPACTS

The process of creating a data warehouse environment at NSWCDD has not always been smooth and several problems, obstacles, and impacts have been experienced along the way. The IS organization realized early on that not only were they implementing a new technology, but they were also creating the potential for tremendous change within the business, user community, and IS organization. Resistance to change has been a major obstacle for the IS organization to overcome.

Technically, the IS organization has faced many internal challenges during their data warehouse experience. The skills required to develop and support the data warehouse environment are fundamentally different than those related to legacy systems. New development methodologies and technical capabilities had to be developed by the IS organization in order to support the requirements associated with the data warehouse. Prior to the development of the data warehouse, legacy systems development and maintenance was a "way of life" for the IS organization. The IS staff felt very comfortable with the legacy system technologies, philosophies, and customer base. Careers had been established supporting legacy systems and not every employee was anxious to venture into a new environment. Not only were new technical skills required but a knowledge of the business and a understanding of how the business will utilize the data became essential. This shift in focus from technology to business has not been easy for some IS employees. Along with the new skills, new customer base and new focus, the IS organization has changed their philosophies associated with managing and supporting the data warehouse environment. Customer support has become a critical skill within the IS organization and knowledge of business data has become vital in order to support this function. Customer support now requires the attention of our best analysts instead of the lesser skilled personnel traditionally associated with legacy system support. This has created additional difficulties internal to the IS organization.

A key philosophy behind the Corporate Database concept is to "empower" the end user so they can satisfy their own dynamic information requirements. IS personnel have found this goal to be somewhat threatening and difficult to accept. They have spent their careers providing users with canned information and some are concerned that their skills and abilities will not be required if end users are trained to develop their own queries and reports. At the other end of this spectrum, end users have spent years relying on the IS organization to provide them with information and they are having some difficulty being empowered to satisfy their own requirements. This has become a constant struggle for the IS organization: what data and information should be provided as canned capabilities inherent to the data warehouse and what data and information should be provided by the end user of the data warehouse?

End users have experienced additional difficulties adjusting to the skills and knowledge required to effectively access data within the data warehouse. Corporate Database users span the entire enterprise and they have very different levels of desk top computing skills, data knowledge, and business knowledge. Each of these skills are essential to data warehousing. As a result, some have embraced the data warehouse concept and others have continuously resisted it. The IS organization has been required to spend a considerable amount of time and resources helping users transition to the data warehouse environment. In addition, IS management has spent considerable time working "damage control" created by end users who have become frustrated due to their inability to properly utilize the system. Negative feedback to top managers by end users who do not have the required business knowledge and skills to effectively utilize Corporate Database has been a major issue for the entire IS organization.

Top management support for Corporate Database seems to ebb and flow over time. There is substantial understanding and support for the importance of the data warehouse but, top management has not ingrained its capabilities into their management processes. Deficiencies in end-user skills are often blamed on the data warehouse and negative end users comments about the system are the ones that seem to have a "lasting impact" on top management. When things are going good, the IS organization is recognized as being "new and improved" but when things are rumored to be going bad (real or perceived), they think of us once again as the old IS organization of the past. New ideas and business needs have a tendency to generate heavy discussion and renewed interest in Corporate Database; however, the tendency to revert to business as usual is still very strong. Many opportunities exist to reengineer and streamline certain business practices as a result of Corporate Database, however; most of the reengineered processes and costs savings have occurred internal to the IS organization. External recognition for the data warehouse efforts at NSWCDD has helped the IS organization to gain internal support and recognition for their efforts.

PLANNED EVOLUTION

A major cornerstone to successful data warehousing evolves around the strategies for continued data warehouse evolution. Nothing could have prepared the IS organization for the impacts associated with evolution of the data warehouse. The data warehouse evolution process naturally placed them in all phases of the data warehouse life cycle at the same time. As a result, it didn't take long to realized that with each new increment of the data warehouse, increased complexity occurs. One of the toughest decisions in the evolution process has been knowing when to evolve the system with new data and capabilities and when to wait for the user base, IS organization, and business to catch up. As a result, the evolution process has not just become a technical and management issue, it has also become a political issue for the IS organization. IS management find themselves constantly doing one of two things: (1) either marketing and selling for continued support of existing capabilities or (2) attempting to "control" demand for new capabilities.

Business demand and corporate information requirements will be used as drivers to determine the evolution of the NSWCDD data warehouse. It is expected that future evolution will be centered around the following categories: (1) evolving the data, (2) evolving the users, (3) evolving the IS organization, (4) evolving the business, and (5) evolving the system functionality. Data expansions will continue to occur across internal NSWCDD business areas. The benefits of providing external data to the enterprise will be explored by providing DOD budget information and other external data sources that may prove to be of business benefit. Additional users will be added as the data within the data warehouse is expanded. Improved analytical capabilities for end users will continue to be a major focus and the IS organization will continue to improve their overall support infrastructure for the data warehouse. Additional executive information and decision support capabilities will be provided to help top management begin to derive benefits from the data warehouse.

OBSERVATIONS AND SUMMARY

Data Warehousing is much like participating in a triathlon; it requires a multitude of different skills to implement and support, and it's definitely a game of endurance. To the dismay of most IS professionals, we believe that data warehousing is less about technology and more about creating change within the IS organization and throughout the enterprise. Success related to data warehousing will not and can not occur within weeks or months; it must evolve over time. The success of your data warehouse will not be as much a result of the technologies you utilize to support the data warehouse but will ultimately be determined by the ability of your end users to access and utilize the data warehouse. Great technical implementations will be doomed to failure if users can not utilize the provided capabilities. We feel the challenge to IS management is related to taking the right risks, the ability to accept and support change, the ability to explore possibilities, and the desire to occasionally venture into the unknown. You must not only do these things within your IS organization, but you must also help the business accept these challenges. When Tom Landry (the former coach of the Dallas Cowboys) said, "Coaching is about making men do things they don't want to do in order to accomplish the things they want to do," he provided inspiration to all IS organizations attempting to support data warehousing activities. We have certainly learned that Data warehousing is not for the weak of heart or for those who prefer guaranteed success before accepting the challenge. For those willing to accept the challenge, Data warehousing can provide tremendous business advantages and creates the opportunity for business change.

Corporate Database has become an integral part of the NSWCDD business environment and will continue to provide business benefit to the Division as we continue to downsize and reduce internal costs. Support and demand for the data warehouse increases as users become better accustomed to the system and more familiar with manipulating data. As a result of Corporate Database, NSWCDD is positioned to become more competitive in today's changing business environment and will be better positioned to face the new business challenges of tomorrow.

Alarming Profits at Harris Semiconductor: A Case Study

Mark W. Poole

Harris Semiconductor

INTRODUCTION

The demand for Harris Semiconductor's integrated circuits grew substantially in the period of 1993 to 1995, to the point where factories were operating at full capacity. With more demand than supply for many of the products, factory throughput became a significant constraint to profitability. Several initiatives were implemented to improve factory productivity, one of which was the integrated yield management (IYM) system. IYM provides a data warehouse of manufacturing information along with an alarm system that quickly identifies desirable and undesirable changes in the factory that may impact throughput, and therefore, profits.

This chapter will discuss the Harris Semiconductor IYM system development initiative, the system capabilities, and how IYM fits into the definition of a traditional data warehouse. This includes the client/server architecture, system features, database design and performance issues, problems encountered, and successes that would be pertinent to other data warehouse projects.

WHY DATA WAREHOUSING?

In 1993, the Gartner group forecasted that ninety percent of all information processing organizations would be pursuing a data warehouse strategy in the next three years. Gartner had determined that many companies were rich in operational data but poor in their capability to gain decision support information from it. The operational data that runs the business from day to day cannot answer the questions frequently asked by management without reorganization, consolidation, summarization, and company-wide snapshots at various points in time. Harris was one of these companies with mountains of operational data that lacked methods for realizing its full potential. It was also determined that critical information should be Alarmed automatically rather than "found" through traditional ad-hoc data mining and data reduction efforts.

The Goals of the IYM system were very consistent with those of a traditional data warehouse:

- provide decision support information not currently available in the operational databases
- maintain 10 years of historical decision support information
- remove the impact of decision support on operational databases
- automatically identify significant changes in the factory
- provide a single source for decision making
- provide consistent answers
- provide a common access method to the warehouse and operational data
- provide "Best Practices" analysis tools

The traditional data warehouse is subject oriented, integrated, time-variant, nonvolatile, intended for decision support usage, and resides on a single stand-alone hardware platform. Each of these characteristics will be discussed regarding their relationship to the Harris Semiconductor IYM system implementation.

Subject Orientation

Harris manufactures integrated circuits at several facilities throughout the world, for use in the commercial and military markets. Each manufacturing site is primarily concerned with the performance of only the operations that are performed there. In many cases the products then move to another facility for further processing. The local Ingres operational databases contain the measurement information specific to that site, organized by manufacturing area and product. These databases identify "measurements" at that site. Harris needed a repository for summarized yield information by facility, period, product and process, in order to answer frequently asked manufacturing questions about overall facility, product, and process performance over time. The orientation of this information is time-based "Yields," "Products," and "Personnel." For this reason the IYM system was developed to routinely extract, calculate, and maintain Yield history information for each facility, the processes at each, and individual products in a process. The Ingres operational databases (at each site) maintain the daily detail information for the many operations, while the IYM Ingres warehouse maintains the summarized yields and the world-wide product/personnel relationships.

The Data Warehouse Is Integrated

Historically the integration of data from operational sources into decision support warehouses has been the most difficult part of the project. This was also true for Harris. A diagram of the data sources is shown in Figure 13–1.

Like any other data warehouse, the IYM system receives its data from many sources. Each of these required SQL software to move the data from its original location into the warehouse. Some of the facilities have Digital Equipment VAX/

VMS work-in-process software that tracks the production lots as they move from operation to operation. Nightly extracts were developed to move part of the desired information into the IYM system. Other Harris facilities (acquired within the last few years) have Hewlett-Packard-based software that performed the lot-tracing functionality. These systems also required that extracts be developed to move the desired information into IYM.

Figure 13–1:   IYM Data Sources

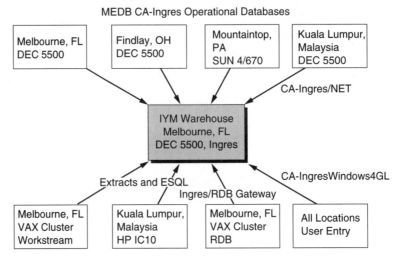

At one facility, lot movement information is loaded into a Digital Equipment VAX/VMS Relational Database (RDB). Access to this information was provided through the CA-Ingres Gateway product and the IYM graphical user interface (discussed later). The gateway allows any CA-Ingres tool to access the RDB information as if it were an actual remote Ingres database. This capability saved months of work that would have been required if extracts would have been used.

A portion of the summarized information originates from the manufacturing hardware. Some vendors calculate lot-based statistics while the operation is taking place. Where this occurs, software was developed to collect this information and automatically load it into IYM system on a periodic basis. Each source has its data converted into a Harris-defined standard input file so that a single data-loading program could be used for these sources.

Lastly, some of the data is maintained by selected users. This would include yield forecasts for future periods and product/personnel assignment information. Harris developed character and GUI-based screens to provide the data-entry interfaces, utilizing Ingres "roles" to handle the security requirements.

IYM also requires access to a SUN/Oracle database that contains lot-traceability data. This functionality is made available using either an Ingres Gateway or ODBC connectivity.

The Data Warehouse Is Time-Variant

The operational databases are organized by manufacturing area, product names, and lot identification (lotid) numbers. In every case the lotid is part of the primary key. Date information is then associated with the lotids. The data warehouse, however, is organized by manufacturing area and periods of time, with the manufacturing period in the primary key. The records indicate a summarized view of the factories at some point in time. The operational databases maintain 6 months of the measurement detail information, the warehouse maintains 10 years of the summarized data.

The Data Warehouse Is Non-Volatile

Updates, Inserts, and Deletes frequently occur in the operational environment on a record-by-record basis, when production lots must be retested or data entry errors are corrected. The summarized IYM yield information, however, is only loaded and then accessed. It accurately represents a snapshot of the factory at a period of time, and that view will never change. Only the product/personnel assignment information may be changed.

The Decision Support Users

The operational systems are used by the engineering community to determine relationships between measurements taken early in the manufacturing process and performance parameters measured later on. The summarized yield information within the IYM system, however, is being accessed by many levels of management in several organizations, to determine overall performance of manufacturing lines as a whole and the facilities that own them. All of the IYM users can access both the operational and summarized information via the IYM graphical user interface.

The Graphical User Interface

Access to the operational data at each facility and the summarized data warehouse information is provided through a graphical user interface developed using the Computer Associates Windows4GL and Ingres/Net tools. The IYM graphical user interface provides transparent connectivity to any of the operational databases or the data warehouse from a workstation, X-terminal, or a personal computer with an x-terminal emulator package. A remote login (telnet, rlogin, etc.) to a dedicated application server provides the GUI capability. The IYM system and graphical user interface allow the users to do any of the following:

> Analyze yields and standard performance metrics for facilities, processes, or products for any Harris location, for user-specified periods of time
>
> Query and statistically analyze the manufacturing operational data originating at any Harris location
>
> View the Alarm System statistics, configuration, and historical information
>
> View the product/personnel relationships for all products
>
> View product specification information

These capabilities are provided to the user without their having to know where the data resides. The interface utilizes lookup tables that indicate the source of the operational or decision support data. If the user desired to view and analyze yield information, a connection is made to the yield server. If operational data from a particular location is desired, the appropriate connection is made to make that data available.

The Alarm System

It was identified early in the design process that the IYM system needed to quickly identify when a change (desirable or undesirable) occurred in either the operational or warehouse data. With capacity-constrained factories, the strategic processes and products cannot tolerate unnoticed changes, and "bad" products must be identified as soon as possible. The Alarm system was developed to provide this functionality, and proved its value only one week after it was implemented into production.

IYM "key users" identify which data elements should be monitored by the Alarm System. The IYM interface allows these individuals to establish a new alarm, indicating who will be responsible (the "owner") for "clearing" it when it gets triggered, and who should receive e-mail when this happens.

The IYM data loading processes determine if data that is to be loaded is associated with an established alarm. If so, information about the newly loaded data gets staged into "to be processed" tables in the operational and warehouse databases. A separate UNIX "Alarm Server" routinely connects to each database to determine if there is a new alarm-based data to process. When this occurs, the Alarm Server then retrieves the required data across the network to local disks where the statistical methods are applied. This client/server methodology minimizes the impact of the Alarm processing on the databases, and allows for a centralized administration of the statistical software.

Harris developed the statistical algorithms internally, considering the possibilities for non-normal parametric and summarized data distributions. All "trigger points" for the alarm system are statistically based from historical information, with sophisticated methods for cleaning the incoming data. A minimum number of data values must be present before an alarm calculation will occur.

The Alarm System can identify shifts in distributions, outliers, and trends in the data. When this occurs, electronic mail is sent to the distribution list for the assigned alarm, indicating the alarm condition. The triggered alarm is registered in the IYM system and will stay in an "uncleared" state until the owner clears it and provides an explanation as to why it may have occurred. This "probable cause" and all historical Alarm information is available online for all IYM users to review. The users can also view and analyze the data that caused the alarm to trigger using one of the many data analysis tools.

In the first week of implementation, the Alarm system alerted an engineer that a particular production batch had parametric distributions that were significantly different than historical information. The engineer quickly identified that the batch had not been processed properly, leading to the discovery that other batches had also been misprocessed. This early identification of the problem saved Harris many hours of wasted processing time and scrapped product. Since the implementation of the Alarm system in November of 1994, many manufacturing problems have been quickly identified and resolved, saving Harris enormous amounts of money and allowing the company to increase the factory throughput.

Database Design Issues

The query and reporting requirements associated with the summarized data often mandate that non-normalized tables be provided, and that redundancy be used to increase query performance. A normalized table design for the yield information could have included a column to indicate the manufacturing area associated with the yields (facility, area, product, period, yield). This table was horizontally fragmented to improve query performance, resulting in separate tables for each manufacturing area (facility, period, product, yield).

It was also determined that many of the user queries would involve a wildcard after the fifth character of the product field, since the product information may be associated with an entire family of part types. Queries of this kind became unacceptably long as the database and its usage grew. To remedy the problem, a separate, indexed field was created to represent the first five characters of the product field.

IYM System Architecture

The IYM system utilizes a client/server architecture that specifies separate UNIX servers for different tasks. There are application servers, database servers, the Alarm server, and user clients.

Every Harris location has a UNIX application server that provides the user directories, IYM interface, data analysis tools, and third-party UNIX utilities. These application servers are a mixture of DEC Ultrix and SUN Microsystems Solaris platforms. Each factory location will also have a UNIX Ingres database server for the operational data. These SUN and DEC platforms are configured and specifically tuned for data loading processes, data administration, and user queries against the Ingres databases. The summarized yield data, product information, and product/personnel relationship data are stored on another Ingres database server at the corporate headquarters in Melbourne, Florida. The UNIX Alarm Server is also located in Melbourne. The users at each location perform a remote login to one of the application servers to invoke the graphical user interface, displaying the screens on their client UNIX Workstation, X-terminal, or Personal Computer. The Ingres/NET middleware provides the transparent access from the application servers to each of the database, warehouse, and alarm server systems.

This task-specific architecture provides an extremely flexible environment for growth and change and allows each system to be configured and tuned to the specific task. If, for example, an application server can no longer handle the user load, another could be added, possibly NFS-mounting the required disk of executables from the existing application server. New versions of the IYM interface or third-party tools only need to be installed on the application servers, rather than on a large number of user systems. A diagram of the IYM system architecture can be seen in Figure 13–2.

LESSONS LEARNED

Data warehouses don't have to be planned projects with budgets. An internal need arose for summarized yield information, there were hardware and programming resources available, so it happened. The result is a system that has become the world-wide source for the manufacturing yield data. If a data warehouse is built and marketed well, the users will come to it and support the enhancement process because it will provide decision support capabilities not available in any other system.

Figure 13–2:   IYM Architecture

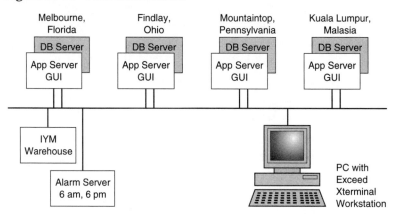

The yield information originally resided on a UNIX system that was intended to only act as an application server. The usage and size of the yield information grew much faster than expected, forcing the migration to a separate server.

All users of the system can view and analyze the data using the graphical user interface. They also have SQL access due to a proliferation of the SQL tools in earlier years. The latter provides the ultimate flexibility to the select few who feel they need it, but they frequently issue queries with wildcards on nonindexed fields, impacting everyone else on the system. Eventually the SQL access must be disabled, but this can only be done after screens can be built to provide the same (controlled) capabilities that they have in SQL.

Many of the required analyses also need to be available from the command line or in a batchmode. Reports such as "Yields for Process XYZ for the last 6 periods" will be frequently executed. The users don't want to enter the system and work their way through several screens to request this standard report. This functionality can be provided through shell scripts that prompt for the required information and automatically print to a selected printer.

Once everyone determined that the data is available and reliable, they wanted to extract it and feed their organization-specific reports. Tools must be available to allow this data extraction, otherwise they expect the organization that developed the warehouse to do it for them. The IYM system provides the capability to extract any user-defined dataset into a tab-delimited file so that they can apply their personal analysis software as needed.

When first implemented, few users believed the yield numbers being displayed because they didn't know what method was being used to calculate them. The interface had to be modified to offer a Help Screen that described the calculation methods. Only then did the users understand and trust what they were viewing.

RESULTS

Common Metrics

The integration effort required that each facility agree on common metrics for performance, and that standards for certain data elements (product names, measurements) be defined. Yield calculations, for example, were performed differently at many of the Harris locations, and each believed theirs to be the right way. The IYM integration team had to bring the appropriate organizations together to determine a standard method for the yield calculations. The users could then depend upon consistent and meaningful answers to the yield questions.

Increased Communication

The multi-facility IYM implementation brought to light many issues that had previously been unrevealed. All locations can view the performance of remote facilities and their processes, and how performance has changed over time, knowing that the standard metrics are being applied. Engineering communities from all sites are communicating more, sharing their experiences regarding problem identification and resolution. There is a greater sense of being part of a worldwide yield improvement team rather than an individual plant.

Improved Engineering Efficiency

Prior to IYM, engineers at each facility would spend part of their time developing analysis software, duplicating the work that was being performed at the other sites. The IYM team worked with all locations to determine the "Best Practices" for yield analysis and then integrated them into the system. After this was done, the engineers spent more time in problem resolution activities rather than in software development. The usage of the common tools also allows them to better communicate about the results of their analyses.

SUMMARY

The IYM system has significantly increased Harris Semiconductor's manufacturing decision support capabilities, removed much of the decision support burden from the operational systems, and helped to improve the overall factory throughput. It provides the functionality of a traditional data warehouse but removes the need for ad-hoc data mining in order to determine if critical changes have occurred.

The easy access to accurate, summarized, time-based information in a central location as well as complete access to the operational data has improved interplant communication and yield improvement efficiency. The establishment of standards and common statistical analysis functions provided great returns.

The Alarm System proved to be a critical element in the early identification of changes in the manufacturing processes. Its usage and capabilities are expected to grow dramatically over the next few years. The user community continually invents additional ways to apply the Alarm System technology to other areas of the factories.

The Ingres database and tools from Computer Associates have worked exceptionally well over the years. The Ingres/NET software made client/server database implementations completely painless, and the Windows/4GL tool (now renamed OPENROAD) provided fast prototyping and powerful GUI system development. The ability to transparently query remote databases and switch from one to another within the same session make the system appear as one central source for all of the operational and decision support data. Users can answer many questions much faster than before and do it within one environment rather than having to access many systems.

Index